Ethnography and the Corporate Encounter

Studies in Public and Applied Anthropology

General Editor: **Sarah Pink,** University of Loughborough, and **Simone Abram,** Town and Regional Planning, University of Sheffield

The value of anthropology to public policy, business and third sector initiatives is increasingly recognized, not least due to significant innovations in the discipline. The books published in this series offer important insight into these developments by examining the expanding role of anthropologists practicing their discipline outside academia as well as exploring the ethnographic, methodological and theoretical contribution of anthropology, within and outside academia, to issues of public concern.

Ethnography and the Corporate Encounter

Reflections on Research in and of Corporations

Edited by

Melissa Cefkin

Berghahn Books
New York • Oxford

First published in 2009 by
Berghahn Books

www.berghahnbooks.com

Library of Congress Cataloging-in-Publication Data

Ethnography and the corporate encounter : reflections on research in and of
corporations / edited by Melissa Cefkin.
    p. cm. — (Studies in public and applied anthropology)
  Includes bibliographical references and index.
  ISBN 978-1-84545-598-9 (alk. paper)
  1. Business anthropology 2. Corporate culture. I. Cefkin, Melissa.
GN450.8.E87 2009
306—dc22

                                                          2009013508

British Library Cataloguing in Publication Data

A catalogue record for this book is available from the British Library

Printed in the United States on acid-free paper

978-1-84545-598-9 hardback
978-1-84545-777-8 paperback

CONTENTS

———⊙⊙⊙———

CULTURE AND CORPORATE EPISTEMOLOGIES

ANOTHER LOOK: COMMENTARIES FROM
CORPORATE RESEARCH AND THE ACADEMY

Figures and Tables

—⊶∝∝∞⊷—

Chapter 1

INTRODUCTION
Business, Anthropology, and the Growth of Corporate Ethnography

Melissa Cefkin

A relentless quest for innovation, improvement, and change—in short, "the new"—characterizes the steady march of corporate and organizational efforts of all kinds. In the latter part of the twenty-first century, a confluence of social, economic, and cultural dynamics, glossed by such terms as *globalization,* the *new economy, knowledge work, customer-centered business, mass customization,* and the *information age,* cast a particular hue on that quest. A pursuit desiring of a more nuanced grasp on the varieties of human experience both exposed by and driven through these dynamics, within this context anthropological perspectives and the application of ethnography to business and organizational actions have emerged as a favored source for this understanding. Ethnographic researchers, many of them anthropologists, have "entered the corporation," invited there to influence the organizations' understandings, and effectiveness and profits, to be sure, of their customers, their employees, and the social and cultural worlds they inhabit. Attesting to this interest, a steady stream of journalistic reportage on the phenomena of ethnographic work in corporate and public sector enterprises has appeared, going so far as to suggest that "anthropologists are now regarded as a necessity at such firms" ("Off with the Pith Helmets" 2004).

Growing out of an intermittent history of prior interactions between anthropology and the business world, I believe that a confluence of recent developments points to the emergence of a nascent canon of corpo-

Notes for this chapter begin on page 28.

rate ethnography. The drive anthropologically oriented researchers fee to work deep within the engines of the business sector is now being matched by corporations who seek to actively engage ethnographic work as a part of their strategic and operational efforts. This interest is not restricted to for-profit businesses. Not-for-profit and governmental enterprises are getting into the act as well.

The experiences of practitioners who perform this work promises valuable insight on these dynamics and on the cultural, social, and economic worlds the organizations they work with produce and inhabit. Practitioners' experiences also provoke consideration about the effect of ethnography in business, about the role those who engage in and with it play, and about the value, practice, impact, and quandaries of producing particularly situated ethnographic understandings as the basis for action in the corporate sector. As described below, numerous sites for this deliberation are beginning to emerge. And yet, answering the questions raised by this realm of work will be neither simple nor straightforward, requiring evaluation through both the kind of perspective afforded by an ethnography of the ethnography in and of industry as well as through the reflections of practitioners themselves. The contributors to this volume engage, in bits and pieces, in both such examinations. Our aim is to identify and sharpen the questions raised by this realm of work and to advance an understanding of the role of ethnographic work in industry and its effect on both organizations and in intellectual traditions of cultural analysis.

This book explores anthropological relations within organizations for whom, and with whom, ethnographic work is conducted. Examined from the perspective of anthropological researchers engaged to influence organizational decisions and actions, the volume explores how sites of research are construed and experienced as well as how practitioner-researchers confront questions of their own positioning. The authors reflect on their struggles to prompt different ways of thinking, knowing, and doing in these organizations. Proceeding by way of descriptions of particular projects, practices, and subjects of the researchers' work, the volume also broadens the aperture to consider how ethnographic work in industry is in dialogue with broader social and cultural discourses. Aware that their anthropologically inspired work is positioned within powerful sites of socio-economic production, the authors commit to exploring the meanings of their work within traces of traditions of critical inquiry. Neither a "how-to" book in applied anthropology, nor one of angst-ridden hand wringing about practitioners' moral and political complicity, the aim of this volume is, nonetheless, to explore and expose the very complex conditions of this work.

At a time when cultural analysts, perhaps anthropologists in particular, are voicing renewed concern for the value, impact, and representation (or lack thereof) of their work to matters of social import, this volume contributes to ongoing explorations of the positioning of cultural researchers vis-à-vis those they work with and through as well as in regard to broader forces of social production. That the contexts of inquiry are business and organizational settings is, on this front, simply a matter of locating the work; the thoughts contained in these explorations can be productively engaged by anyone interested in issues of anthropological relations in contexts of ethnographic study and their implications to knowledge production. Readers particularly interested in business and organizational sites and applications of ethnography (including those currently or potentially participating in it) can additionally expect to gain insight onto contemporary business practices, epistemologies, and ideologies (see especially chapters 2 and 7) and can expect to learn about corporate anthropology and the many ways it is performed (see especially chapters 3 and 4 for descriptive accounts.) Indeed, the business and organizational contexts of these examinations and the fact that the authors are themselves active participants in them adds a significant set of dimensions to these concerns. Accordingly, the volume invites more incisive examination and discussion about issues of representation, efficacy, and positioning among the growing community of ethnographic practitioners directly involved in corporate and organizational worlds. Finally, the many interested (and non-anthropologically trained) business colleagues of such ethnographic practitioners may expect to find value in these discussions as well, both broadening and deepening their understanding of the perspective of ethnographic work in industry and the hopes and worries their ethnographic collaborators bring to it.

Just as ethnographic practitioners in industry contexts are particularly situated within the everyday sites of their work, this work emerges as well out of particular histories. Below I provide a fuller account of recent developments and situate these developments in both disciplinary and social historical trajectories. I conclude by outlining the structure and contents of the volume more fully.

Recent Developments: Convergences Toward a New Corporate Ethnography

Refractive of the online communities, user-driven content sites, and digital social-networking forums many business anthropologists are hired to research and advise on, numerous blogs, user groups, and websites have emerged to join and service the growing set of people engaged with corporate ethnography. Indicative of the increased energy invested in and attention to corporate ethnography is the vibrant Yahoo discussion group,

Anthrodesign. Started in 2002,[1] Anthrodesign has grown by word of mouth from its original six members to over fifteen hundred by the autumn of 2008. In addition to regular calls for advice and information seeking, participants on the list frequently engage in active and lengthy discussions and debates around the nature of the ethnographic enterprise in commercial and organizational settings and its relationship to other fields of practice and academic disciplines. Similar forums exist within social networking sites such as Facebook and Linked In.

The flourishing interest and activity in the area of corporate ethnography is also mirrored in institutional placements. Figures indicate that more than half of anthropology PhDs are employed in ways other than traditional higher-education teaching positions (Bennett et al. 2006; Rylko-Bauer, Singer, and Willigen 2006). Many maintain membership in professional associations such as the American Anthropological Association (AAA), who estimates that more than 20 percent of its membership in 2005 was employed outside academia (Bennett et al. 2006), the Society for Applied Anthropology (SfAA), the European Association of Social Anthropologists (EASA), and the Association for Social Anthropology (ASA) in the United Kingdom. At the same time, a large number of scholars and practitioners from other fields—not just from within the social sciences and humanities (such as sociology or cultural studies) but also design and technical fields—are developing expertise in ethnographic research.

Stirrings of Corporate Ethnography

Where are all these ethnographically oriented practitioners employed? Many can be found in the numerous management consultancies, design firms, market research companies, marketing agencies, and small think tanks that were established and grew in the 1980s, 1990s, and 2000s. Firms focusing on everything from strategy consulting to product and system design to market research to change management boast of their ethnographic and anthropological approaches and capabilities. They may employ anthropologists, include various forms of ethnographic research techniques in their tool kits, and articulate their guiding perspectives in terms at least partially derived from ethnography and anthropology.[2]

Mid-sized and large corporations also participate in this dynamic. In the US,[3] the hiring of Eleanor Wynn and then Lucy Suchman in the late 1970s into Xerox's famed research lab, the Palo Alto Research Center (PARC), is commonly pointed to as the initiation of an active pursuit by companies to hire anthropologically trained ethnographers directly into research and product development labs. Xerox stood out into the 1990s for its concentration of ethnographic researchers across its research labs in California,

New York, and Great Britain (employing about eleven researchers engaged in and capable of ethnographic studies, nine of them PhD anthropologists or sociologists[4]), as well as for the notable output of anthropological research publications which continues to this day.[5] Other large corporations, too, began hiring anthropologists and others with ethnographic research expertise. General Motors, Hewlett Packard, Kodak, Motorola, Sun Microsystems, and others have had or continue to have anthropologists on their payrolls. In the late 1990s, the "fast five" internet consulting firms such as Scient, Viant, and Razorfish were in a race to bring ethnographers in-house. Sapient Corporation triumphed in this competition by acquiring eLab, a research and design consultancy profoundly guided by anthropological and ethnographic methods and sensibilities[6] in 1999. After the acquisition, Sapient's Experience Modeling function grew to employ (prior to the dot-com bust of 2001) no fewer than 23 PhDs in anthropology and closely aligned disciplines, and over 120 people worldwide with ethnographically informed research capability. In the 2000s, Intel has similarly been notable for its large concentration of anthropologists, some of whom hold significant strategic and organizational roles in the company. As of the fall of 2006, fifteen of the twenty-four or so researchers with ethnography as a part of their training and responsibilities held PhDs in anthropology, and *Technology Review* gleefully (and over-ambitiously, as it turned out) reported in 2006 that Intel was "in the process of hiring more than 100 anthropologists and other social scientists to work side by side with its engineers" (Fitzgerald 2006). Microsoft, too, has brought on numerous anthropologists and ethnographic researchers in both their research and product divisions, with about twenty practitioners as of the fall of 2006 (seven with PhDs in anthropology). Other high-tech firms such as IBM, Yahoo, and Google have hired anthropologists (albeit in single-digit numbers) and developed ethnographic capability in-house. Similarly, several government research labs, such as NASA and Sandia, have brought anthropologists in-house to work in labs or in organizationally focused roles as ethnographers and scholars, while others, such as the Department of Veterans Affairs, actively work with ethnographic consultancies on organizational matters.

Independent research firms, often operating from a mix of grant funding and contracted research, have also participated in this growth of corporate and organizational ethnography over the last several decades. Notable among them and paralleling the history of anthropology and ethnography at Xerox PARC was the not-for-profit Institute for Research on Learning (IRL). Founded in 1986 through seed funding from The Xerox Foundation, IRL's aim was to rethink learning by providing a deeper understanding and appreciation of the sociality of learning contexts and practices. The methodological and epistemological foundations of IRL's approach were strongly informed by ethnographic and anthropological principles, most evidently through the work of the anthropologist and social-learning theorist Jean Lave done in conjunction with the IRL researcher Etienne Wenger (1991). Many of IRL's full-time and contract members over the decade and a half of its existence were anthropologists and the institute maintained a strong connection to PARC throughout this time.[7]

Emerging Institutionalization

The nascent institutionalization of a new corporate ethnography is also being signaled from within the academy. In the United States, several departments of anthropology have formulated specializations responsive to this current confluence of events. Wayne State University offers a doctorate with a concentration in business and organizational anthropology (BOA),[8] while San Jose State University launched a master's degree in applied anthropology in 2006 to prepare people as researchers, administrators, and program developers for public- and private-sector organizations.[9] The anthropology department at the University of North Texas also has a concentration in business anthropology.[10] Yet further academic groups are forming throughout Europe and the UK with a focus on anthropology and ethnography for enterprises. Among these are the User Centered Design group at the Mads Clausen Institute for Product Innovation at the University of Southern Denmark, which offers a concentration in design anthropology, and the London-based Incubator for Critical Inquiry into Technology and Ethnography (INCITE) program. Founded in 2001 in the sociology department at the University of Surrey in the UK and now housed at Goldsmiths University, INCITE actively works across anthropology-, cultural-, and gender-study programs as well as with researchers in the private sector.[11] Moreover, anthropologists worldwide have been actively hired into or affiliated with other university departments with strong relations to the corporate world such as business,[12] computer science and informatics,[13] and design.[14]

Scholarly production in the form of conferences and publications further signals the emergence of a canon of new corporate ethnography. A number of books that address aspects of this growing field have been published since the early 2000s, including Susan Squires and Bryan Byrne's *Creating Breakthrough Ideas: The Collaboration of Anthropologists and Designers in the Product Development Industry* (2002), Ann Jordan's *Business Anthropology* (2003), Sarah Pink's *Applications of Anthropology* (2006), and Brian Moeran's *The Business of Ethnography* (2005) and *Ethnography at Work* (2006). Patricia Sunderland and Rita Denny's *Doing Anthropology in Consumer Research* (2007) is a notable recent contribution to the field.

Sunderland and Denny provide a valuable primer for clients and others (among them anthropologists and aspiring practitioners themselves) for gaining a deeper understanding of what cultural analysis is and what it offers (resonating in particular with Martin Ortlieb's contribution in this volume in teasing out notions of culture at play in corporate contexts). By way of description of an awareness-building exercise they use with clients, and more generally throughout the essays and examinations offered in the book, they elegantly demonstrate how the very foundations and approaches of the questions being asked and the understandings being sought in anthropologically informed ethnographic studies differ from those motivated through psychology, the discipline and orientation more well-entrenched in organizational settings.

A larger, longer-standing core of anthropological works, much of it done at the cusp of research and consulting or applied projects, addresses related themes and topics and informs today's practitioner-oriented ethnography in and of industry. These include studies of organizations and workplaces (Aneesh 2006; Baba 1991; Batteau 2000; Dubinskas 1988; Garsten 1994; Hamada 2000; Kunda 1992; Traweek 1988); consumer and brand studies (Malefyt and Moeran 2003; McCracken 2005, 2006); computing, information and communication technologies, including the prominent domain of human-computer interaction (Bell 2006; Bell, Blythe, and Sengers 2005; Blomberg 2005; Crabtree 2003; Garsten and Wulff 2003; Hakken 1999, 2003; Hakken and Andrews 1993; Heath and Luff 2000; Jordan 1996; Luff, Hindmarsh, and Heath 2000; Nardi 1996; Nardi and O'Day 1999; Sellen and Harper 2002; Star 1995); and work, work practices, and the cultural construction of professional identities (Barley and Kunda 2004; Barley and Orr 1997; Blomberg and Henderson 1990; Blomberg, Suchman, and Trigg 1996, 1997; Casey 1995; Darr 2006; Darrah 1996; Darrah, Freeman, and English-Lueck 2007; English-Lueck 2002; Forsythe and Hess 2001; Orr 1996; Sachs 1995; Schwarz 2003; Schwarz, Nardi, and Whittaker 1999; Suchman 1987). Moreover, research journals both within anthropology and those published in other fields and through other kinds of professional associations, such as Computer-Human Interaction (CHI), Computer-Supported Collaborative Work (CSCW), Association for Computing Machinery (ACM), and the American Management Association (AMA), regularly publish works addressing the methods, findings, and contributions of ethnographic research in such areas of technology design, marketing, and organizational dynamics.

Finally, reflective of the growing commitment of participants in and around these areas of work to examine and advance the theoretical, methodological, and disciplinary formations of the new corporate ethnography, the Ethnographic Praxis in Industry Conference (EPIC) has been held annually (and produced published conference proceedings) since 2005.[15] Its aim is to provide both a critical and celebratory space for a concentrated examination of work in this area. Rick Robinson inaugurated the first conference with a cautious provocation toward disciplinary formation, challenging participants with the assertion that "application of methodology to an arena doesn't make a domain, or a discipline. Theory debate does" (2005: 2). The participants in that debate, as Robinson suggests and Jeanette Blomberg (2005) further explores, consist of a particular blend of people across a range of disciplinary backgrounds and practice orientations, from anthropology and sociology to design, computer-human interaction, psychology, business, and more. Among and between this group of varied and hybrid participants and their business interlocutors, "ethnography" itself acts as a boundary object around which participants communicate (Wakeford 2005). As a corporate anthropologist I may be trying to understand, for example, the way that financial constructs and the hyper-rationalized ways in which they are represented and managed informs a worldview and set of practices against which sales representatives of a global firm negotiate their role and participation in the firm's business and the global economy more generally (Cefkin 2007; Cefkin, Thomas, and Blomberg 2007). My business counterparts may see my ethnographic work as a useful effort in gaining sales representatives' insight on the value, use, and function of the firm's tools and processes by engaging directly in their worlds. In both cases, ethnography functions as a legitimate rubrique through which a particularly situated local culture is understood, its relations to broader socioeconomic dynamics are explored, and considerations for change are based.

What is to be learned from the encounters of anthropologists and other ethnographic researchers in the organizational contexts in which they operate? What do these encounters offer traditions of critical inquiry? As a canon continues to form, it is essential that what comes of this activity and the questions and challenges it raises are critically examined. This book explores the insights gained from people working from ethnographically informed perspectives within and about business enterprises. Moving beyond the often facile, curiosity-framed slant posed by the kinds of journalistic treatments found in the popular press, the authors here take a serious look at the subjects and dynamics that comprise organizational practices and corporate developments, considering these arenas as powerful sites of knowledge production and as sites catalyzing decisions and actions complexly affecting broad swaths of contemporary society globally.

Each of the authors draws on their experience as a practitioner. Denied the critical distance of an outsider on the corporate and organizational dynamics they examine, the contributors all draw on work undertaken directly for and with business stakeholders and clients, stakeholders and clients who expect to be able to act on the produced results. This requirement for direct relevance and impact positions the work in ways not always demanded of cultural analyses. This domain of work also encourages, if not requires, a rethinking of the meaningfulness of the methods to be used in these collaborative work settings and has provided a rich space for the learning of how to do fieldwork in dynamic, complex contemporary settings. It has further engendered new forms of ethnographic writing and representation as practitioners' ethnographically informed work products ("deliverables") encompass everything from PowerPoint presentations to video ethnographies to project reports. Indeed, this volume itself is suggestive of such changes. Readers may note, for instance, the relatively fewer number of citations found in some chapters as compared to more traditional academic texts. One reviewer of the volume suggested this signaled not a paucity of content, theoretical development, and value, but rather a categorical innovation. Rising to the challenge posed in traditions stemming from the anthropological rethinking of the 1980s, to work toward a more strongly engaged and collaborative ethnography (Fischer 2003; Marcus and Fischer 1986), it is my belief that the combination of these perspectives—that of ethnographic researchers *from deep within* and *as active participants in* the engines of corporate and organizational life— offers a unique stance from which the discipline of anthropology and other intellectual traditions of social and cultural inquiry can learn as they strive to understand and advance their impact in the world.

Situated Engagements: How Did We Get There?

Contemporary cultural production happens across mobile and transformed locations. As such, it draws attention to the varying subject positions of actors, including the ethnographer, in those sites.

> In contemporary multi-sited research projects moving between public and private spheres of activity, from official to subaltern contexts, the ethnographer is bound to encounter discourses that overlap with his or her own. In contemporary field of work, there are always others within who know (or want to know) what the ethnographer knows, albeit from a different subject position, or who want to know what the ethnographer wants to know. (Marcus 1995: 97)

Douglas Holmes and George Marcus have recently extended Marcus' articulation to other dimensions of meaning construction. Their notion of the "para-ethnographic" embodies

the conception that the traditional subjects of study have developed something like an ethnography of both their own predicaments and those who
have encroached on them, and that their knowledge practices in this regard
are in some sense parallel to the anthropologist's and deserving of more
consideration than mere representation in the archive of the world's peoples
that anthropologists have created. (2006: 35)

Chris Darrouzet, Helga Wild, and Susann Wilkinson (chapter 3) reveal
how this impulse is at work inside a large US healthcare organization.
They suggest that "as we become used to the idea of ethnography as a
distinct modality for puzzling things out in situations of complexity, it becomes clearer that ethnography is also what it has always been: a mode of
relating to others." This positioning of an ethnographic sensibility within
organizational sites of contemporary life holds promise that the new corporate ethnography can actively occupy the kind of strategic terrain demanded by the complexities of the early twenty-first century.

Disciplinary Contexts

That actors in the business community know or want to know what the
ethnographer knows, and that they are looking to apply the "distinct modality" of understandings that ethnography offers, is not entirely new. Anthropologists and other ethnographically oriented social scientists have
worked in the business sector in previous times dating at least to the early
1930s in the United States (Baba 2006) and the late 1940s in the United
Kingdom (Mills 2006). The engagement of anthropologists in other organizational apparatus such as governmental and non-governmental organizations (NGOs) is even lengthier and better known, constituting the
traditional mainstay of the sub-discipline of "applied" anthropology. That
history—together with trenchant critiques of the close relationship between the early development of the discipline and colonialism as well as
concerns about applications of anthropological knowledge under certain
conditions of development work—continues to inform both intellectual
and ethical concerns of applied ethnographic and anthropological work.
This history and critique is extensive and has been treated elsewhere (Baba
2006; Mills 2006; Pink 2006; Rylko-Bauer, Singer, and Van Willigen 2006;
Strathern and Stewart 2005; West 2005). Indeed, while the interventionist
dimension of applied anthropology frames and encompasses the kind of
work performed in the new corporate ethnography, this arena of study
draws as much or even more from other intellectual trajectories. Suggestive of such threads of influence, but by no means exhaustive, a brief outline of some of these influences follows.

Much ethnographic work in and for businesses and organizations has been concentrated on the intersecting arenas of workplace and consumer studies.[16] An antecedent to current workplace anthropology is marked by the Hawthorne studies (Baba 2006) and related projects in both the US and Europe. Prompted by the dominance of large-scale, densely populated work facilities common to manufacturing, such studies were interested in examining and experimenting with forms of labor, environmental, and organizational design. The anthropological dimensions of the studies commonly concerned cultural—in the sense of national, ethnic, and occupational—aspects of organizational forms and examined how varying organizational and work environments meshed with cultural forms to produce differing outcomes in such areas as worker satisfaction and productivity.

Workplace and work practice studies of the 1980s, 1990s, and 2000s have also been informed both conceptually and in terms of participants by the sub-field of the anthropology of work.[17] Patricia Sachs, for instance, an early and key participant in the new corporate ethnography, received her PhD in economic anthropology from the Graduate Center CUNY with June Nash as her advisor, while the studies of Jean Lave (Lave and Wenger 1991) focused on occupational identity and the intersection between practice and learning had a direct bearing on the establishment of the Institute for Research on Learning where many ethnographic studies of the workplace were conducted throughout the 1990s. Marietta Baba's pioneering organizational studies (1988, 1991, 1998, 2005, 2006) together with other researchers of organizations (see, for example, Tomoko Hamada and Willis Sibley's 1994 edited volume *Anthropological Perspectives on Organizational Culture*) have impacted the development of workplace studies, as have critical studies of industry and labor, particularly as focused in the area of globalization. Especially notable have been developments in the area of science and technology studies, or STS (including, for instance, the work of Diana Forsythe [2001], Karin Knorr-Cetina [1999], Bruno Latour [1987; Latour and Woolgar 1986], and Susan Leigh Star [1995, 1995]), which continue to impact workplace studies of practicing corporate ethnographers in rich and compelling ways.

The historical trajectories intersecting in ethnographic studies of consumption and consumer practices are similarly varied. One thread enters by way of social and cultural analyses of material culture (Appadurai 1986; Miller 1998, 1998, 2001; Slater 1997) drawing on interests in the ways that objects and artifacts are invested with and manipulated for meaning, function, and power. Symbolic and linguistic anthropology (particularly semiotic analysis) together with interests in visual anthropology have had notable impact in consumer-focused work, particularly in their application to marketing, product design, and advertising. The reigning paradigm of research framed through psychologically oriented approaches in brand and marketing studies has recently been challenged, particularly in the face of globalization and broader awareness to the emergent nature of social forms. Anthropological thinking and interest in cultural analysis has both prompted and responded to this rethinking (Malefyt and Moeran 2003; Sunderland and Denny 2003, 2007).

While numerous theoretical, conceptual, and methodological dimensions are shared in common and underlie these dual threads of workplace and consumer studies, here I would like to call attention to two in particular: theories of practice and orientations to design. In many ways, the notion of "practice" forms the third leg of a stool, together with "ethnography" and "culture," upon which much of this work sits. Informed through trajectories ranging from attention to performance and self-presentation found in the symbolic interactionism of Erving Goffman (1956, 1961, 1967, 1974) to both Michel de Certeau's (1984) and Pierre Bourdieu's (1984, 1990) notions of everyday practice and *habitus*, theories of practice have provided ethnographers in industry a theoretically nuanced yet empirically resonant object of analysis by which to frame and ground their work. The notion of practice is used across consumer and workplace studies variously to index: the way objects and tools are used; descriptions of everyday performances of work and consumption; and the informal more generally, particularly distinctions between "processes," idealized types of practice envisioned through often overly linear branching and step-wise process diagrams, and practice, a notion reserved for the messy, non-linear, and varied way things unfold (Bishop et al. 1994). In the survey-saturated world of corporate enterprise, where people's perceptions are solicited through already constituted frames of understanding, attention to the messiness of what people do and the way things actually transpire as culturally informing and constituted continues to have significant impact.

Much work in the areas of end-user and consumer research has been done in the service of industrial and product (including interactive) design.[18] The ethnographic dimension brings with it a view to understanding users' — or potential users'[19] — situations of use, motivations, practices, and sociocultural contexts through ethnographic field studies and informed by a frame of interest somewhat broader (and sometimes deeper) than the immediacy of the kinds of user studies more commonly conducted in human-factors engineering, marketing, or usability studies. From early on, the participatory design movement, with its roots in Scandinavian trade union–backed efforts to prompt meaningful worker participation in dynamics affecting worker's lives and extended to other areas of community participation, influenced approaches undertaken in both organizational transformation and product design. Ethnographic researchers at PARC, for instance, worked hand-in-hand with potential users and designers of new technologies while the success of eLab built on the vision of its founders and practices encountered at the Doblin Group (another design consultancy) as to the potential of collaborations across different client and stakeholder groups. Many ethnographically informed workplace interventions dovetail with the original Scandinavian goals of worker empowerment, as evidenced, for example, in the work of the consulting firm Water Cooler Logic Inc. (see chapter 3) which grew out of the Institute for Research on Learning (IRL) and works to actively involve participants in all aspects of research design, execution, and implementation.

These varying areas of focus deriving from both workplace and consumer studies point to the range of roles occupied by corporate ethnographers. Many perform organizational work as advisors on corporate structure, work design, and day-to-day workplace operations working in the areas, for instance, of organizational development and management consulting. Often the work of anthropologists is as suppliers of insight on the consumers of the enterprises' products and services and is performed in conjunction with interactive and product designers, for example, or as market researchers. Each of the contributors to this volume has done work framed by either one or both of these foci and the cases discussed here reflect those efforts.

Socioeconomic Contexts

Socioeconomic dynamics of the last quarter of the twenty-first century reveal compelling indicators as to why anthropological and ethnographic consumer and workplace studies have gained visibility and help explain the rise of the new corporate ethnography. Technological developments together with changes in policy and practices governing labor structures and the organization of work have contributed to the ability to transform from mass production to both mass customization and niche-market production. Aided notably by the growth of the internet together with changes in regulation and trade, processes of supply and demand have dispersed globally in ever-dynamic ways, enabling new and expanding channels of development, dissemination, and commerce. Existing markets have both shrunk and expanded, and new markets have emerged. The inflection of varying "cultural" (for example, national, ethnic, sub-cultural) influences in networks of production and consumption has converged with identity marketing to focus attention on new culturally defined markets. Enterprises' awareness of their existing or potential global reach has more generally become an area of concern and attention. Developments internal to organizations, such as, for example, the increasing mobility and dispersion of labor forces, have also added to this awareness.

The internet boom and dot-com era fueled a hyper-orientation to the centricity of "the customer," now imagined to be able to access an ever-increasing array of products and services from which to fulfill their needs and desires and who thus possesses the power to be increasingly more selective and demanding in their consumption choices. Ethnography and the perspective of anthropological research has been positioned commercially as a powerful means of tapping into a better understanding of both these shifting labor markets and the "new" consumer. It is also seen as a route to more fully understand sociocultural market contexts in which consumers together with the organizations themselves intersect.

An example of this confluence between market dynamics and the promise of ethnographic work is in the area of experience marketing and design. The 1980s and 1990s were marked by appropriations of elite cultural styles, products, and services by the middle class and a mainstreaming of design. The notions of "experience marketing" and "experience design" arose in tandem with this shift, focusing attention less on the uniqueness of a particular product or service and more on the overall experience of the engagement a customer would have in procuring and consuming a product or service. Ethnographers were particularly drawn on here for their attention to process and change and to their perceived ability to tap into deeper underlying dimensions of even mundane experiences, a capability often mis-perceived as either a simple positivist viewing of "the real" or as an intuitive ability to see the un-seeable, thus eliding the anthropological frame of interpretation that asks how specific cultural meanings attach to and are embedded in social practices and structures that traverse time and place.

An additional socioeconomic dimension relevant to the rise of the new corporate ethnography is the increasing predominance of the services economy. Until recently, the prevailing engines of first world and global economies were the structures and processes of production, and the giants of economic agency, industrial and manufacturing companies. In contrast to systems of manufacturing, services depend on a more tightly bound interdependence between production and consumption. That which is generated emerges only by way of cooperation between producer and consumer and only through processes which unfold over (greater or lesser) durations of time. As was indicated in the rise of experience marketing, this, too, has lead to organizations' increased attention to processes of consumption and has refocused attention beyond the design of the product. Indeed, product sales are often driven by the services to which they provide access (consider, for example, how mobile phones are given away in order to get people to sign on to a particular cellular service). Moreover, the construction of work in services is highly performative and relational. As I have suggested elsewhere (Cefkin 2006), what is important is not just what people produce but how they do so; the customer is increasingly buying a set of ongoing relations and interactions through which service will be rendered. Interest in an anthropological take on this interactional space stems from the sense that an ethnographic sensibility can help to better understand and enhance this dynamic. This is evidenced most strongly, perhaps, in the interests of International Business Machines Co. (IBM). In 2003 IBM launched a new research group (which I joined in 2004), Almaden Services Research, explicitly focused on providing a deeper research-based understanding of services. This was prompted by the fact that by the mid 2000s more than half of IBM's revenue and employee base worldwide was based in services (for example, consulting, application management, and outsourcing). Unique in the history of IBM, the Almaden Services Research group has included social scientists whose work continues to focus on social-scientific understandings of work and organizations beyond the more narrowly directed attention to the construction and design of technical systems. This group includes anthropologists and others with ethnographic research expertise to provide examinations particularly suited for understanding the extenuated, collective, and co-constructed aspects of services. Recognizing the unique confluence of approaches needed to better understand the nature of services, Almaden Services Research has been at the forefront of helping drive the development of a new area of academic study known as Services Science Management and Engineering, or SSME (Maglio et al. 2006; Spohrer et al. 2007; Spohrer and Riecken 2006).

This growing focus on research on services comes on the heels of the proclaimed "new economy" of the late 1990s and early 2000s and suggests that the business sector has been going through a rethinking phase of its own, one particularly framed around notions of value. Reconsideration of the foundations and expressions of value has played out at the micro-level in the daily experiences of actors within corporate and organizational domains just as it has in the annals of the business press. In his ethnographic study of two new media companies over the cusp of the heights and initial fall of the dot-com era, Andrew Ross (2003) observed a scene that speaks to this rethinking in the New York offices of Razorfish (in which one of Ross's key informants herself held an advanced degree in anthropology). Triggered by the report of lowered customer satisfaction ratings, during an office meeting a heated discussion ensued. The debate volleyed between those who suggested that clients were failing to recognize the true value of their products (a stance held chiefly by designers), and those who argued that they must consider factors beyond their ability to provide the best or coolest designs (the stance held predominantly by strategists). The discussion quickly turned into a charged reflection, tagged by one of their members as a culture war of their own, on their own contested positions and relationships.

Such queries, worries, and hopes reflect a twinned set of questions emergent from a socioeconomic history that puts labor at the core of wealth production: What acts or occurrences add or create value and who are the agents of those acts? As Ross's illustration suggests, on the ground the debate unfolds something like this: Designers make the images and structures that form the interfaces directly perceptible to users through sight, touch, smell, or sound. Technologists bring these images into existence through writing code or manipulating materials. Undeniably, these people make things, leaving behind tangible instantiations of their labors. Strategists, planners, and researchers, however, suggest, prompt, promote, or refine ideas that underlie or support these instantiations, but they do not build things in the same sense. At some level their services are secondary to the production of things, raising questions of whether their labor creates value. And yet, whether something is worth bringing into existence to begin with, whether it is likely to have value to the user and/or the business, is something conceptualized or validated through strategy and research. Thus those engaged in these practices understand themselves to be producers as well, indeed often arguing that they are the true producers of *value* as opposed to just *things*.

The new economy was heralded as an era in which the fundamentals of business value were primed for reconfiguration. New descriptors—the "attention economy" (Davenport and Beck 2001), or the "experience economy" (Pine and Gilmore 1999)— were coined, modifying the nature of the economy. In the heyday of the dot-coms, revenues and profits were downplayed in the equation of value. Instead, "brand-equity," "mind-share," "intangible assets," and "social or intellectual capital" were touted as supplementing, if not actually replacing, the telos of revenue and profits. For instance, traditional accounting models built around discreet "outputs," and their consumption or purchase, were rethought in an effort to capture latent or potential value. New organizational designs, software code, brands, and ideas in development were recognized to have value even prior to their resulting in more revenue (if they ever they did) and formed key parts of firms' portfolios of intellectual property. The growth of the domain of "user experience," a significant area of work for corporate anthropologists (pointed to in the works of Flynn and Ortlieb in this volume), also arose hand-in-hand with this rethinking.

Arguing that the new economy has led to transformations, however uneven and unstable, Melissa Fisher and Greg Downey (2006: 4) have assembled a set of rich ethnographic examinations into the "mutually constituting relations between technology and social change, the cultural foundations of the economic 'material,' and the subtle ways that social relations affect business both at the helm as well as the frontiers of the New Economy." While all but disappeared from Wall Street discourse and from the pages of the business press, the new economy, if not a harbinger of the complete overthrow of business fundamentals, has produced symbolic and conceptual shifts that continue to give rise to new considerations of the means (if not the ends) of business and organizational existence.

The active inclusion of anthropologically informed work in business enterprise factors into these transformations. The contributions to this volume point to how the value of these efforts is understood by corporate ethnographers' business counterparts. They are also suggestive of where and how their efforts become embedded in business and organizational practices becoming part of a broader market dynamic. Critical examination of the practices and dynamics at play must be an ongoing part of the development of this emergent field of study.[20] There is a specific and continuing need to examine not only how the new corporate ethnography is being inscribed into the discourses and external positioning of the organizations and businesses the work supports, but how that inscribing in turn informs and shapes the work that is done.

Charged Engagements: What Are We Doing There?

The work of ethnographers in industry stands in interesting relation—in ways to be probed, clarified, and sharpened—to that of other anthropologists and ethnographers of contemporary sites of knowledge production and market processes. Surely the congresses of the European Union attended by Doug Holmes (1993), the Harvard-based string theorist interviewed by Mazyar Lotfalian (2004), and the movers and shakers of Wall Street and global trading firms as encountered by any number of anthropologists (Fisher 2006; Fisher and Downey 2006; Ho 2005; Knorr-Cetina and Preda 2005; Zaloom 2004, 2006) are every bit as powerful and provocative as the practicing corporate ethnographers' network-mediated global sales offices, off-shore software development cubicle farms, downtown-loft design firms, or high-security manufacturing plants. The stance of the corporate anthropologist/ethnographer, though, is unique in that it combines ethnographic examination with application; as practitioners, corporate anthropologists actively enter into and become accountable to the productive processes of the settings and subjects of their ethnographic work.

Underlying the contributors' examinations are questions of how they, as ethnographic researchers in corporate and organizational settings, are positioned within the contexts in which they operate.[21] With varying degrees of directness, the contributors all grapple with the question of what they are doing "there," what the commercial, political, and social functions of their being there are? These deceivingly simple questions are in fact inquires of multiple facets. While at times poignantly probed (chapter 6), the contributors avoid the kind of self-flagellating hindsight marked by the mea culpa tone sometimes found in the work of academic scholars who have ventured into such waters and then retreated to the presumably unsullied grounds of academia (Scaglion 2005). Nor do the contributors claim the stance of those whose applied work has been undertaken as a means of gaining access to or financing research intended primarily for an academic audience, an audience quite other than the sponsors and participants of the study. Rather, understanding that as with research of any kind their efforts may become implicated in interests and processes not fully of their making, the contributors, nonetheless, chose to act from within, pursuing ongoing and repeated participation in business and organizational settings as employees, contractors, and consultants.

In all areas of research, whether for primarily academic, policy, or commercial interests, issues of ethics abound. Ethical issues infuse every aspect of corporate ethnography as well, from the very constitution and formation of the research agenda to the nature of fieldwork encounters. Some of these questions take on a significantly different caste from those of their academic counterparts, others are entirely the same. Ethnographers in industry must contend with consideration of what happens when the participants engaged in their ethnographic forays and about whom they may gain potentially powerful and dangerous knowledge are also their coworkers? What happens when results and outcomes of the work lead to results that the ethnographer may desire as well as others that they don't (chapter 6)? And when their efforts and results are embedded in global systems of capitalism far beyond their ability to control?

I ask "What are we doing there?" neither to voice a sense of wonderment nor as a prelude to a defense of the work, but rather to push toward a deeper consideration of what comes of our being there. The authors provide insight into what actually goes on in the new corporate ethnography; that is, what they literally *do*—the kinds of problems they address, the effort and activity it involves, the people they work with, and the insights and results they produce. Brigitte Jordan (chapter 4), for example, offers a particularly descriptive example of the arc of a corporate research project focusing on chip-plant manufacturing operations. But more importantly, by exposing their work and their own queries and reflections, the authors open up the terrain in ways that allow us to begin to more fully explore varying affects of such work; to explore what impact it has on the people, thinking, and practices of those contexts, on understandings of contemporary capitalistic enterprise, and on disciplines of social and cultural inquiry. The authors grapple with their thinking in these areas in bits and pieces and through encounters with and examinations of specific nodes of organizational existence. We witness their efforts and struggles to convey different ways of thinking about meaning and knowledge construction, to draw attention of processes of human interaction, and to recognize and account for the impact of structural, ideological, and environmental factors on peoples' actions and beliefs and those of the institutions and organizations they inhabit. While Martin Ortlieb (chapter 7) explicitly examines renderings of the notion of culture by both anthropologists and their business collaborators, all the chapters bear witness to the ways in which the authors operate from a perspective consistent with an anthropological view of culture not as a "variable" but as "relational … elsewhere … in passage … where meaning is woven and renewed" (Fischer 2003: 7), as concerning difference, "but [where] the differences are no longer taxonomic; they are interactive and refractive" (Appadurai 1996: 60). Resonating with A. Aneesh's strong claim (and overly singular sense of what counts as engagement) that "disengagement is merely a form of unfavorable engagement" (2006: 96), the authors in this volume reveal a willingness to, if not a bias for, laboring to bring their thinking into the moments and contexts in which the organizations themselves operate. In these contexts, others may hold, and may hold dearly, views quite opposite those of the anthropologist (for instance, precisely the view that culture is something knowable and manageable, that it precisely is a variable that can be dialed up or toned down so as to sell more, work better, or add more to the bottom line).

That explorations of the social functions of ethnographic practitioners' roles and actions in business and organizational contexts underlie the examinations assembled here reflects an arena of practitioners' preoccupation and may well be indicative of the anxieties of early disciplinary formation. Indeed, this volume grew out of an effort to hold a dialogue across varying constructions of corporate ethnographic work. Held as a conference panel, the dialogue was meant to explore what can be learned from considerations and comparisons of work focused on consumers, with that focused on workplaces. While overlapping significantly in terms of practices, clients, working conditions, and the consultative nature of their work, workplace and consumer projects also raise some divergent practical and conceptual considerations and enable pursuit of somewhat differing sets of questions. As the organizer for this panel, I had envisioned a more modest examination of parameters and dimensions of these intersecting but not precisely identical arenas of work.[22]

It quickly became apparent, however, that the main preoccupation for panelists and audience members alike was not working out the similarities and differences in conceptualizing and engaging workplace and consumer studies, but in teasing out an understanding of what goes on vis-à-vis those through whom and with whom the work is conducted, the firms and organizations corporate ethnographers work in and for. The panel expanded from a focused comparison of the practitioners' ethnographies of consumer and employee practices and of workplace or market dynamics to a broader ethnographic exploration of the sites and conditions of ethnographic knowledge production in business and organizational domains.

Questions of positioning are sensitive at any time, but perhaps ever more so in the politically charged war-time climate of the 2000s, and in the context of a technologically saturated era where mobile, interpenetrating extrapolations and uses of information and surveillance prompt heightened concern about rights and obligations. This volume is being produced, indeed, just as anthropologists are debating anew the role and responsibilities of the anthropological community concerning the service of anthropologists in military efforts. Critical reflection on issues of positioning also emerge from the intellectual and methodological trajectories of anthropology's own history, echoing the project of disciplinary rethinking catapulted most famously in the 1980s by the publications of *Anthropology as Cultural Critique* (Marcus and Fischer 1986) and *Writing Culture* (Clifford and Marcus 1986). These pivotal works themselves grew out of a moment of heightened anthropological interest in the constructs of their own production, exposing, in the manner of Clifford Geertz (1973), the interpretive and textual nature of their endeavors and seeking to recognize the role of their interlocutors and silenced partners in the construction of those interpretations (Crapanzano 1981, 1990; Rabinow 1977). Indeed, one manifestation of tensions over issues of positioning has been the assertion of varying claims as to how to appropriately *name* anthropological engagements and the positions that anthropological investigators occupy vis-à-vis their research sites and communities. From the semiotically biased notion of "dialogue" (Crapanzano 1990; Dwyer and Muhammad 1982; Fischer and Abedi 1990; Maranhäo 1990; Tedlock and Mannheim 1995) to the politically potent notion of "complicity" (Marcus 1997), anthropologists and other field-based social science researchers have advanced various means of identifying the stance of the researcher/participant. Notions of advocacy (Fortun 2001; Rylko-Bauer, Singer et al. 2006), collaboration (Lassiter

2005; Schensul and Schensul 1992), participation (Darrouzet, Wild, and Wilkinson, chapter 3; Blomberg and Henderson 1990), and engagement (Eriksen 2006) figure prominently in these configurations.

In preparing for a grounded theory-based doctoral study of the organization in which she is employed, Lisa Kreeger, following Sandra Harding (1991), aptly notes, "As an insider to the larger business domain, a critical reading of what is going on can be seen as 'traitorous'" (2007: 19). Ethnographers in industry, I believe, must ask whether the particular set of conditions we work within suggests the potential for a different set of designators to speak of our positionality.[23] Anthropologists have both embraced and demonstrated anxiety toward hopes that by participating in powered social arenas in new ways, critically engaged researchers might advance much needed understanding and impact on challenges, both grand and subtle, facing the contemporary world (Fischer 2003, 2007; Gusterson 2006; Marcus and Fischer 1986; Strathern and Stewart 2005). Anthropologists of industry pursue their hopes of having a significant impact by working both inside and outside and collaboratively with others in organizations and enterprises fueling global socioeconomic dynamics. There as producers, designers, solution providers, advisers, and provocateurs, the efforts of corporate and organizational ethnographers are expected to be productive for those sites. They quite literally work *in* them and *for* them; they don't "just" study them. Reminding us of the perils of representing the always only partial understanding we gain in the field and the ethical dilemmas attendant to these choices, Françoise Brun-Cottan (chapter 6) articulates a concern evocative of the tight-rope that ethnographic practitioners' must navigate in these efforts:

> If we are to embody and advance our own discipline's evolution, there is an imperative need for us to maintain mindful vigilance regarding our principled placement between informants and employers. There is a risk in helping industry commodify results of ethnographic studies into goods and services. That risk is the commoditization of anthropology such that only immediately expedient methods signify. Increasingly the value of findings derived from fieldwork is acknowledged but there is a desire for us to leave the messiness of individuals and contexts—including the messiness of consequences for study participants and informants—in the field. I suggest that traveling further along those convenient oversights would be a loss for both industry and for anthropology.

Perils exist. Ethnography risks both exoticization and commoditization (Suchman 2000). The highly compelling and commercially expectant hope that ethnographers offer access to an unfettered truth, to "the real"—real people, real problems, real motivations—is a constant risk, a "success disaster," as Brun-Cottan so evocatively articulates. So too is the naturaliza-tion of ethnographic work such that, as Dawn Nafus and ken anderson have suggested, "our data and our representations of data produces a lin-earity of truth effects" that "down play much of the 'real' work that goes into producing an ethnographic representation" (2006: 249). Accounting for these challenges, understanding the work they do for *and* against the promise of the new corporate ethnography, is part of the work that must be done. By working at the heart of the complex, multi-disciplinary, tech-nologically, and conceptually advanced contexts that earlier helped give rise to the rethinking project of anthropology and the human sciences, eth-nographers in industry hold the promise of fulfilling demands for deeper engagement and impact.

Seeing and evaluating that impact may be perceived as a challenge as ethnographers in industry do not produce ethnography qua ethnography as their primary mode of production. George Marcus locates the ability of the ethnographer to reestablish their ethnographic authority, to bring forth their ethnographic positioning, in the writing of ethnography. "Only in the writing of ethnography, as an effect of a particular mode of publica-tion itself, is the privilege and authority of the anthropologist unambigu-ously assumed" (1995: 97). Corporate ethnographers, on the other hand, are more likely to produce ethnographically sensitive "deliverables" framed not only by their interests in richly exposing and representing the cultural dynamics and social actors pertaining to their focus of study, but also by concern for the interpretation and use of such research, whether in the form of recommendations, concept designs, requirements, critiques, or assessments.[24] As Robinson notes, "In applied work … we don't just reconcile our conceptualizations to the 'facts' or the observations we've made, but we must reconcile the models that we build or employ with the models of the people or institutions on whose behalf we are doing this investigation" (2005: 4). Nafus and anderson (chapter 5) offer a nuanced examination of efforts to promote this reconciliation in practice. Rather than focus on the authoritative representations of knowledge contained in final works (reports and other deliverables), they instead explore how cer-tain kinds of knowledge are co-produced with other (non-social scientist) business counterparts (here, namely designers) along the way.

These reconciliations and negotiations happen, as Robinson reminds us, from particular spaces. Michael Fischer's evocations around ethnographic encounters as happening within and opening up a "third space between the desires of empire (of control) and the defense of the oppressed" (2003: 8) is suggestive of the promise the new corporate ethnography may hold in reformulating ethnographic if not anthropological praxis. Grappling with such a "third space," Donna Flynn's exploration (chapter 2) of the "political economy of design" reveals how the collaborations that practicing ethnographers participate in become a lens for understanding how the objects of their collaborative productive efforts become "products of corporate contestation" within "landscapes of production." Resonating optimistically with the potentiality of such efforts, Fischer claims that "anthropology's challenge is to develop translation and mediation tools for helping make visible the difference of interests, access, power, needs, desire, and philosophical perspective" (2003: 3). As Flynn's work and that of the other contributors to this volume suggest, this call for the active mobilization of ethnographic insight across boundaries and audiences dovetails squarely with the space of work of the corporate anthropologist. Indeed, the aim of producing "translation and mediation tools" to help make differences visible might just as well have been the desire expressed by the business-counterparts with whom corporate ethnographers' engage. It is in this space that the new corporate ethnography promises a new footing.

The New Corporate Ethnography

The chapters which follow provide readers a view onto unique realms of research, original insights on corporate and organizational life, and renewed considerations of the negotiation of anthropological relations and knowledge. The core topics of concern for this volume are to expose anew questions of how ethnographers are positioned in their contexts of work and to open up consideration of the opportunities and quandaries the emerging field of corporate ethnography illuminates for traditions of critical cultural analysis. These questions underlie and cut across each of the chapters below. Students and academia-based cultural analysts desiring to gain insight into how the new corporate ethnography is performed and what it looks like may wish to pay particular attention to chapters 3 and 4, both of which offer rich descriptions of differing approaches to ethnographic work in organizational contexts. Non-anthropologists, including the general business reader, may find chapters 2 and 7 especially valuable in introducing them to underlying perspectives and concepts such as the notion of culture and conceptions of expertise core to anthropological ways of knowing. Readers may also find particular interest in the specific topics the cases expose—from computer documentation (chapter 2), healthcare operations (chapter 3), global chip manufacturing (chapter 4), and website strategy and design (chapter 7) to concepts and theories of complexity (chapter 3), memory and materiality (chapter 5), recipient design (chapter 6), and culture (chapter 7).

Specifically, the remainder of this volume is organized into five sections. The next four sections, made up of contributions by key practitioners of anthropologically and ethnographically informed work in enterprise settings, explore a range of organizational sites and practices and provide insight into how researchers who have worked as commissioned producers of ethnographically derived insights, problem solving, and advice giving for businesses and other organizations encounter and engage these sites of organizational practice. The first section, "Encounters with Corporate Epistemologies," introduces the reader to how anthropologists' ways of knowing intersect with some of the dominant epistemologies within the corporate terrains of their work. In chapter 2, "'My Customers are Different!': Identity, Difference, and the Political Economy of Design," Flynn works from a particular workplace interaction to a broader examination of the political economy of production. Her launching point is a story of trying to get her ethnographically produced and anthropologically informed results regarding the use of product documentation by particular sets of users adopted by affiliate colleagues at Microsoft. Reminiscent of the "Do artifacts have politics?" debate in social studies of science and technology (Joerges 1999; Latour 2004; Pfaffenberger 1992; Winner 1980), Flynn exposes the (often-implicit) debates and negotiations around kinds of expertise—insider-outsider, user-observer, designer-researcher, engineer-anthropologist—that underlie and become embodied by the things that get produced. Moving beyond consideration of the politics inherent in producer-consumer relations, Flynn examines the politically charged dynamics among and between producers through sensitive attention to the ways in which varying positionalities, including that of the ethnographer, play out on the ground. She argues that "[t]he shape of collaborations—flavored by constructs of identity within the corporate entity, rules and patterns of interaction, and individual and group competitions over resources—thus becomes a potent lens for understanding how the things that we are building become products of corporate contestations."

The second section, "Doing Anthropology in Corporate Contexts," consists of two chapters which pay particular attention to ways of performing ethnographic engagements in organizational settings and to the work anthropologists' perform in organizational environments. In chapter 3, "Participatory Ethnography at Work: Practicing in the Puzzle Palaces of a Large, Complex Healthcare Organization," Darrouzet, Wild, and Wilkinson describe their multi-year engagement with the Veterans Health Administration (VA) in the United States as anthropological consultants who offer a highly participatory approach to organizational interventions. Focusing on a particular project concerning bed control and patient discharge, they reveal a rich and complex terrain in which participants in those settings aim to "puzzle out" an understanding of their organizational context and the actions and shifting meanings of themselves and others within it. Framing their exploration through notions of complexity, the authors depict how they apply their particular ethnographically informed approach to dealing with and even recognizing benefit from the instability and indeterminability of the context. Their work, they suggest, helps move the puzzling-out that people are always already doing (and which they reveal through a multi-perspectival, Rashamon-effect view of how individuals occupying different subject positions and roles view the work of bed control and patient discharge) into a socially and dialogically mediated forum.

In chapter 4, "Working in Corporate Jungles," Jordan takes readers on a journey to Intel's chip-manufacturing factories in Costa Rica and Malaysia and then follows the course of the project, from early discussions with the corporate stakeholders through rounds of fieldwork (first by Jordan alone, and then together with her collaborator, Monique Lambert) through to analysis and examination of particular facets of how the plants function. Through a fascinating focus on the unit of the "lot" as a particular assemblage and vehicle for transporting product, Jordan provides a view as to how particular units of examination and analysis can frame particularly productive inquires. Jordan pays particular attention to the form ethnographic research takes in such applied, corporate contexts and provides a welcome description of just what this kind of work (particularly of the workplace variety) can entail and the challenges it raises.

The third section, "Refractions of Anthropological Ways of Being and Knowing," includes two chapters that reveal the authors' confrontations with the foundational perspectives and motivations of ethnographic practice refracted through their encounters with other ways of knowing and being. In chapter 5, "Writing on Walls: The Materiality of Social Memory in Corporate Research," Nafus and anderson offer a sensitive and detailed portrayal of a particular kind of ethnographic knowledge production used in organizational settings. They look at the practice of externalizing and inscribing research "datum" onto various visual forms, describing, quite literally, "writing on walls." They offer a self-reflective examination of their own process of grappling with how to make sense of the effect of exposing photographs, maps, and various forms of words and captured utterances (namely, quotes from research participants, summary notions of the researcher, emergent themes) on physical displays. They consider the embodied space of the performance of anthropological work in corporate settings, settings where the authority of the work cannot lie simply with reporting findings (however critical and provocative) but must instead be advanced through ongoing acts of production. By way of this examination, they reflect on the discursive orthodoxies of their own anthropological backgrounds as revealed through encounters with business counterparts whose conceptions of what counts as valuable differs significantly from their own.

Drawing on principles of interaction, Brun-Cottan in chapter 6, "The Anthropologist as Ontological Choreographer," recounts poignant stories of fieldwork in workplace settings to expose the difficulties not only of coming to an understanding of the motivations and personhood of those encountered in the doing of the work, but of knowing how to account for those selves in the context of multiple and conflicting interests. Brun-Cottan presents her concern less as challenge brought on by the particular commercial and organizational contexts of this work, recognizing but not dwelling on the limitations imposed by the contexts of work (she remarks, "it is unfortunate that these accounts tend not to conform to bulleted items and decision trees") and more as a provocation to practitioners themselves to continue to bring forward the grounded basis of the work and the subtleties and richness of ethnographic insight ("we must agitate!").

In the fourth section, "Culture and Corporate Epistemologies," we return to the question of how the cultural analyst encounters competing frames of reference and other ways of knowing common to corporate environments. Chapter 7, Ortlieb's "Emergent Culture, Slippery Culture: Conflicting Conceptualizations of Culture in Commercial Ethnography," examines how the notion of culture is conceptualized in business environments where ethnographers commonly intersect. He posits that many actors in business settings conceive of culture as, however difficult to pin down ("slippery"), ontologically grounded and fixed. This is a view upheld by treatments of the notion of culture common to organizational studies. Many corporate anthropologists and ethnographers, on the other hand, reject such inclinations to reify what is essentially an abstraction, holding instead a view of culture as "emergent." His upbeat assessment is that businesses are beginning to see and value this emergent view, in part due to the translation and interpretation efforts of their resident anthropologists and in part due to the exigencies they face as they operate across increasingly multi-local and globalized settings. While Ortlieb's efforts to illustrate these shifts themselves itself runs the risk of becoming subject to new forms of essentializing (for example, "the global" as a difficult to pin down but ultimately identifiable entity), he puts his finger on the pulse of a key dynamic underlying the current interest in ethnographic work in industry and his contribution illuminates the kinds of significant issues at stake in the emerging canon of the new corporate ethnography.

Readers will undoubtedly find additional areas of overlap and intersection, as well as unique insight and provocation, among these six chapters. In the fifth and final section of the volume, "Another Look: Commentaries from Corporate Research and the Academy," two commentators provide their own interpretations of the emergence of the new corporate ethnography as read through the contributions here. In this section, the opportunities and challenges raised in the prior sections are considered from two distinct vantage points—corporate research and the academy—each with its own stake in and relevance to the issues at hand. Underlying this book are questions of how anthropologists and others working from interpretive social-scientific, specifically ethnographically informed, perspectives are located in the contexts in which they operate. The two commentators consider how they are located in broader social and intellectual arenas, considering and engaging the opportunities and challenges raised in the chapters taken as a whole. In chapter 8, "Insider Trading: Engaging and Valuing Corporate Ethnography," Blomberg clearly writes from the inside, from the perspective of someone long participating in and confronted by the sites, dynamics, and quandaries illuminated by the contributors. Pushing and pulling on themes addressed in the introduction as well as the prior chapters, she focuses on the question of how the efforts of corporate ethnographers should be read and valued. Writing as an academically based anthropologist, Fischer, in chapter 9, "Emergent Forms of Life in Corporate Arenas," pans out further, offering an engaging romp, or as he suggests, a hyperlinked set of "pop ups" and animations, of connections he sees between the space of the new corporate ethnography and concerns and interests of other areas of social and cultural study. Appearing to read the pieces as much as ethnographic data of their own as for the questions raised and arguments formulated by the authors, Fischer's meta-ethnographic take on the space of the new corporate ethnography thus provides a fitting end-point to this exploration of the emergent space of ethnography in and of industry by pointing not to closures, but to the new openings it promises.

Signaled by recent convergences of interest and activity in the area of ethnographic work *in* business and organizational contexts, *of* their actions and reach, and *for* their consideration and use, the new corporate ethnography creates an opportunity to identify new cultural understandings. The contributions to this volume offer rich and provocative glimpses of some of these new cultural understandings. Specifically, however, this volume is dedicated to the view that as this field continues to grow and develop it is imperative that practitioners in this domain together with their interlocutors identify and address questions of where it is going and what it produces. Questions of the nature of anthropological relations resulting from the corporate encounter and of the social functions performed by this work remain at the core of that questioning. It is into that core that this work proceeds.

Acknowledgments

Writing is a remarkably social act, no matter how isolated and singular the author's own inscriptions emerge. This is perhaps particularly so for a work that covers the scope of a terrain as wide, broad, and fluid as this one. For their influences and traces in this work I happily owe a debt of thanks to a great many people. The anonymous reviewer provided not only insightful comments but clear suggestions for improvement as well. I completed this effort while at IBM Research and I thank the organization and particularly my colleagues there for their support and patience as I cajoled this project into being. I have had the great fortune to work under the leadership of some of the known luminaries of anthropology and of this emerging domain—Maria Bezaitis, Jeanette Blomberg, Michael Fischer, Brigitte Jordan, George Marcus, Patricia Sachs, Rick Robinson, and Marilyn Whalen—and from them I have gained enormously, both in ideas and in friendship. It has been my honor to have worked alongside and learned from a great number of inspiring colleagues. I regret only that they are too many to list here. My thanks go out particularly to each of the contributors to this volume, to Rick Robinson for conversations in the early formulation of this volume, and to Lisa Kreeger and Melissa Fisher for enriching and enlivening this journey. My deepest gratitude goes to Mazyar Lotfalian, who has sustained me and challenged me as I encountered the joys and confusions encountered along the many pathways of these efforts.

Notes

1. Anthrodesign grew out of email communications among practitioners following a 2002 panel at the American Anthropological Association meeting. The panel was organized by Natalie Hanson, who also established and moderates the group. In a message to the listserv several years into the establishment of the group, Hanson reflected that the list has served as a bridge between those who had been doing this kind of research for years, and "newbies like myself that were learning 'our' institutional history and trajectory through the telling of stories." (Hanson 2006)

2. The list of strategy, marketing, design, and consulting firms professing an orientation informed by ethnographic if not anthropological principles and/or some degree of ethnographic expertise is extensive and constantly shifting. Neither is this development limited to the United States—firms can be found notably in the UK and Denmark, as well as Canada, Mexico, Spain, Japan, and elsewhere.

3. While several indicators to practices and developments outside the United States are included throughout the volume, the perspective of the authors remains largely, though not exclusively, US-centric. A counterpart examination from other parts of the world would be most welcome.

4. The questions of who "counts" in this designation is emblematic of the multi-disciplinary and shifting nature of this emerging domain, as practitioners prepared in ethnographic research may come out of disciplines other than anthropology or sociology and often combine ethnographic methods with other forms of research and analysis. These numbers were provided by trained anthropological practitioners in these settings according to the standards they use in naming their capabilities.

5. Two books, Lucy Suchman's *Plans and Situated Actions* (1987) and Julian Orr's *Talking About Machines* (1996), represent defining theoretical and ethnographic explorations in the arenas of work-practice studies.

6. eLab was a research and design planning consultancy founded by Rick Robinson, a University of Chicago PhD social scientist, together with the designer John Cain and another former business partner, Mary McCarthy. Robinson had designed a unique program of study at the University of Chicago, working closely with the psychologist Mihaly Csikszentmihalyi to apply thinking from anthropology and cultural theory to issues of creativity (see, for instance, Robinson and Hackett 1997). eLab "develop[ed] theories and methodologies to understand meaningful behavior patterns" (Robinson and Hackett 1997: 11) by employing ethnographic research and design principles to understanding and innovation. Robinson, Cain, and their colleagues over the years at the Doblin Group, eLab, and Sapient contributed considerably to the development of current norms and forms of ethnographically oriented strategy and design consulting.

7. John Seely Brown, who became Xerox's chief scientist, created the vision for IRL, while George Pake, the retired first director of PARC, served as its inaugural director. The anthropologist Brigitte Jordan, who pioneered the use of interactive (collaborative) video analysis labs as a key mode of ethnographic data analysis while a professor at Michigan State University and with whom Lucy Suchman began to work while a graduate student early in her time at PARC, was a lead researcher in the area of workplace studies and maintained a joint appointment between PARC and IRL. Over the years, several other researchers spent time at both of organizations.

8. Wayne State has offered its business concentration in anthropology since 1985. The program was founded by Marietta Baba, who went on to become the dean of social sciences at Michigan State University, and at the time of publication is directed by Allen Batteau. The program focuses on cultural dimensions of global business and industry and its faculty members continue to do research in a wide range of corporate and industrial settings.

9. The program at San Jose State University is designed to prepare graduates as practitioners and is organized around particular skill (for example, ethnographic research, evaluation, program planning) and content (healthcare, business and industry, immigration services) areas. Two of the program's lead faculty, Charles Darrah and Jan English-Lueck have been involved in a long-term ethnographic study of families in the region, known as the Silicon Valley Cultures Project.

10. Anthropology at the University of North Texas is an applied department with a specialization in business anthropology. Faculty includes Ann Jordan and Christina Wasson, who focus on both organizational culture and change as well as consumer studies, user-centered design, and human-computer interaction, globalization, and communication.

11. The sociologist Nina Wakeford established the Incubator for the Critical Inquiry into Technology and Ethnography (INCITE) in 2001. INCITE's highly experimental and experiential work focuses on "social research of new technologies, particularly from an analytically critical or skeptical perspective" (Wakeford 2003: 229) with the aim to create "interprofessional hyperlinks" (234) with designers, technologists, other researchers, and government and corporate stakeholders. For a fuller treatment of INCITE's back-

ground, focus, and work, see Wakeford's "Research Note: Working with New Media's Cultural Intermediaries" (2003).

12. The dean of the social sciences, Marietta Baba (PhD, Wayne State University), is also affiliated with the Eli Broad College of Business at Michigan State University. Dr. John Sherry (PhD, University of Illinois, Urbana-Champagne) is a professor of marketing at the Mendoza College of Business at Notre Dame University. Brian Moeran (PhD, SOAS, University of London) is the Director of the Creative Encounters Research Program and on faculty at the Copenhagen Business School.

13. David Hakken (PhD, The American University) is a professor of infomatics at Indiana University and Bonnie Nardi (PhD, University of California at Irvine) is professor of informatics at UC Irvine.

14. Jamer Hunt (PhD, Rice University) was a faculty member and director of the industrial design program at the University of the Arts in Philadelphia before becoming director of interdisciplinary graduate initiatives and associate professor of design at Parsons: The New School for Design. Elizabeth (Dori) Tunstall is in the School of Art and Design at the University of Illinois at Chicago.

15. EPIC was conceived by ken anderson at Intel and Tracey Lovejoy at Microsoft with input and support from a number of other leaders of this domain. An international, peer-reviewed conference, the forum brings together social scientists, computer scientists, designers, marketers, and academics to discuss recent developments and future advances in ethnographic research in and for corporations. The conference is sponsored through the National Association of Practicing Anthropology (NAPA) and American Anthropological Association (AAA), and receives financial sponsorship from numerous large and small companies. Proceedings (anderson and Lovejoy 2005, 2006; Cefkin and anderson 2007; Cefkin and Cotton 2008) are published through the American Anthropological Association and available through AnthroSource (www.anthrosource .net).

16. Focus on workplaces or consumers can (but doesn't necessarily) suggest differing analytical frames (for example, organizational structures or consumption practices) and can require differing practical considerations for conducting studies (for example, different ways of accessing participants or differences in the applicability of popular culture as a source of research) and is not a matter of categorical or always clearly delineated differences. One operative, albeit imperfect, definitional contrast is between workplaces as sites where the focus of the research concerns participants acting for and from within organizational boundaries and studies of consumption and market practices where the actors are viewed primarily as consumers outside the institutional confines of the invested parties. From the point of view of the organizations requesting the work, it is often simply a difference of research focused internally on their employees and organization, or externally on the customers and/or potential end-users of their products and services.

17. See June Nash's article (1998) and others in *The Anthropology of Work Review* for a critical appraisal of work in this area.

18. Christina Wasson (2000) provides a useful review of the taking-up of ethnographic work, specifically in the field of design circa 2000.

19. The notion of "user" is a highly contested one as it predefines people's subject positioning as always already in reference to product or technology. Debates about appropriate terminology are frequent. Nonetheless, it remains the most broadly used shorthand to designate people of interest in relationship to the studies under question.

20. Lessons should be learned from the analyses of how anthropological discourse is taken up and deployed by development and environmental organizations. For example, Paige

West offers a nuanced and penetrating analysis of how anthropological terms and rhetoric are co-opted by an environmental NGO in Papua New Guinea in order to make a case for the indigenous populations as a "threat" to the environment. Her argument goes beyond these points, moreover, to show how this co-optation in turn impacted her own ethnographic inquiry (2005).

21. Andrew Strathern and Pamela Stewart (2005) pose questions of positioning as concerns anthropologists acting as consultants in the context of development projects. Focusing a lens on the position of these anthropologists vis-à-vis their academic contexts, they provide useful insight into professional concerns—particularly regarding constraints on publishing—faced by academic researchers who engage in consultancy work. While contributors to the present volume do not address these concerns directly, their work is suggestive of the new, emergent forms of ethnographic writing that are arising in response to internal and external audiences.

22. The session took place at the Society for Applied Anthropology annual conference in 2005. I organized and chaired the two-part panel entitled "Workplace and Consumer Studies: A Dialogue." Additional presenters in this session included: Jeanette Blomberg, Francoise Brun-Cottan, Melissa Fisher, Donna Flynn, Natalie Hanson, Brigitte Jordan, Martin Ortlieb, Rick Robinson, Patricia Sacks, Ari Shapiro, and Elizabeth Tunstall.

23. It is worth noting that the term *practicing*, as an identifier for much of this kind of work (the term defaulted to here and one adopted by the sub-section of the American Anthropological Association, the National Association for Practicing Anthropology, or NAPA), focuses on extra-academic applications of anthropological work. Like the more long-standing term *applied*, however, it does little to distinguish the activity of those engaged in this arena from others and is unavoidably tautological—what anthropologist doesn't practice their anthropology?

24. A significant, if largely unrecognized, form of knowledge production among practitioners are project reports (see, for example, Aronson et al. 1995; Bishop et al. 1994; Brun-Cottan et al. 1991). In many ways project reports are more liberated in form and function from that of a primarily academic text and many increasingly take the form of a combination of written report and multi-media format, offering a vibrant arena for experimentation with forms of knowledge production and expression. Resonating with terrain explored by Nafus and anderson in this volume, Sunderland and Denny (2007) offer significant insight into the construction of such reports and the intellectual work they are designed to effect in the corporate context.

References

anderson, ken, and Tracey Lovejoy. 2005. *Ethnographic Praxis in Industry Conference Proceedings*. Ethnographic Praxis in Industry Conference, Seattle, WA. American Anthropological Association.

———. 2006. *Ethnographic Praxis in Industry Conference Proceedings*. Ethnographic Praxis in Industry Conference, Portland, OR. American Anthropological Association.

Aneesh, A. 2006. *Virtual Migration: The Programming of Globalization*. Durham, NC: Duke University Press.

Appadurai, Arjun. 1986. *The Social Life of Things: Commodities in Cultural Perspective*. Cambridge/New York: Cambridge University Press.

———. 1996. *Modernity at Large*. Minneapolis, MN: University of Minnesota Press.

Aronson, Meredith, et al. 1995. "Reflections on a Journey of Transformation: Learning, Growth, and Change at Xerox Business Services." IRL/XBS Systemic Assessment Project, Final Report. *Technical Reports*. Palo Alto, CA: Institute for Research on Learning.

Baba, Marietta L. 1988. "Anthropological Research in Major Corporations: Work Products of the Industrial Domain." *Central Issues in Anthropology* 7(2): 1–17.

———. 1991. "The Skill Requirements of Work Activity: An Ethnographic Perspective." *Anthropology of Work Review* 12(3): 2–11.

———. 1998. "The Anthropology of Work in the Fortune 1000: A Critical Retrospective." *Anthropology of Work Review* 18(4): 17–28.

———. 2005. "To The End Of Theory-Practice 'Apartheid': Encountering The World." *Ethnographic Praxis in Industry Conference Proceedings*, 205–17. American Anthropological Association.

———. 2006. "Anthropology and Business." In *Encyclopedia of Anthropology*, Birx, ed., 83–117. Thousand Oaks, CA: Sage Publications.

Barley, Stephen R., and Gideon Kunda. 2004. *Gurus, Hired Guns, and Warm Bodies: Itinerant Experts in a Knowledge Economy*. Princeton, NJ: Princeton University Press.

Barley, Stephen R., and Julian E. Orr. 1997. *Between Craft and Science: Technical Work in U.S. Settings*. Ithaca, NY: IRL Press.

Batteau, Allen. 2000. "Negotiations and Ambiguities in the Cultures of Organization." *American Anthropologist* 102(4): 726–40.

Bell, Genevieve. 2006. "No More SME from Jesus: Ubicomp, Religion and Techno-spiritual Practices." *Ubicomp Conference Proceedings*, 141–158. Springer-Verlag Berlin.

Bell, Genevieve, Mark Blythe, and Phoebe Sengers. 2005. "Making by Making Strange: Defamiliarization and the Design of Domestic Technologies." *ACM Transactions on Computer-Human Interaction* 12(2): 149–73.

Bennett, Linda, et al. 2006. Final Report: Practicing Advisory Work Group (PAWG). American Anthropological Association.

Bishop, Libby, et al. 1994. "A Learning Organization in the Making: A Report on the Work-Practice and Design Project at the Xerox CAC in Dallas." *Technical Report*. Palo Alto, CA: Institute for Research on Learning.

Blomberg, Jeanette. 2005. "The Coming Of Age Of Hybrids: Notes On Ethnographic Praxis." *Ethnographic Praxis in Industry Conference Proceedings*, 67–74. American Anthropological Association.

Blomberg, Jeanette, and Austin Henderson. 1990. "Reflections on Participatory Design: Lessons from the Trillium Project." *Proceedings of CHI '90 Human Factors in Computing*, 353–359. Association for Computing Machinery (ACM).

Blomberg, Jeanette, Mark Burrell, and Greg Guest. 2003. "An Ethnographic Approach to Design." In *Human-Computer Interaction Handbook: Fundamental, Evolving Technologies and Emerging Applications*, Sears and Jacko, eds., 965–84. Philadelphia, PA: Lawrence Erlbaum Associates.

Blomberg, Jeanette, Lucy Suchman, and Randy Trigg. 1996. "Reflections on a Work-Oriented Design Project." *Human-Computer Interaction* 11(3): 237–65.

———. 1997. "Back to Work: Renewing Old Agendas for Change." In *Computers and Design in Context*, Mathiassen, ed., 201–38. Cambridge, MA: MIT Press.

Bourdieu, Pierre. 1984. *Distinction: A Social Critique of the Judgement of Taste*. Cambridge, MA: Harvard University Press.

———. 1990. *The Logic of Practice*. Stanford, CA: Stanford University Press.

Brun-Cottan, Françoise, et al. 1991. "The Workplace Project: Designing for Diversity and Change" (videotape). Palo Alto, CA: Palo Alto Research Center (PARC).

Casey, Catherine. 1995. *Work, Self, and Society: After Industrialism.* London/New York: Routledge.

Cefkin, Melissa. 2006. "Cultural Transitions—WWMD? Ethical Impulses and the Project of Ethnography in Industry." *Ethnographic Praxis in Industry Conference Proceedings,* 166–176. American Anthropological Association.

———. 2007. "Numbers may Speak Louder than Words, but is Anybody Listening? Rhythms of Sales Pipeline Management." *Ethnographic Praxis in Industry Conference Proceedings,* 187–199. American Anthropological Association.

Cefkin, Melissa, and ken anderson. 2007. *Ethnographic Praxis in Industry Conference Proceedings.* Ethnographic Praxis in Industry Conference, Keystone, CO. American Anthropological Association.

Cefkin, Melissa, Jakita O. Thomas, and Jeanette Blomberg. 2007. "The Implications of Enterprise-wide Pipeline Management Tools for Organizational Relations and Exchanges." *Proceedings of GROUP '07,* Sanibel Island, FL. 61–68. Association for Computing Machinery (ACM).

Cefkin, Melissa, and Martha Cotton. 2008. *Ethnographic Praxis in Industry Conference Proceedings.* Ethnographic Praxis in Industry Conference, Copenhagen, Denmark. American Anthropological Association.

Certeau, Michel de. 1984. *The Practice of Everyday Life.* Berkeley, CA: University of California Press.

Clifford, James, and George E. Marcus. 1986. *Writing Culture: The Poetics and Politics of Ethnography.* Berkeley, CA: University of California Press.

Crabtree, Andy. 2003. *Designing Collaborative Systems: A Practical Guide to Ethnography.* London/New York: Springer.

Crapanzano, Vincent. 1981. *The Hamadsha.* Berkeley, CA: University of California Press.

———. 1990. "On Dialogue." In *The Interpretation of Dialogue,* Maranhao, ed., 269–91. Chicago, IL/London, University of Chicago Press.

Darr, Asaf. 2006. *Selling Technology: The Changing Shape of Sales in an Information Economy.* Ithaca, NY: Cornell University Press.

Darrah, Charles N. 1996. *Learning and Work: An Exploration in Industrial Ethnography.* New York: Garland Publishing.

Darrah, Charles N., James M. Freeman, and J. A. English-Lueck. 2007. *Busier Than Ever! Why American Families Can't Slow Down.* Stanford, CA: Stanford University Press.

Davenport, Thomas H., and John C. Beck. 2001. *The Attention Economy: Understanding the New Currency of Business.* Boston, MA: Harvard Business School Press.

Downey, Greg, and Melissa Fisher. 2006. "Introduction: The Anthropology of Capital and the Frontiers of Ethnography." In *Frontiers of Capital: Ethnographic Reflections on the New Economy,* Fisher and Downey, eds., 1–30. Durham, NC/London: Duke University Press.

Dubinskas, Frank A. 1988. *Making Time: Ethnographies of High-Technology Organizations.* Philadelphia, PA: Temple University Press.

Dwyer, Kevin, and Faqir Muhammad. 1982. *Moroccan Dialogues: Anthropology in Question.* Baltimore, Johns Hopkins University Press.

English-Lueck, Jan. A. 2002. *Cultures@Silicon Valley.* Stanford, Calif., Stanford University Press.

Eriksen, Thomas Hylland. 2006. *Engaging Anthropology: The Case for a Public Presence.* Oxford/New York: Berg.

Fischer, Michael M. J. 2003. *Emergent Forms of Life and the Anthropological Voice.* Durham, NC: Duke University Press.

———. 2007. "Culture and Cultural Analysis as Experimental Systems." *Cultural Anthropology* 22(1): 1–65.

Fischer, Michael M. J., and Mehdi Abedi. 1990. *Debating Muslims: Cultural Dialogues in Postmodernity and Tradition*. Madison, WI: University of Wisconsin Press.

Fisher, Melissa. 2006. "Navigating Wall Street Women's Gendered Networks in the New Economy." In *Frontiers of Capital*, Fisher and Downey, eds. 209–36.

Fisher, Melissa S., and Greg Downey, eds. 2006. *Frontiers of Capital: Ethnographic Perspectives of the New Economy*. Durham, NC/London: Duke University Press.

Fitzgerald, Michael. 2006. "Intel's Hiring Spree." In *Technology Review*. Cambridge, MA: Massachusetts Institute of Technology.

Forsythe, Diana, and David J. Hess. 2001. *Studying Those Who Study Us: An Anthropologist in the World of Artificial Intelligence*. Stanford, CA: Stanford University Press.

Fortun, Kim. 2001. *Advocacy after Bhopal: Environmentalism, Disaster, New Global Orders*. Chicago, IL: University of Chicago Press.

Garsten, Christina. 1994. "Apple World: Core and Periphery in a Transnational Organizational Culture," x, 250. Stockholm: Stockholm University, Department of Social Anthropology.

Garsten, Christina, and Helena Wulff. 2003. *New Technologies at Work: People, Screens, and Social Virtuality*. Oxford/New York: Berg.

Geertz, Clifford. 1973. *The Interpretation of Cultures*. New York: Basic Books.

Goffman, Erving. 1956. *The Presentation of Self in Everyday Life*. Edinburgh: University of Edinburgh, Social Sciences Research Centre.

———. 1961. *Encounters: Two Studies in the Sociology of Interaction*. Indianapolis, IN: Bobbs-Merrill.

———. 1967. *Interaction Ritual: Essays in Face-to-Face Behavior*. Chicago, IL: Aldine Publishing Co.

———. 1974. *Frame Analysis: An Essay on the Organization of Experience*. New York: Harper & Row.

Gusterson, Hugh. 2006. "Where Are We Going? Engaging Dilemmas in Practicing Anthropology." *Anthropology News* 47(5): 26–26.

Hakken, David. 1999. *Cyborgs@cyberspace? An Ethnographer Looks to the Future*. New York: Routledge.

———. 2003. *The Knowledge Landscapes of Cyberspace*. New York: Routledge.

Hakken, David, and Barbara Andrews. 1993. *Computing Myths, Class Realities: An Ethnography of Technology and Working People in Sheffield, England*. Boulder, CO: Westview Press.

Hamada, Tomoko. 2000. "Anthropological Praxis: Theory of Business Organization." *National Association for the Practice of Anthropology Bulletin* 18(1): 79–103.

Hamada, Tomoko, and Willis E. Sibley. 1994. *Anthropological Perspectives on Organizational Culture*. Lanham, MD: University Press of America.

Hanson, Natalie. 2006. Email to Anthrodesign (anthrodesign@yahoogroups.com).

Harding, Sandra. 1991. *Whose Science? Whose Knowledge? Thinking from Women's Lives*. Ithaca, NY: Cornell University Press.

Heath, Christian, and Paul Luff. 2000. *Technology in Action*. Cambridge/New York: Cambridge University Press.

Ho, Karen. 2005. "Situating Global Capitalisms: A View from Wall Street Investment Banks." *Cultural Anthropology* 20(1): 68–96.

Holmes, Douglas R. 1993. "Illicit Discourse." In *Perilous States: Conversations on Culture, Politics, and Nation*, Marcus, ed., 255–81. Chicago, IL/London: University of Chicago Press.

Holmes, Douglas R., and George E. Marcus. 2006. "Fast-Capitalism: Para-ethnography and the Rise of the Symbolic Analyst." In *Frontiers of Capital*, Fisher and Downey, eds., 33–57.

Joerges, Bernward. 1999. "Do Politics Have Artefacts?" *Social Studies of Science* 29(3): 411–31.

Jordan, Ann T. 2003. *Business Anthropology.* Prospect Heights, IL: Waveland Press, Inc.

Jordan, Brigitte. 1996. "Ethnographic Workplace Studies and Computer Supported Coopera-tive Work." In *The Design of Computer-Supported Cooperative Work and Groupware Systems,* Shapiro, ed., 17–42. Amsterdam: North Holland/Elsevier Science.

Knorr-Cetina, K. 1999. *Epistemic Cultures: How the Sciences Make Knowledge.* Cambridge, MA: Harvard University Press.

Knorr-Cetina, K., and Alex Preda. 2005. *The Sociology of Financial Markets.* Oxford/New York: Oxford University Press.

Kreeger, Lisa D. 2007. "Inside Outsourcing: A Grounded Theory of Relationship Formation within a Nascent Service System," 214. PhD thesis, Antioch University. Seattle, WA.

Kunda, Gideon. 1992. *Engineering Culture: Control and Commitment in a High-Tech Corporation.* Philadelphia, PA: Temple University Press.

Lassiter, Luke E. 2005. *The Chicago Guide to Collaborative Ethnography.* Chicago, IL: University of Chicago Press.

Latour, Bruno. 1987. *Science in Action: How to Follow Scientists and Engineers Through Society.* Cambridge, MA: Harvard University Press.

———. 2004. "Which Politics for Which Artifacts?" *Domus.*

Latour, Bruno, and Steve Woolgar. 1986. *Laboratory Life: The Construction of Scientific Facts.* Princeton, NJ: Princeton University Press.

Lave, Jean, and Etienne Wenger. 1991. *Situated Learning: Legitimate Peripheral Participation.* Cambridge/New York: Cambridge University Press.

Lotfalian, Mazyar. 2004. *Islam, Technoscientific Identities, and the Culture of Curiosity.* Lanham, MD: University Press of America.

Luff, Paul, Jon Hindmarsh, and Christian Heath. 2000. *Workplace Studies: Recovering Work Practice and Informing System Design.* Cambridge/New York, NY: Cambridge University Press.

Maglio, Paul, et al. 2006. "Service Systems, Service Scientists, SSME and Innovation." *Com-munications of the ACM* 49(7): 81–88.

Malefyt, Timothy Dewaal, and Brian Moeran, eds. 2003. *Advertising Cultures.* Oxford/New York: Berg.

Maranhão, Tullio. 1990. *The Interpretation of Dialogue.* Chicago, IL: University of Chicago Press.

Marcus, George E. 1995. "Ethnography in/of the World System: The Emergence of Multi-Sited Ethnography." In *Ethnography Through Thick and Thin,* Marcus, 79–104. Princeton, NJ: Princeton University Press.

———. 1997. "The Uses of Complicity in the Changing Mise-en-Scene of Anthropological Fieldwork." In *Ethnography Through Thick and Thin,* Marcus, 105–31. Princeton, NJ: Princ-eton University Press.

Marcus, George E., and Michael M. J. Fischer. 1986. *Anthropology as Cultural Critique: An Ex-perimental Moment in the Human Sciences.* Chicago, IL: University of Chicago Press.

McCracken, Grant David. 2005. *Culture and Consumption II: Markets, Meaning, and Brand Man-agement.* Bloomington, IN: Indiana University Press.

———. 2006. *Flock and Flow: Predicting and Managing Change in a Dynamic Marketplace.* Bloom-ington, IN: Indiana University Press.

Miller, Daniel. 1998. *Material Cultures: Why Some Things Matter.* Chicago, IL: University of Chicago Press.

———. 1998. *A Theory of Shopping.* Ithaca, NY: Cornell University Press.

———. 2001. *Consumption: Critical Concepts in the Social Sciences.* London/New York: Rout-ledge.

Mills, David. 2006. "Dinner at Claridges? Anthropology and the 'Captains of Industry,' 1947–1955." In *Applications of Anthropology: Professional Anthropology in the Twenty-first Century,* Pink, ed., 55–70. New York/Oxford: Berghahn Books.

Moeran, Brian. 2005. *The Business of Ethnography: Strategic Exchanges, People and Organizations.* Oxford/New York: Berg.

———. 2006. *Ethnography at Work.* Oxford/New York: Berg.

Nafus, Dawn, and ken anderson. 2006. "The 'Real' Problem: Rhetorics of Knowing in Corporate Ethnographic Research." *Ethnographic Praxis in Industry Conference Proceedings.* 244–258. American Anthropological Association.

Nardi, Bonnie A. 1996. *Context and Consciousness: Activity Theory and Human-Computer Interaction.* Cambridge, MA: MIT Press.

Nardi, Bonnie A., and Vicki O'Day. 1999. *Information Ecologies: Using Technology with Heart.* Cambridge, MA: MIT Press.

Nash, June. 1998. "Twenty Years of the Anthropology of Work: A Critical Evaluation." *The Anthropology of Work Review* XVIII(4).

2004. "Off with the Pith Helmets." *The Economist,* 11 March.

Orr, Julian E. 1996. *Talking About Machines: An Ethnography of a Modern Job.* Ithaca, NY: ILR Press.

Pfaffenberger, Bryan. 1992. "Technological Dramas." *Science, Technology & Human Values* 7(3): 292–312.

Pine, B. Joseph, and James H. Gilmore. 1999. *The Experience Economy: Work is Theatre & Every Business a Stage.* Boston, MA: Harvard Business School Press.

Pink, Sarah, ed. 2006. *Applications of Anthropology: Professional Anthropology in the Twenty-first Century.* Studies in Applied Anthropology. New York/Oxford: Berghahn Books.

Rabinow, Paul. 1977. *Reflections on Fieldwork in Morocco.* Berkeley, CA: University of California Press.

Robinson, Rick E. 2005. "Let's Have A Conversation: Theory Session Introductory Remarks." *Ethnographic Praxis in Industry Conference Proceedings,* 1–8. American Anthropological Association.

Robinson, Rick E., and James P. Hackett. 1997. "Creating the Conditions of Creativity." *Design Management Journal* 8(4): 9–16.

Ross, Andrew. 2003. *No-Collar: The Humane Workplace and its Hidden Costs.* New York, NY: Basic Books.

Rylko-Bauer, Barbara, Merrill Singer, and John Van Willigen. 2006. "Reclaiming Applied Anthropology: Its Past, Present, and Future." *American Anthropologist* 108(1): 178–90.

Sachs, Patricia. 1995. "Transforming Work: Collaboration, Learning, and Design." *Communications of the ACM* 38(9): 36–44.

Scaglion, Richard. 2005. "From Anthropologist to Government Officer and Back Again." In *Anthropology and Consultancy: Issues and Debates,* Stewart and Strathern, eds., 46–62. New York/Oxford: Berghahn Books.

Schensul, Jean J., and Stephen L. Schensul. 1992. "Collaborative Research: Methods of Inquiry for Social Change." In *Handbook of Qualitative Research in Education.* LeCompte, Millroy, and Preissle, eds., 161–200. San Diego, CA: Academic Press.

Schwarz, Heinrich. 2003. "Mobile Workplacing: Office Design, Space and Technology." In *New Technologies at Work: People, Screens, and Social Virtuality,* Garsten and Wulff, eds., 91–117. Oxford/New York: Berg.

Schwarz, Heinrich, Bonnie A. Nardi, and Steve Whittaker. 1999. *The Hidden Work in Virtual Work.* International Conference on Critical Management Studies. Manchester.

Sellen, Abigail J., and Richard Harper. 2002. *The Myth of the Paperless Office.* Cambridge, MA: MIT Press.

Slater, Don. 1997. *Consumer Culture and Modernity.* Cambridge: Polity Press.

Spohrer, Jim, et al. 2007. "Steps Towards a Science of Services." *Computer* 1: 71–77.

Spohrer, Jim, and Doug Riecken. 2006. "Introduction to Special Issue on Services Science." *Communications of the ACM* 49(7): 30–32.

Squires, Susan E., and Bryan Byrne. 2002. *Creating Breakthrough Ideas: The Collaboration of Anthropologists and Designers in the Product Development Industry.* Westport, CT: Bergin & Garvey.

Star, Susan Leigh. 1995. *The Cultures of Computing.* Oxford/Cambridge, MA: Blackwell.

———. 1995. *Ecologies of Knowledge: Work and Politics in Science and Technology.* Albany, NY: State University of New York Press.

Strathern, Andrew, and Pamela J. Stewart. 2005. "Anthropology and Consultancy: Ethnographic Dilemmas and Opportunities." In *Anthropology and Consultancy: Issues and Debates,* Stewart and Strathern, eds., 1–23. New York/Oxford: Berghahn Books.

Suchman, Lucy. 1987. *Plans and Situated Actions: The Problem of Human-Machine Communication.* Cambridge/New York: Cambridge University Press.

———. 2000. "Anthropology as 'Brand': Reflections on Corporate Anthropology." Lancaster: Centre for Science Studies, Lancaster University.

Sunderland, Patricia L., and Rita M. Denny. 2003. "Psychology vs. Anthropology: Where is Culture in Marketplace Ethnography?" In *Advertising Cultures,* Malefyt and Moeran, eds., 187–202. Oxford/New York: Berg.

———. 2007. *Doing Anthropology in Consumer Research.* Walnut Creek, CA: Left Coast Press.

Tedlock, Dennis, and Bruce Mannheim. 1995. *The Dialogic Emergence of Culture.* Urbana, IL: University of Illinois Press.

Traweek, Sharon. 1988. *Beamtimes and Lifetimes: The World of High Energy Physicists.* Cambridge, MA: Harvard University Press.

Wakeford, Nina. 2003. "Research Note: Working with New Media's Cultural Intermediaries." *Information, Communication & Society* 6(2): 229–45.

———. 2005. "Craft, Value, and the Fetishism Of Method." *Ethnographic Praxis in Industry Conference Proceedings,* 75–80. American Anthropological Association.

Wasson, Christina. 2000. "Ethnography in the Field of Design." *Human Organization* 59(4): 377–88.

West, Paige. 2005. "Environmental Non-governmental Organizations and the Nature of Ethnographic Inquiry." In *Anthropology and Consultancy,* Stewart and Strathern, eds., 63–87. New York/Oxford: Berghahn Books.

Winner, Langdon. 1980. "Do Artifacts have Politics?" *Daedelus* 109(1).

Zaloom, Caitlin. 2004. "The Productive Life of Risk." *Cultural Anthropology* 19(3): 365–91.

———. 2006. *Out of the Pits: Traders and Technology from Chicago to London.* Chicago, IL: University of Chicago Press.

ENCOUNTERS WITH CORPORATE EPISTEMOLOGIES

Chapter 2

"MY CUSTOMERS ARE DIFFERENT!"
Identity, Difference, and the Political Economy of Design

Donna K. Flynn

There has been a growing literature over the past two decades on the complex dynamics of organizational culture, examined from both within and outside of anthropology. Critical questions around definitions of organizational culture, analytic and disciplinary approaches to understanding it, and the complex social interactions that shape it have been explored (Baba 1989; Jordan 1989, 1994; Ortlieb chapter 7, this volume). Large organizations are complex checkerboards of boundaries defining social groups, missions, loyalties, and individual success. Tomoko Hamada has suggested that the study of organizational culture "is in a way an inquiry into the political processes of social relationships from individual members' viewpoints" (1989: 5). As someone who is both an active agent within (as employee) and an active analyst of (as anthropologist) those political processes within a product development company, I explore questions around how competitions and cooperation are reproduced within the organization and ways in which they become both embedded in processes of design and projected onto the outside world of customers. Weaving together strands of organizational analysis, cultural analysis, and material culture, I shine an ethnographic lens on an ethnographic effort within a corporate context of product development. Cultural meanings imbue boundaries of power and difference that are entrenched and scattered across layers of people, processes, and products that comprise so much of organizational structure. At Microsoft Corporation, these "three Ps" are recognized "webs of significance" (Geertz 1973) within everyday

---

Notes for this chapter begin on page 56.

management practices, and are often used as organizing principles for an individual's annual performance commitments. The ebb and flow of social relationships across organizational boundaries and specific meanings attached to individual and group success play a dynamic role in interpretations of innovation. Through a critical examination of what Cefkin calls in this volume "corporate epistemologies" and with a specific focus on dynamics of identity and expectation within a specific site of design, I hope to reveal how everyday patterns and practices set the stage for ways in which organizational histories become embedded in the objects we create and produce.

Field Story: "My Customers are Different!"

To begin with a story from the field, early in my career at Microsoft I was a member of a design team within a development team for servers. The primary products I supported were spread across three families of servers enabling messaging, database management, and business services. As the team's official "ethnographer," my role was to conduct field research on relevant topics to inform development of all three of these product families. Our customers and end-users were professionals in information technology: administrators who supported the installation and maintenance of networks, developers who build programs to run on the networks, and executives driving decisions to purchase and deploy IT systems.

At that time, there was a business goal to cut production costs by moving 80 percent of product documentation away from paper and CD formats to the web. There were many questions about how this "80/20 rule" might impact customers, and widespread recognition that we had very little knowledge about how our customers actually used our server documentation. Working closely with key internal clients who created product-documentation and support resources for the three server families, I designed and led a field research project exploring this issue. How are IT professionals currently utilizing server documentation? How do usage patterns vary across IT roles (administrator versus developer), across business size, or type of business? When do they utilize print versus web-based documentation? What are key pain points, un-met expectations, and un-articulated needs? What are opportunities for providing a more effective set of resources to customers while still cutting costs of production?

In brief, we identified three primary modes of interaction with documentation, shaped by customers' specific goals as related to server implementation cycles (for example, deployment vs. maintenance), the type of information they sought (product overviews vs. step-by-step guides), and the preferred channels for seeking that information (books vs. white papers). We then mapped current support resources to this model, identified gaps and opportunities, and made specific recommendations for improving the entire customer experience with documentation. We also found that these patterns were generally *independent* of type of server, business size, or type of business. This seemed quite logical to many of us: IT professionals developed practices for finding information and support resources based on the nature of the problem they were solving, not based on whether the server was for messaging, data management, or e-commerce.

My focus here is not on the actual findings of this project, but on the way in which my internal clients received—and resisted—the conclusion above that documentation-usage practices were independent of the type of server. Overall, the findings were well-received and became a primary input to the redesign of web-based documentation for our IT professional customers. But they were also met with strong and vocal pockets of resistance—including by some colleagues who had participated in the study design and data collection but were ultimately unhappy with the conclusions and outcomes.

One of the most common challenges I heard was based on assumptions of irreconcilable difference between customers of different types of servers, or between specific types of IT professionals:

"These are not customers of my type of server. ... My servers, and my customers, are different!"

"You did not look at all the different kinds of database administrators. ... My customers are different!"

"Your sample size is too small and does not represent all our customers. ... My customers are different!"

Although we could not cover the entire range of customers, due to resource and time constraints, we did carefully design a study that covered a broad range of representative and high-priority types of IT professionals. Given the clear consistency across this range, we were quite confident that interaction with server documentation was characterized more by shared behaviors than by specific behaviors, and that the primary factor shaping these patterns was server implementation cycles over time, rather than type of server.

Nevertheless, I was struck by the vehemence of many against this finding. Now, looking back, I can see that this was in some ways my initiation into a deeply embedded organizational discourse, "my products/my customers are different," which pervades product teams across Microsoft.

This is in stark contrast to the customers' perspective of "I'm managing this network of different servers, and I need to get them all working together." In the customers' eyes, it is not about this type of product versus that type of product, it's about Microsoft products. But organizational boundaries, internal competitions for resources, and corporate reward systems repeatedly result in the unfortunate consequence that we force our customers to navigate varied and complex resources siloed by product, or even by feature sets within a product. So why do teams cling so strongly to insistence of difference over common experience? I believe some understanding of this can be uncovered through a web of histories and practices that shape an organizational culture that prioritizes the parts over the whole.

Culture of Individualized Innovation: Constructs of Difference within the Corporation

And so, like many other Microsoft stories, it all begins with one man. The mythical history of Bill Gates creating the next revolution in work practices seeps into unsuspecting nooks and crannies of the organization. Like many effective leaders—of companies, states, or social or political movements—"billg" is able to capture fascination by being both larger-than-life and utterly human.[1] His offices are cordoned off on the top floor of a centrally located building with unobstructed views of Mt. Rainer and the Cascades, and guards are posted around his parking spaces all hours of the day. At the same time, any employee can email him, and may very well get a personal reply. Face-to-face or presenting to small groups, he can be self-deprecating and humorous; presenting to large forums he actually seems diminutive; but there is also some truth to hallway rumors of his tendency to strike with ruthless and biting criticism in strategy reviews.

There are many directions we could take in deconstructing billg's influence on Microsoft's corporate culture. What I want to focus on here is how his personal history and accomplishments have shaped expectations of innovation inside Microsoft. Contrary to business theories that chart successful innovation as an achievement of collaboration within creative environments, innovation at Microsoft is for the most part defined as an individualized accomplishment. Today's innovators are expected to develop and discover in front of their computers, largely behind closed doors of separate offices. Microsoft's campus consists of rows and rows of nearly identical offices flanking narrow hallways, disorienting in their sameness. Open, collaborative spaces for interacting with peers and spontaneous discussion exist primarily when teams temporarily commandeer a corner of a hallway or empty office.[2] As archaeologists well know, the magnitude of the effect of material spaces on our lived experiences is too often undervalued. I am reminded of this when I compare how jarring the spaces were to me when I first came to Microsoft, to how accustomed I have become to them now.

Social rules of course overlay the ways in which we navigate our material worlds. One of the unspoken and yet deeply embedded social rules inside Microsoft is around competition. Although we all belong to smaller teams situated within product groups situated within divisions, this sense of competition begins at the individual level. Success is frequently defined in terms of individualized innovation: the perceived ability of an individual to develop something different that results in positive gains for the business group. I quickly learned that individuals who can successfully create a public perception of having an impact—whether or not they actually did—were rewarded, while the work of other individuals quietly making real impacts was undervalued. One of the ways this plays out is in very visible interpersonal interactions, as individuals jockey for leadership in meetings, aggressively critique one another, or use email as a tool for public pronouncements and building constituencies close to circles of power.

A key practice for reinforcing the primacy of individual accomplishments and instilling the urgency to excel is the annual rite of passage at review time. As annual reviews approach, a sense of trepidation often becomes palpable. Careers can be quickly destroyed, and the margin for error is minute. In 2006 the company introduced a major overhaul to the review system in response to employee feedback and in an effort to soften the hard edges of the competitive system. Until then, scores were assigned to individuals within a five-point scale, on a half-point basis. However, the real range of acceptability was within one point: a score of three for satisfactory performance was an eye-raising review (consistent "three-performers" risked being managed out), and scores of four and a half or higher were awarded only in rare cases of exceptional impact.[3] While many companies incorporate some element of team-based performance into reviews, Microsoft has no such practices and for the most part focuses rewards on individual achievements.

Competitive expectations extend outward from individuals to product teams. Managers and executives, for example, are appropriately held accountable at review time for performance of their teams. Cross-group collaboration across the company is often viewed as a distracting risk to achieving product development milestones and team success. As product groups progress on their own cycles and drive toward their own release dates, individuals' commitments are prioritized based on team needs. Work plans and time allotments are focused on product silos, and poor knowledge management systems inhibit efficient sharing of intellectual capital and development efforts across teams and across the company. Any cross-group collaboration must ultimately be measured in terms of the end-impact on one's specific product. Even for those of us committed to the value of collaboration, it can be difficult to realize in an environment where our individual activities and time is consistently prioritized based on the needs of our product team rather than for the benefit of the larger, holistic corporate entity.

This tension between competition and collaboration runs throughout a myriad of work practices across Microsoft—from individualized planning and execution without being "slowed down" by too many other stakeholders to the broader phenomenon of parallel development of similar solutions for identical target markets by multiple teams across the company. Progress has historically been defined as personalized impact, and the duplication of individuals and teams solving the same problems and creating mirrored solutions in different parts of the company are excused as necessary messiness in the pursuit of innovation. While the organizational consultant part of me sees myriad opportunities for streamlining efficiencies, the embedded employee-anthropologist part of me understands that our motivations are rooted in a climate of individualized innovation and we are all seeking in some small way to recreate and relive the historical triumph of billg.

The Persona Phenomena: Constructs of Difference between Customers

Personas are archetypal representations of a group of customers or users. Since Alan Cooper popularized them with his 1999 book *The Inmates Are Running the Asylum,* personas have become "best practice" tools across product design and development for providing concrete representations of the behaviors, characteristics, and needs of customers or users (see also Pruitt and Adlin 2006; Pruitt and Grudin 2003). As archetypes, effective personas distill a vast amount of quantitative and qualitative data into consumable and imaginable representations of customers. In their best incarnations, they successfully condense this data into a definable set of customer behaviors and scenarios that can be easily digested by a number of types of roles across an organization. Personas come alive with a name and a face, and visual storytelling around personas infuses the data with humanity and personality, a critical methodological device for educating technical minds about the everyday worlds of real people.

Personas succeed by establishing a sense of intimacy between customers and corporation. When this intimacy is established, and all the key stakeholders of a product or marketing team feel they share a familiar relationship with the people that the personas represent, they can be enormously effective tools for driving agreement around value propositions and functionality for a product. They provide a common language for large divisions and small teams to talk about target customers, and can influence tactical planning around feature specifications, guide prioritization processes for functionality within specific releases, and inform marketing communications. A more intangible benefit has been their effectiveness in getting people across the company to simply think from the customer perspective. Personas at Microsoft are on a first name basis, and across the company you can hear developers, program managers, testers, marketing managers, and executives asking "What does this do for Melissa, or Abby, or Marco?" In a culture where user researchers are called engineers, this is a relatively large feat for encouraging intellects to think beyond the code.

As personas have proliferated across the company, we have also seen some of the dangers of their misuse. One risk we have seen is the way in which their names can become mere checklists on product specification documents without having any real impact on how teams are thinking through the design problems that the persona frames for the product. The reductionist nature of personas—always providing a neat encapsulation of complex experiences into a set of statistical data, descriptive soundbytes, and day-in-the-life stories—is at the heart of their ability to impact development and marketing teams but can also become a danger if personas alone are relied upon to educate stakeholders about their customers. They are a single tool within a rich user research toolbox, and should never be developed or used in isolation from other tools. Distilling complexities of multiple types of customers into a handful of personas defined by bullet points can be a misleading oversimplification of diverse behaviors when utilized in an isolated manner without the depth and perspective that other types of data and models can provide. When combined with other methods for developing customer insights—such as segmentations, scenarios, task flows, behavioral analysis, opportunity mapping, quantitative measurements, and, of course, ethnographic storytelling—personas can be enormously effective in helping to educate and orient a large product team around a common goal.

One way in which teams have countered the reductionist drawbacks of personas is through the production of large sets of multiple personas. But having too many personas can dilute their impact, resulting in a confusing maze of multiplicity with no clear prioritization to guide decisions being made at all levels of the product development organization. It can also counteract that sense of intimacy and familiarity which is the cornerstone of their effectiveness. I have sat through persona reviews that covered more than twenty-five different types of IT professionals, leaving everyone around the table confused about the kinds of customer needs and characteristics they should think about most with regard to their product.

Increasingly embedded use of the archetypes has also had another, unexpected effect: that of reinforcing rigid concepts of who your customer is and—just as important—who your customer is not. Let's return to my field story: during the time that I was on the server team, researchers and designers dedicated to each of the server product groups were in the process of creating and evangelizing separate sets of personas. Unique sets of IT administrator, developer, and business manager personas were being created for each of the three families of servers in my division, as well as for other server families in other divisions. While there are some good reasons to develop separate personas for database administrators versus messaging administrators, doing so also builds constructs of difference between customer types that can become barriers for recognizing common aspects of experience. The independent creation of personas by different teams—rather than borrowing and building upon already existing models—also results in constructs with overlapping characteristics wrapped in very distinct representations with different names and faces. There may be common threads lying under the surface, but the differences are canonized in the ways in which teams own and identify with the characters.

This canonization of difference between types of servers and types of IT roles as constructed by the personas was partly shaping the resistance of some stakeholders to my ethnographic findings that usage of product documentation was independent to type of server or type of IT role. The key stakeholders for my documentation research project—who represented all three server groups—were adopting and building a sense of ownership over separate sets of personas as "their" customers. These personas were concrete representations of the boundaries between servers and IT roles and did not adequately represent shared experiences. Product development organizations tend to be characterized by close affinities between team, product, and customer/user. Teams are identified by the products that they build, which in turn are largely driven (or at least should be) by the customers/users. In an environment where notions of difference between product-defined teams are elevated and honored, expectations of difference between customers of this and that product can be falsely reinforced. Amidst a background of proliferating product-focused personas, the widespread discourses over customers-as-personas were unintentionally reinforcing differentiation between customers at the expense of common experiences. Thus my finding that type of product was *not* a critical factor in determining customer behaviors with regard to product documentation was a perspective that also directly contradicted deeply embedded practices of team differentiation and identity. In this light, the repeated refrains that "my customers are different!" are redolent with assertions of the unique, individualized value of the product team as well as the customer.

I must end this discussion of personas with a brief, confessional detour: I have had a deep skepticism of personas for years—until recently. After leading my team in my current division through a long and in-depth persona-development process and launching these new personas to our division, I have learned first-hand the positive power that robust, effectively communicated personas can have in shaping both strategic direction and tactical decisions. Our personas—and the value propositions they represent—rapidly made their way into strategy discussions at the highest levels of the company, becoming a discourse between our vice presidents, presidents, and our CEO in discussions about target markets, product direction, investments of resources, and channel strategy. At the same time, they are being used by all levels of the organization—program management, developers, testers, content publishers, user experience, and marketing—to frame the everyday tasks and decisions of product development. As I continue to see the manifold impacts, my skepticism is being reframed and focused more specifically into vigilance at the ways in which personas are developed, communicated, and integrated across a product development process.

"I am my Customer": Dialectics of Identity and Difference between Corporation and Customer

Many of the managers across the server product team in my field story came from an IT background and have played roles as administrators or developers in server support groups in earlier stages of their careers. With extensive experience and long histories with their product, a number of key stakeholders for my server documentation study felt a deep sense of affinity with the customers for whom they were developing product. Quite literally, many of them felt like they *were* their customers and didn't hesitate to tell me this. They found it disdainfully amusing that a technical neophyte and relative outsider such as myself could actually teach them something new about their highly technical customers. The strong sense of identification that my colleagues shared with their customers became a concrete challenge to my efforts to evangelize new perspectives and opportunities based on ethnographically-derived insights. I began to understand on a deeper level the ways in which dynamics of identity and group member-ship can play a critical role in the adoption of ethnographic knowledge.

In this particular story, a triangular dialectic of identity and difference between product managers (my internal clients), IT professionals (our customers), and the design anthropologist (myself) shaped the ways in which ethnographic knowledge was circulated and adopted within the organizational setting. Each set of players had a slight but significantly different perception of these relationships, defined both by positioning of self and assumptions of the other. In one corner, product managers si-multaneously emphasized personal affinities with "their" customers as well as differences between their customers and customers of the "other" products (see figure 2.1). As discussed in the context of personas, such distinctions between my/your customer extend constructs of difference between product-based groups within the organization onto the people for whom the products are being designed. Moreover, the product manag-ers' perceived social distance between themselves and the design anthro-pologist—a non-technical outsider—is actually greater than the perceived distance between themselves and their customer.

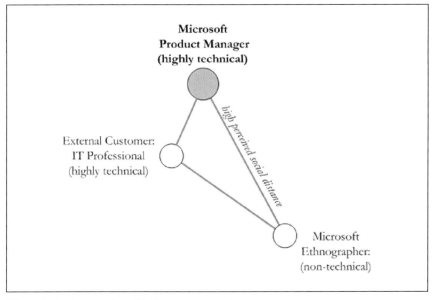

Figure 2.1. Perspective of technical product manager.

This is reflective of a rather widespread organizational tendency across Microsoft product teams to imagine customers as shadows of ourselves and to design products based on the ways in which we ("Microsofties") like to use them. It is a common joke within the company's user-experience community that Microsoft builds products for Microsoft. Indeed, a large part of the role of ethnographers and other user-experience and customer-facing professionals across the company is to reinforce vigilance against these kinds of laissez-faire assumptions about customer needs, technology uses, and behaviors. Corporate executives recognized the tenaciousness and dangers of such an inward focus in the late 1990s, launching a series of initiatives to increase the primacy of the customer across multiple levels of business strategy and product development. These strategic shifts by leadership have created more opportunity for ethnography to integrate into the organization, but in the trenches there remain extensive challenges around evangelizing against product decisions based on false assumptions about customers.

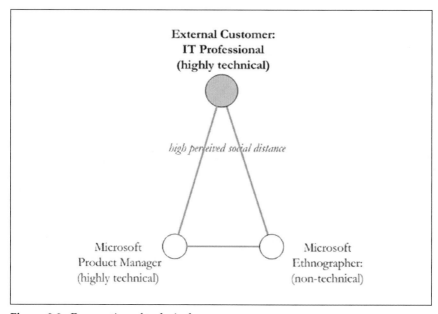

Figure 2.2. Perspective of technical customer.

From the customers' perspective in the triangular dialectic (see figure 2.2), the social distance between themselves and a product manager is greater than the distance between myself (design anthropologist) and a product manager. To the customer, we both represent and embody Microsoft. The organizational boundaries within which we operate may create certain efficiencies for processes of production and measuring profit, but rarely do they reflect the ways in which people actually integrate products into their everyday lives. While distinctions between *my* customer and *your* customer might be imbued with meaningful separations within the organization, the people who encounter the products we build consider themselves, quite simply, as Microsoft's customers. They likely use multiple types of Microsoft products in their everyday life, and the most common way for them to experience the constructs of difference between customer/product/team across our company is through breakdowns of interoperability and integration across our products. Customers with whom I have direct contact and interaction perceive me as a representative of Microsoft—someone who can carry messages about their holistic needs and experiences back to the entire company—rather than a representative of a single product team.

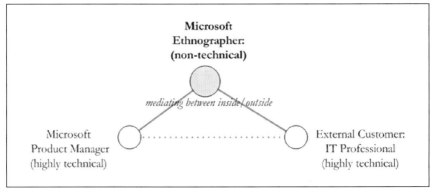

Figure 2.3. Perspective of ethnographer.

From my corner of the triangle, I recognize that I am at once part of the organizational whole while at the same time, with respect to the product managers, a non-technical outsider (see figure 2.3). It is precisely this liminal positioning and my expertise in social analysis which allows me to take a step backward and see different kinds of cross-cutting boundaries being drawn between all the players. I can articulate common experiences and aspects of shared identity, enumerate various contextual factors that shape those, and elucidate potential impacts on business value. But I am also an embedded member of the organizational group, and the heart of my work is to educate my internal clients about our customers. Within this shifting dialectic of positioning of self and assumptions about others, one of my greatest challenges is to reduce the perceived distance between myself and my internal clients to be able to effectively evangelize ethnographic insights to the organizational collective, gently reshape their assumptions about the customer, and improve the customer's experiences with our products.

The Political Economy of Design, and the Design Ethnographer[4]

In his introduction to the Theory section of the 2005 Ethnographic Praxis in Industry Conference (EPIC), Rick Robinson points out that evolution of our discipline lies in our ability to engage in conversations about the work we do and the spaces within which we do it, and thus to develop stronger, homegrown theoretical frameworks. In her introduction to this volume, Cefkin points to the promise these conversations hold for understanding dimensions of knowledge production where ethnographic work is present, and the promise that our work in corporations presents for opening up this thinking. The varied voices of this volume represent a lively dinner party of engaged dialogue for our discipline as we forge our way forward through the tangles of theoretical relevance of corporate ethnography.

Here I have explored some of the complex relationships that shape the conversation among the relevant parties that Robinson identifies: the ethnographic practitioner (myself), clients (my product team), participants (our customers), and other interested theorists (you, as the reader; and other authors). The core question I have examined in this field story is how perceptions of identity—as formulated through organizational and personal histories, individual interactions, shared meanings and experiences, and assumptions of the "other"—among and between this cast of characters can ultimately shape the ways in which knowledge is applied and embodied in the things that we are building.

Also at EPIC, Kris Cohen (2005) raised our attention to the politics of design in his analysis of the ways in which design research constructs relationships between the Who (user) and the What (product) by defining exclusionary frameworks for how people should/could relate to products; indeed, the construction of personas represent a very concrete example of this. But, as Robinson points out, there is more than one Who in this conversation (see also Brun-Cottan, chapter 6, this volume). The politics of design extend beyond the exclusions we impose upon the consumers of the things that we build and also encompass the exclusions—and inclusions—among the people and groups who are building the products. In organizational contexts, "collaborations" are the alliances and political bondings that are forged on both individual and group levels to achieve the ends of production (see also Lovejoy and Steele 2008). So here I want to politicize the notion of collaboration: collaboration is as much about exclusion as about inclusion, and alliance-building is a potent tool for negotiating access to resources, elevating status, and augmenting power. Within an organizational structure that exalts and rewards individualized innovation, alliances are developed to serve corporate ends through individualized successes. The shape of collaborations—flavored by constructs of identity within the corporate entity, rules and patterns of interaction, and individual and group competitions over resources—thus becomes a potent lens for understanding how the things that we are building become products of corporate contestations.

The shape of collaborations within which we, as ethnographic practitioners, are enmeshed inside corporate contexts define the ways in which we approach our objects/subjects of study, and the ways in which we must produce and circulate knowledge that ultimately finds its way into the end-results of our business. The final product embodies more than constructed relationships between the subject and object; it also embodies constructed relationships among the various parties creating the object, and all the organizational complexity and messiness within which they (we) are situated in the context of production. More specifically, how does the shape of collaboration in product development define and become embedded within the objects we produce? How can we look at the successes and failures of our products and see the organizational outlines of the teams and relationships within which we are situated as we create those products? By extending a Marxian lens to the arenas of production of our twenty-first century information technology age in which we ourselves are actively participating, we can see anew the ways in which familiar social analysis frameworks reveal hidden dynamics that shape our experiences. The life of a thing (Mintz 1985; Appadurai 1986) is as revealing to follow from its conception as a kernel of an idea through to its commercialization in the market as it is in its travels post-commercialization between markets, owners, and contexts of usage. My assertion here is rather simple: I am merely pointing out the affinities—and potential for further exploration—between some longstanding theoretical perspectives of material culture with our contemporary roles as creators of material culture.

As active agents within the process of production, it might be more fruitful to focus our lenses on the political economy of design—the ever-shifting landscapes of ideologies, power, and competitions between individuals and groups within the sites of design and development that directly or indirectly define what will be created for consumption by the imagined users. Our work is not only about understanding the "landscapes of possibility" (Cohen 2005) for consumers and the objects we design, but identifying and understanding the continually shifting landscapes of production through which the landscapes of possibility will ultimately be interpreted and distilled to operational and productized outputs (see figure 2.4). If we recognize that one of our strongest advantages in the corporate field is our ability to be both liminal to and embedded within this political

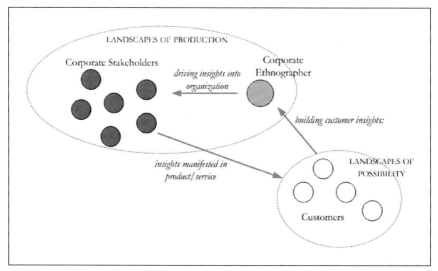

Figure 2.4. Flows of knowledge.

economy, our power as ethnographers lies in being able to reframe priorities, values, and even relationships within those landscapes of production.
Through effective integration of ethnographic knowledge into production
processes, we can help redraw boundaries of exclusion/inclusion between
corporation and customer; and by applying our skills in effectively moving across social boundaries and bridging social distance, we can redraw
boundaries of exclusion/inclusion within the landscape of production.

Practicing ethnographers in industry become accustomed to the challenge of illustrating ethnographic value to clients and colleagues, and we
tend to develop our own personal toolboxes of metaphors, explanations,
case studies, and models for effectively communicating how ethnographic
insight can lead to business value. Ethnography in industry contexts is
unfortunately too often defined in terms of its data-collection methodologies—the practice of understanding people within their own cultural and
physical contexts. I believe that the critical struggle we face in practicing
ethnography is less about the migration of data-collection methodology,
and more about the production, dissemination, and adoption of ethnographic knowledge throughout the discourses and processes of our applied contexts. Anyone can collect data within customer contexts using
our methodological tools, but our ethnographic and analytical lens in
interpreting that data and developing deep, holistic insights to customers and products are what define our value apart from our usability and
market-research colleagues. By thinking critically about some of the specific dynamics surrounding the ways in which our work succeeds—and

fails—at this endeavor, we should be able to develop more-sophisticated tools for effectively integrating ethnographic knowledge into the dominant discourses of production. We are doing ethnography to have an impact, and our successes can only be measured by the ways in which we impact the people, processes, and products—the "three Ps"—that our lens is focused on.

Notes

1. While this book was in press, Bill Gates retired from his everyday responsibilities at Microsoft to focus his time on The Bill and Melinda Gates Foundation.
2. In the past year, a handful of design teams have procured funding and support to renovate some or all of their allotted real estate into open-space working environments designed to encourage a climate of iterative and creative collaboration. Across our vast campus, these spaces still constitute a renegade exception to the norm, and represent less than one percent of the company's employees and square footage.
3. It remains to be seen whether the new performance rating system, which is based on a simpler ranking of three levels characterized by words instead of numbers, will resolve some of the issues it intends to target.
4. At other points in this story I have described myself as a design anthropologist, because my background as an anthropologist is deeply held as a part of my own professional and personal identity. I could alternatively describe myself as a business anthropologist, consulting anthropologist, symbolic anthropologist, economic anthropologist, development anthropologist, or applied anthropologist depending on the context of my career stage, projects at question, or audience. Leaving aside my own constructs of identity, I do recognize that the ethnographic enterprise is no longer the sole realm of anthropologists, and that it has been and will continue to be enriched by the perspectives of practitioners with a wide range of backgrounds.

References

Appadurai, Arjun. 1986. *The Social Life of Things: Commodities in Cultural Perspective.* Cambridge: Cambridge University Press.

Baba, Marietta. 1989. "Organizational Culture: Revisiting the Small Society Metaphor." *Anthropology of Work Review* 10(3): 7–10.

———. 2001. "Uniting Theory and Practice in American Corporations." *NAPA Bulletin* 20(1): 104–6.

Cohen, Kris R. 2005. "Who We Talk About When We Talk About Users." *Ethnographic Praxis in Industry Conference Proceedings,* 9–30. American Anthropological Association.

Cooper, Alan. 1999. *The Inmates are Running the Asylum: Why High Tech Products Drive us Crazy and How to Restore the Sanity.* New York: Macmillan.

Geertz, Clifford. 1973. *The Interpretation of Cultures.* New York: Perseus.

Hamada, Tomoko. 1989. "Perspectives on Organizational Culture." *Anthropology of Work Review* 10(3): 5–7.

―――. 2000. "Anthropological Praxis: Theory of Business Organization." *NAPA Bulletin* 18(1): 79–103.

Jordan, Ann. 1989. "Organizational Culture: It's Here, but is it Anthropology?" *Anthropology of Work Review* 10(3): 2–5.

―――. 1994. "Organizational Culture: The Anthropological Approach." *NAPA Bulletin* 14(1): 3–16.

Lovejoy, Tracey, and Nelle Steele. 2008. "Effectiveness through Partnerships: Navigating the Shifting Landscape of Partnerships to Influence Product Development," in Briody and Trotter (eds): *Partnering for Organizational Peformance.* Lanham, MD: Rowman and Littlefield.

Mintz, Sydney. 1985. *Sweetness and Power: The Place of Sugar in Modern History.* New York: Penguin Books.

Pruitt, John, and Tamara Adlin. 2006. *The Persona Lifecycle: Keeping People in Mind Throughout Product Design.* Amsterdam: Elsevier Inc.

Pruitt, John, and Jonathan Grudin. 2003. "Personas: Practice and Theory." ACM published paper, online at http://research.microsoft.com/users/jgrudin/publications/personas/Pruitt-Grudin.pdf.

Robinson, Rick. 2005. "Let's Have a Conversation: Theory Session Introductory Remarks." *Ethnographic Praxis in Industry Conference Proceedings,* 1–8. American Anthropological Association.

DOING ANTHROPOLOGY
IN ORGANIZATIONAL CONTEXTS

Chapter 3

PARTICIPATORY ETHNOGRAPHY AT WORK
Practicing in the Puzzle Palaces of a Large, Complex Healthcare Organization

Christopher Darrouzet, Helga Wild, and Susann Wilkinson

> Water Cooler Logic helped us see the jigsaw puzzle from the top,
> not just from the side, where we're usually positioned.
>
> —chief of staff for clinical affairs at a large VA medical center

Introduction: Puzzlers One and All

For the past ten years the authors of this chapter have been conducting what are often called "action research and learning projects" in large organizations. Our work maps onto the broad landscape of *workplace consulting*, of which there are nearly as many varieties as consultants. We work on invitation from management within an organization to assist on special initiatives and projects.

We have made the "ethnographic impulse" one of two key impulses driving both our methods and the practical phases of the intervention process we stage in most of our projects (the second impulse is participatory design). In this respect we belong to the small community of consultants to large organizations—which includes a number of contributors to this volume—who work out of an ethnographic anthropological frame. How we do this work—using a participatory mode in the ethnographic phase as well as in the design phase—and how our principal clients assess its value, are the main themes of this chapter.

Notes for this chapter begin on page 92.

We make a three-fold claim about this work: first, that the social and cultural work-world spaces of very large, complex, far-flung, multiple-sited organizations are vast cultural and practical worlds fully understood by no one, but are, at the same time, worlds that many actors are constantly attempting to "puzzle" out. In recent years, most of our work has taken place in one such huge, complex organization: the US Department of Veterans Affairs, Veterans Health Administration (DVA/VHA, usually referred to as "the VA"; it will be profiled later in the chapter). Our second claim is that these types of organizations are ripe for ethnographic anthropology, which is especially effective at puzzling complexity borne of human interactions and human projects. Third, we claim that among the different ethnographies, our specific variation, participatory ethnography, is especially well suited to large, massively complex organizations.

As consultants to large organizations, we share with other contributors to this volume the fieldwork sites and subject matter situated at the other end of the spectrum of what people usually associate with cultural anthropology. We also work this side of the great change in ethnographic anthropology that got underway in the early 1980s and included a major refiguring of a founding concept of the modern age, culture, as well as of ethnographic methodology. As George E. Marcus and Michael M. J. Fischer put it in the introduction to the second edition of *Anthropology as Cultural Critique: An Experimental Moment in the Human Sciences*, a leading text in both recognizing and fomenting this sea change, "No longer, then, is the project of anthropology the simple discovery of new worlds, and the translation of the exotic into the familiar, or the defamiliarization of the exotic. It is increasingly the discovery of worlds that are familiar or fully understood by no one, and that all are in search of puzzling out" (1999: xvii).

Road Map for Chapter

In the first section of this chapter we hope to accomplish two things. First, we outline what we mean by *participatory ethnography*. We emphasize the way in which we bring staff over to the ethnographer's perspective and role, to work alongside us, the professional ethnographers, as "para-ethnographers." Secondly, we relate our approach to the "puzzling" work of people in complex organizations. We invoke the notion and concept of "complexity" to explain why understanding *of* these organizations is not achievable, at least not comprehensively or permanently, but that creating understanding *in* the organization is a daily necessity for many, maybe all, of its members.

The idea of complexity underwrites much of our work in conceptual and theoretical terms, though we rarely mention this underwriting directly in our project work. Here, we highlight complexity and several of its meanings, from ordinary language to the adoption of the term by the "complexity sciences" (particularly chaos theory) to the discourse of complexity emerging in social psychology and anthropology. We argue that the situation of complexity needs to be recognized as the empirical and epistemological background of most ethnographic anthropological work.

We treat theory and concept matters, however, only briefly—enough to point out the underpinnings of our work. In the second section we describe one of our projects as an abridged case study to provide a grounded view of what we do and how we do it. We focus on the ways in which our interventions provide a performative context for staff in the local sites to engage in this ethnographically inspired work of puzzling out their experiences and responsibilities in the organization. The project we feature is "bed control and patient discharge," a topic encompassing difficult, core issues in virtually all large, in-patient medical facilities.

Between the first and second sections is a brief overview of the healthcare division of the Department of Veteran Affairs ("the VA"), the meta-site of many of our project engagements over the past eight years.

Why Everyone Is an Ethnographer

This metaphor of puzzles and of puzzling things out is an apt one for ethnography. Not only do Marcus and Fischer use this metaphor—and we know that they are attuned to the question of metaphor and tropes in ethnographic writing and thinking—but so did one of our astute VA hosts, quoted at the top of the paper. Puzzling captures what is common to the efforts of lots of different people in large-scale, complex organizations. Many of the diverse and diversely positioned subjects in large organizations labor at puzzling out how these organizations work and why; how to navigate them; how to live, work, and realize themselves in them.

Puzzlers operating within these organizations range from senior executives to strategic planning groups, to directors and managers working in scores of different professional realms and grades within the organization. But puzzling does not stop there, for if it did, these organizations would collapse (do collapse, sometimes). One finds clusters of staff "out there," on the frontlines, working daily to figure out what their part of the puzzle might look like. Typically they are being told what it should look like by supervisory, managerial, directorial, and executive-level puzzlers (with puzzling going on at each level in the "Russian doll" hierarchy of puzzlers.) But these designated-puzzlers' views, with their professed understanding of "the big picture," are seldom detailed enough (or even correct enough) to serve staff in the local clusters busy addressing the variability and uniqueness of their issues and concerns.

At the frontlines of these organizations, we find that people often have few beside themselves and their own group to turn to to make sense of their situation or to comply with their ethical and organizational commitments. In the absence of detailed-enough instructions or compelling-enough reasons, they invent their practices on an as-needed basis, resolving issues brought to them by colleagues or clients as best they can, and adjusting their own sense of the world on the basis of feedback and resistance from their surroundings.

Some of them begin to look more closely into what *others* nearby are doing. In stepping back and out from the confines of their stations to engage others nearby, they are adopting a mode of puzzling that reaches toward the "ethnographic." In other words, their existential situation drives them already into a stance akin to ethnography. These puzzlers are candidates for the relatively new notion of the *para-ethnographer*. Currently under construction within anthropology, this notion is derived from the experiences of professional ethnographers who encounter more and more people in field settings and host communities who possess an ethnographic consciousness or analytical framework. (Melissa Cefkin [chapter 1, this volume] reviews Marcus and Holmes's original notion of the "paraethnographic".)

As we become used to the idea of ethnography as a distinct modality for puzzling things out in situations of complexity, it becomes clearer that ethnography is also what it always has been: a mode of relating to others. Ethnography is not defined merely by who is relating to whom, but by the quality of the relation and the perspectives adopted. Ethnography's accepted strengths in gathering and analyzing information ("from the natives' point of view") are also far from the whole story. Ethnography is a means of establishing relations, relations through which positional knowledge of a certain ethnographic kind gets formed. This knowledge may be brought back (or not) into the ongoing discourses near the scenes of its creation, discourses, *and* courses of action that have preceded the ethnographic project and will succeed it. All ethnographic projects, in our view, should be regarded ultimately as "interventional," some far more pointedly so with respect to near-term, near-sited interests than others.

Marcus has described the phenomenon of para-ethnography in a way that provides an opening for the kinds of consulting we do as "Water Cooler Logic" in organizations: "Paraethnographies are, in other words, already out there. What they need is an anthropological staging, a mise-en-scène, to give them articulation within the complex discourse on the nature and operation of the contemporary" (2006: 8).

Staging activities as part of the intervention so that a relatively disciplined ethnographic modality can emerge is a good way of thinking about Water Cooler Logic (WCL). WCL helps build collective systems of meaning, sometimes stopping short of complete consensus, but always ending up with a communal conceptual landscape on which people can locate their and others' positions. This agreed-upon conceptual space then serves as a basis for joint decisions about future actions. Such newly constructed collective understandings can, in the short run, address and alleviate the challenges of everyday operations.

Behind these practical efforts stand the assumptions and insights from discourse theory—discourse understood in the most general term as *social action*—which claim that communicative action is possible and can accomplish a transformation and convergence of positions.[1]

"Participatory" Ethnography

Our use of the qualifying term *participatory* is partially synonymous with the more frequently used *collaborative ethnography,* but as the latter has several meanings, it is worth noting which ones we invoke and why we have chosen to call our work participatory rather than collaborative. Melissa Cefkin (chapter 1, this volume) reflects on discussions of various key terms used to describe further the quality of ethnography as a mode of relating—advocacy, complicity, intervention, collaboration, participation. Different forms of ethnographic engagement merit these different qualifiers.

While the notion of collaboration is broad, in recent years it has tended to describe two distinct elements of ethnographic anthropological research. In one, collaboration refers to two or more researchers working together on the same topic, perhaps on the same formal project, and even sharing time in project-aligned or multiple research sites. In David Gellner and Declan Quigley's (1995) collection, *collaborative ethnography* is used to indicate that several researchers worked collaboratively on the caste system of Nepal. More recently, Sylvia Yanagisako and Lisa Rofel (2008) describe a formal research collaboration project on the Italian-Chinese textile industry in the context of the culture of globalizing capitalism. In the first sense, the vicissitudes of collaboration addressed tend to be those of professional co-researchers. (While researcher collaborations in industry are common, university-based, academic anthropology is only now addressing issues ingrained in the decades-long preference that ethnographers work singly in the field, rather than as collaborators on joint fieldwork projects, especially for their thesis work and as junior faculty.) One reason we have chosen to use *participatory* is so as not to confuse it with this first sense of researcher collaboration.

Another sense of collaboration addresses the shift in the conceptualiza-tion and practice of fieldwork relations and methodology toward a more dialogical relationship between researcher and informant; or better, since that relationship has always been dialogical, toward a structure of inter-action that acknowledges the hierarchical frame of ethnographies and makes an effort to counterbalance it. More concretely, "[it] [namely, col-laborative ethnography] begins to depart from traditional ethnographic practices … with its focus on developing interpretations that are collab-oratively derived and writing descriptions that are multi-vocal" (Lassiter 1998: 10). This sense of collaboration certainly applies to our work with staff as para-ethnographers. We also routinely engage persons in our proj-ects as "informants" but these informants are not those whom we refer to as the para-ethnographers on our projects (actually, our para-ethnogra-phers are quite adept at relating to us professionals and to others on the project in both of these roles, switching between para-ethnographer and informant).

The key characteristic of our version of participatory ethnography, then, is the recruitment of staff team members to operate on the researchers' side of the ethnographic work. Having staff work alongside professional, ex-perienced ethnographers as para-ethnographers is different from asking members of one's host community to review representational findings or suggested solutions and different from asking host-subjects to give their input or bless results and recommendations. It is also different, as noted above, from recognizing or problematizing one's host-subject informants as collaborators.

In Water Cooler Logic, this stronger version of participatory ethnogra-phy transfers part of the ethnographic work, as well as the ethnographic authority cultivated in the knowledge constructed and represented, to the host-staff para-ethnographers. Importantly, the same staff that work along-side us in the "fieldwork" phase of a project—what we call the Discovery phase—also work as full participants in the subsequent Co-Design phase. During Co-Design meetings we work over the materials and perspectives gained in the Discovery, writing them up collaboratively into a form of ethnographic writing that serves to guide and inform the design work. Perhaps few mainstream ethnographers would recognize our short-hand, flip-chart/white-board jottings and scribbled models, eventually worked into action plans and reports, as "ethnographic writing," yet these prod-ucts and activities underscore and exemplify para-ethnographers' author-ity. (In this volume, Cefkin [chapter 1], Nafus and anderson [chapter 5], Blomberg [chapter 8], and Fischer [chapter 9], each take up aspects of this issue of the outputs or results of ethnography, expanding on the core no-tion of the *writing* of ethnography. The kinds of ethnographic projects we address in this volume are distinguishable from "research" ethnography in the forms of reflective knowledge-production they result in from field-work, as well as how these results are used.)

We developed our version of participatory ethnography while working as researchers at the former Institute for Research on Learning in Menlo Park, CA, and then with research colleagues in the VA. It evolved from nu-merous practical trials and extended theoretical discussions about ways of using ethnography in organizations. Patricia Sachs was employing this approach even before joining IRL, as were August Carbonella and others. Melissa Cefkin was an active proponent at IRL, while she led the earliest projects with the Department of Veterans Affairs, and obviously, contin-ues to be in subsequent roles.

Introducing Complexity

The concept of *complexity* throws some light on the reasons why many people in large organizations have turned into puzzlers by necessity, and hence, are ready candidates for para-ethnography. They are often affected by the operational difficulties that beset the large organization: the un-availability of applicable clear-cut decisions; the often-conflicted conse-quences of directive actions; the inability of the organizational agent to understand actions from the resultant responses; and the insufficient func-tional coupling among parts.[2] Managers can let these issues blend into the background while maintaining faith in the rational organization, but a frontline person has to find an answer right here, right now, else decisions can't be made, questions won't be answered, claims won't be resolved, and the work of the organization will grind to a halt.

We would also argue that in large organizations, there is a complex-ity problem of a distinctly human, *social* kind—what might be called the problem of continuously emergent cultural-sociality. However much man-agement staff, acting as systems organizers, attempt to arrange things, no one at work (management included) is free of the irrepressible human demands for action, decision, and meaning (or their paired opposites: in-action or inertia, indecision, and ambiguity). These demands emerge from the core of human sociality and insist on mattering. They interfere with attempts to totally rationalize work as systems, processes, resources (in-cluding human), and things. Thus, for instance, no one at work is free of the anxieties and attractions associated with the pull from the local com-munities of practice that always differentiate the organization into distinct groups and networks apart from the formal organization (Wenger 1998: 118–19). No one can escape the way in which others provide critique or affirmation (often implicit and tacit, but sometimes quite explicitly, too) and thereby influence one's own rendering of the world and of one's own self. Many systems thinkers of the organization ignore or marginalize this human social dynamism as much as possible, but it is forever surfacing, skewing, and interfering with the formation of the organization as a stable thing.[3]

The complexity of a large organization as described above utilizes the term and concept in its ordinary sense. It refers to the phenomenon of complexity as a crucial quality or attribute of these organizations. Even in this everyday sense, complexity imparts significant weight, character-izing the situations in which we live and work, and the phenomena we are trying to understand in large organizations, as being anything but straight-forward or readily approachable, let alone easily manageable. However, in addition to this everyday sense of complexity, we also invoke and cite complexity in the newer, more formal sense to which it has lent its name in recent years. We take complexity to be the phenomenon and instances of complexity theories such as "chaos theory" as proposed explanations for the phenomenon, keeping in mind the essential circularity of this conception.

In the last quarter of the twentieth century, the development of the so-called complexity sciences ushered in a new chapter in the saga of the relationship between the positivist, "hard sciences" and the "interpretive sciences." Complexity arrived on the scene in the meta-discourses of our era in the nick of time, rescuing systems thinking from itself as an overly simplified take on the world, or at least of "the organization." Traditional systems theory has been a convenient silent partner in the management business. It theorized the organization in terms of functionality and helped divide it into manageable parts or functional subsystems. It did a good job thereby of justifying, although more by analogy than by logical argument, the need for hierarchical levels of control. It also made a case for the neces-sity of information gathering and feedback from the frontline, though the latter was often ignored in practice.

In the new formulaic organizations are not (static or simple cybernetic) "systems" but "complexities." Complex dynamic systems were first de-scribed in physical settings such as weather patterns or fluid dynamics, where they were innocently amazing: one could not predict when the next drop of water would fall from the faucet, when a sand hill would start to slide, or which path a process would take under specific sensitive condi-tions. Complexity thinking by itself did not have a great deal of impact on the greater world, but it did strike the imagination: What if complex-ity was the diagnostic characteristic for all these other phenomena, which had not been explainable before, and which include, notably, the sociocul-tural ones?

And so they do, in the sense that features and dynamics similar to those uncovered in the physical contexts can be found in sociocultural and organizational contexts as well (Mosko and Damon 2005).

However, systems theory–thinking does not fare as well in explaining how social and cultural factors impact the functioning of the organization. The social and cultural operate largely below the information radar and crosscut the differentiation of the system. And, as we shall note, complexity thinking is an advance on systems theory but most instances of it still do not address human sociality or the concept of the cultural very well. The "social" and "cultural" have remained largely outside managerial concepts of control in any systematic way—because they have always proved too complex.

This left an opening for anthropologists, sociologists, and social psychologists to suggest that their services could be useful. That said, much of the help offered is problematic in that it works out of that earlier analytical frame that anthropology has since retired. In chapter 7, Martin Ortlieb takes on this tension between an older, more static, and reified sense of culture and the more recent, processual analytic. Many clients in organizations have been schooled to think that culture, in the older, reified sense, is "real enough" to be factored in and leveraged in their organizational dynamics. This conviction is not entirely untrue. They would like anthropologists to help them with their (corporate or organizational) culture and society, as it were. It has proved difficult to disabuse people in organizations of this idea, to steer them toward the more difficult way of thinking that characterizes the processual analytic. From the vantage point of the processual analytic, with its robust view of social agency and complexity, the societal and cultural dimensions of organizations are now recognized as operating apart from the formal organizational system. They present an independent and powerful alternative phenomenon to the formal, hierarchical structures and rules. In short, they constitute the "informal" organization, which, as many researchers have said, is nothing other than the social relations among people and the resulting groupings and histories (Wenger 1998: 188–89).

Unfortunately for those who hope that the concept of complexity will serve as a kind of control-systems theory on steroids, complexity also changes the meaning of explanation and affects how we think about prediction and control. While in the traditional (systems theory) sense, explanation indicates that one has gained an understanding of the phenomena to the point that the emergent behavior can be reduced to or even "rebuilt" from underlying causes, this is not the case for the explanations derived from complexity theory. For in those cases the phenomenon to be explained and its explanation are of the same "size" and thus nothing is gained by substituting the explanation for the phenomenon. One just has to embrace the richness and diversity of phenomena.

Thus, the hope that the new notion of complexity and the theories associated with it might help resolve the problems of designing, managing, and controlling organizations turns out to be misplaced. What the sciences of complexity and their discourses do is make the un-resolvable and the indeterminate necessary and constitutive features of the organization. Complexity states that these "systems," among which count organizations-as-corporations, are (a) dynamic, they evolve over time (which is relatively easy to accept); (b) non-linear, that is, they can make unexpected turns in new directions for which nothing will prepare you (that is much harder to swallow for someone charged with delivering specific functions reliably and controlling the performance of the organization); and lastly, (c) their future behavior can't be fully predicted from their present state (which is unacceptable from the viewpoint of the control function of the organization!).[4]

So far these attributes of complexity may seem negative, from, say, a manager's perspective. But this is so *only* if one regards complexity exclusively in relation to a desire to control. If one gives up that impulse, complexity provides instead a window on local sources of organizational creativity.[5] Since complex phenomena in general are richer in possible responses than even the brightest among us can comprehend, and can accommodate changing conditions without waiting for someone in charge to recognize and cognize the problem, it means that many "solutions" are already somewhere, maybe partially, in existence in the system. The seeds for a solution will typically emerge where the problems are most pressing and where the need to come up with an answer presents itself daily. This explains why we have learned that for creating solutions it is important to recruit frontline people as well as supervisors and managers close to the work. Higher-up managers become more useful later when the organization's approval is required to move forward. This feature of the complex organization—call it "emergence"—explains why we consider our kind of problem solving more a discovery of solutions already immanent to the work practice of our clients. Our facilitation aims at releasing the organization's inherent potential, which is why we see ourselves in some profound way as *passive* contributors.[6]

These developments with respect to the concept of complexity are all well and good; however, having invoked complexity and the way in which it has developed into a cluster of "sciences of complexity," we want to step back from seeing these approaches as being useful *directly* in our work and in many kinds of ethnographic anthropology. In fact, we concur with one close reader of complexity theories, Ralph Stacey, that these sciences are mainly important to the social sciences as resources for analogies and metaphors. What is needed, instead, is the development of concepts and discourses on complexity that work well in sociological and anthropological frames and situations.

In one of Stacey's several books tracing his sojourn from management to management studies, through the complexity sciences to clinical group (social) psychotherapy, *Complexity and Group Processes: A Radically Social Understanding of Individuals* (2003), he makes these points in the course of developing his concept and theory of "complex responsive processes" — basically a theory of social interaction, built in the tradition of G. H. Mead (Stacey 2003: 66–69) and informed by basic principles of complexity. Stacey's work is relevant for both the critique of the complexity sciences as they may apply to human social phenomena, and because his theory of complex responsive processes resonates well with current work in anthropology on process, event, encounter, emergence, and the person as agent in, well, highly *complex* social dynamics. Stacey argues that

> complex responsive processes of human relating have the intrinsic capacity to pattern themselves in coherent ways ... [and] that such patterning emerges in narrative forms, which can be described in terms of continually iterated themes patterning the experience of being together. Again by analogy to the complexity sciences, these self-organizing integrative themes perpetually reconstruct the past and in the process of constructing the future. And the future so constructed emerges as both continuity and potential transformation at the same time. The potential for transformation arises because iterative nonlinear interaction has the capacity to amplify small differences. (2003: 327)

We draw attention to his remarks about narrative and the constructed use of the past in the present to situate persons with respect to their future. This is quintessential "sociocultural work," which people perform endlessly (and which is inevitably a part of the Discovery findings in our ethnography). For Stacey, this creation of patterns of meaning that generate understanding emerge in ways that are remarkably like those that emerge in the processes observed in complex phenomena studied in the complexity sciences. Stacey writes elsewhere in *Complexity and Group Processes* about what he judges to be other, key self-organizing themes, besides narrative. They include the power-dynamics of "turn taking/making," a familiar topic from sociolinguistics, and of "associations," which bring into play notions of symbols that processualists in the vein of Victor Turner's work would surely recognize. All of which is to say that "complexity" in human-centered phenomena can be shown to have its analogues to the kinds of factors theorized in the complexity sciences.[7]

Indeed, we need not look outside anthropology to find interest in and development of notions of complexity in human society and culture. Several articles in *The Manchester School: Practice and Ethnographic Praxis in Anthropology* (2006), edited by T. M. S. Evens and Don Handleman, develop the discourse on complexity in a vein familiar to anthropologists. The Manchester School, led by Max Gluckman starting in the 1940s, championed the extended case study or situational analysis as an alternative to mainstream Malinowskian, structural-functionalist anthropology. This argument was largely over the reified sense of society and culture versus a processual one mentioned above. The Manchester School took process, event, encounter, and agency seriously long before "the complexity sciences" arose; however, they did not have the richness of the supporting analogues of contemporary complexity science and discourse to fuel development of their ideas.

In *The Manchester School* Bruce Kapferer writes, "The idea of the situation can be conceived of as a kind of net that the analyst casts over complexity, thereby bringing together a diversity of dynamic and different processes without asserting that in reality they constitute an integrated unity" (in Evens and Handelman 2005: 126). At the start of many of our projects, clients will say, "We have a situation … that needs attention and work; we hear you (WCL Inc.) may be able to help us with it."[8] We are then operating the situation in reverse—by pulling apart the diverse processes that have been identified as part of it without assuming that they form a coherent unit.

For Stacey, as for Gluckman many years before him, the question was: if *this* is how the social and cultural world really is—namely, a maze of complexity, of process and change—what is the best methodology for engaging it? For the Manchester School it is the extended case study or situational analysis, an approach that requires the ethnographer to engage his host-subjects *in step* with their actual, ongoing, or arising issues, concerns, projects, conflicts.

In a very real sense each of our projects in a large organization is an extended case study that actively experiments with the complex setting in which we work, which is, after all, what our client sponsors want us to do in our "interventions": help them experiment with their organization. Ethnography—especially this kind of project-based ethnography—is a good way to do this because it mobilizes and leverages the same kind of puzzling modality that is a key facet of both management and staff in actual organizations, regardless of the brand of ideology of top-down command and control, system and process they espouse.

Stacey provides a summarizing statement of what is needed, and what we try to do in Water Cooler Logic: "The move we want to make, therefore, is away from thinking about the organization as a system, to thinking about organizing as highly complex, ongoing processes of people relating to each other" (2003: 66).

The puzzling of which we speak—this process of sense making and meaning making, which is constantly going on in the organization at all levels—gets propped up in our WCL process and fieldwork method, itself an outcome of our extensive combined theory and practice. The propping-up includes some literal, on-site methodological scaffolding: we negotiate a real space and time for the people on the team to step away from their daily work and reflect on it at some distance. We create a secure space within which people can admit to not knowing or not understanding, and puzzle over how to apply an instruction or regulation. We provide them with a running memory of insights and concerns that gradually grow into a tacit agreement of what criteria the solution has to fulfill or furnishes building blocks for a department-spanning solution. We shepherd the process by creating a balanced playing field among the participants, balanced in the sense of dampening down—but never disqualifying or denying—the sometimes substantial power and personality differences represented on a team (a physician or pharmacist and a clerk for example), all in the service of enabling emergence. In many instances, those higher in the organization's hierarchy look to us expressly to help accomplish this facilitation of power relations in a way that allows for better understanding and communication.

We've learned that our efforts as outsider ethnographers in setting the stage should not obviate, overrun, or *overwrite* the original practice of sense and meaning making and of delivering concrete outcomes to the organization. We cannot proceed with the customary ethnographic approach of thick engagement, followed by translation from afar using concepts distant from the ethnographic context. We must stay local, act more as catalysts in the process, which calls for careful maneuvering by the ethnographer-consultant. Working with staff as para-ethnographers does effect a shift in the center of gravity of ethnographic authority that builds in a project, a shift away from us as the experts and onto the client host team. Just how we do this in actual practice is easier to show in a developed example, which we do below.

But first, it would be helpful to provide a brief overview of the VA for readers who may be unfamiliar with it, or who may harbor fragments of the many cultural memes about the VA that float broadly about in the popular imagination created by the press. The VA is the health care system established originally for the members of the United States armed services, following their discharge. Below is a brief synopsis of the VA's health care system.

"The VA": A Vast, Massively Complex Organization Ripe for Ethnography

> The VA? It's a place where old soldiers go to die.
>
> —staff member with more than thirty years on the job,
> reflecting on how people used to view the VA
>
> In the past decade, largely unnoticed by the public,
> the [VA health care] system has undergone a dramatic
> transformation and now is considered by some to be a model.
>
> —Gilbert M. Gaul, *Washington Post*, 22 August 2005

The VA operates the largest health care system in the United States. In terms of "organizational mass," the VA is also among the nation's largest organizations, governmental or otherwise. The VA is a cabinet level department with an operating budget of ninety billion dollars in 2008 and a staff of over 200,000 employed in three divisions. Of the approximately twenty-seven million living US veterans, more than 80 percent are registered to receive some part of their health care from the VA.[9]

The VA's network of medical facilities is distributed over 1,300 sites of healthcare, including 157 tertiary care hospitals, 862 ambulatory care and community-based outpatient clinics, and 134 nursing facilities. It operates long-term care facilities and programs across the country, including facilities in Alaska, Hawaii, and Puerto Rico, and in other locales where the population density of US veterans warrants it.[10]

The complexities of the VA are manifest to anyone who spends time getting service from or working with the VA. Over and beyond its sheer size is the fact that it is much more than simply a healthcare system for vets. It is also a major training ground for the nation's medical schools, and over half of all medical students rotate through the VA as interns or residents. With its collaborations between VA medical centers and affiliated prestigious private and state medical schools, the VA is also the setting for a significant portion of clinical research in the US.

A significant percentage of VA employees in all ranks and functions are themselves veterans. To them, the VA and its culture are strongly "mission-driven" (their term), meaning that they see their work as fulfilling a social and community function. They are strongly motivated beyond just earning a living and their expressed care for veterans constitutes a key characteristic of "VA culture," a quality of the sociality that is recognizable in the everyday decisions and conflicts.

During the last fifteen years, the VA has undergone revitalization as a healthcare organization. This revitalization story and the realities behind it come complete with its own "hero" (at least in the minds of many VA employees) in former leader Dr. Kenneth Kizer. Under Kizer's leadership the VA turned around many aspects of its operations. By 2005 the VA was seen as having succeeded well beyond the levels at which many people believed a huge governmental organization could succeed. In recent years the VA has emerged as a model of (managed) healthcare organization and delivery. The VA offers an alternative model, distinct from the private sector's, that is a combination of insurance and healthcare delivery. The VA offers something akin to "socialized-medicine" for many veterans.

Our work with the VA grew out of a connection between the Institute for Research on Learning and the VA staff responsible for the dissemination of many educational innovations and, more generally, with "training-up" VA staff to operate in the new modality of a "can-do" organization. These VA leaders recognized that IRL's mantra about work, learning, and change being largely social, informal, and local (or "situated") phenomena fit well with their analyses that traditional approaches were not very effective.[11] Driving our espousal of this deep participatory work was a recognition of how easily and effectively VA staff members could move into and work innovatively in this ethnographic space along with the professional ethnographers, a level of participation that would eliminate many of the vexing problems that can occur when the outside ethnographer works up the knowledge gained into representations, which are then shared, somehow, with someone(s) in the organization and become the basis for implementation by yet someone else.

Bed Control and Patient Discharge: Participatory Ethnography in Practice

Now let us turn to the case study, a close-up look at Water Cooler Logic in practice, with an emphasis on Participatory Ethnography and CoDesign.

A Project Emerges

We had just completed a project at one VA medical center that focused on developing a model for "physician productivity." At the project's final meeting, several high-ranking staff, including the director, the associate chief of staff, the chief resident, the nurse executive, some staff nurses, and others, entered into a frank discussion of their local problems. These

ranged from a bed shortage, to the inability of pharmacy to deal with discharge medications, to logjams in surgery and cardiological procedures,
to more personalized complaints about how residents were performing
and how some attending physicians were not discharging or transfer-
ring patients promptly. Intensive-care nurses added their concerns about
working with staff on the general wards. And the "bed control" nurse
expressed frustration with having to juggle competing demands for beds
in the face of little cooperation and even downright resistance from some
staff. All of these complaints are systemic to the VA's healthcare system
and a function of the size, complexity, and unique institutional position
of the VA.

After everyone had a say, the chief of staff for clinical affairs proposed
that the collection of leaders in the room could at least agree that the central
bottleneck of this conflicted system of patient flow was patient discharge.
He proposed that by working through the WCL process to, as he put it,
"fix the patient discharge process," they would be able to make progress
toward the more intractable issues of bed control. This suggestion was
accepted, even as one high-ranking physician added, "It's not a matter of
fixing the system for patient discharge; we don't have a system."

Within a few weeks we returned and met with our new core team,
composed mainly of staff from the first project. This time, though, our
focus was on puzzling out the confusion of work practices and processes
around patient discharge that involved staff from practically every major
functional area in the hospital.

Staging and Conducting Participatory Ethnographic Moments

When hospital staff talk about *patient discharge,* they refer to the events,
procedures, and policies associated with (a) determining that a patient
is ready, medically, to leave the hospital, (b) the many steps necessary to
implement this decision, including provisions for ongoing care after discharge (such as prescriptions for medication, doctor's appointments, or
home-based nursing care), as well as ancillary, non-medical discharge–
readiness issues such as social-work assistance, family notification, and
patient transport, and (c) the many "in-house" ramifications of a patient
being discharged, which include readying the patient to leave the room
and turning that room around for a new admission.

The suspicion is that too many patients stay in the hospital for too long
after it has been determined—or, more controversially, *could* or *should* have
been determined—that it was medically and socially suitable for them to
be discharged. Historically, veterans did stay in VA hospitals for weeks,
even months, longer than is considered appropriate today. Veterans and

their care providers, however, may have grown used to, and in some situations attached to, the option of longer stays.

So the goal of the WCL project and the charge for the WCL team was to understand how patients are discharged, to uncover the inefficiencies, determine their impact on other concerns such as bed availability, patient transfers, and quality and continuity of care, and design ways to improve the situation. The core team consisted of the chief of staff (for clinical affairs), an MD, his assistant, two nurses from specialty services, the bed control nurse, the center's patient-transfer coordinator, and one WCL researcher. Each of the team members represented his or her own agenda, and to differing degrees, the interests of a professional community or functional unit.

The staging work begins with a day-long "project orientation and planning workshop," a time for the free flow of a multi-vocal conversation among the team members about the topic in its broadest sense. This discussion provides a preliminary setting of the scope of the project work; namely, the places to visit, the functions and practices to understand, the individuals and groups to speak to. The rest of the time is spent preparing them to visit with and relate to others in the organization in a way that emphasizes informal, deep conversation and the observation of how their co-workers go about their work in their everyday settings. To this end, we coach team members on how to see the organization and their colleagues "with fresh eyes" (a phrase we regularly use).

The team goes out—in pairs at first, later often individually—to conduct a friendly examination of the different work settings, practices, and communities. This work constitutes the core of the "ethnographic moments" we effect in our WCL projects. Arranging for our team members to get out of their workplace neighborhoods and into those of others is our version of the basic ethnographic impulse of "going about the world." In this case, the "world" is the work-world of this large, complex organization, and our participatory ethnography invites staff to visit communities within it.

The WCL team visited and talked to staff in the areas they represented, plus staff in pharmacy, on the general medical and surgical patient units, house staff (residents and interns, MDs still in training), and attending physicians. Visits were also made to environmental engineering staff (housekeeping, responsible for maintenance, cleaning rooms, and changing bedding), respiratory therapists, patient transporters, and social workers. Over three days, team members spoke with about fifty staff; some visits were short, lasting no more than twenty minutes, some lasted a couple of hours. Some staff even camped out to talk with staff on the evening and night shifts.

Team members are urged to observe closely how their colleagues arrange and use their workplace, tools, and resources. The observational and participatory elements of the Discovery work are subtle but occasionally give rise to significant insights.[12] We encourage team members to speak with staff in a private setting aside from their workplace. These "short sessions" from the person's work often turned into long interviews that at times astonished the team members in their richness.

Finally, we caution the team members to make sure that the person they are visiting agrees to their being there. They must let the interviewee know that these engagements are entirely voluntary, confidential, and unrelated to an evaluation of their work; that he or she can terminate the interview and observation at any moment with no explanation required.

Each day review and reflection on the Discovery work goes on in regular "huddles"; the first is held after the first or second round of interviews and observations; after that, there are two per day. In these huddles, team members recount details of their visits, providing everyone the opportunity to gain insight into areas they have not visited. Huddles are a first stage of analysis and integration of findings, where overlaps are noted, connections are made, and the different sides and angles reported are sewn together into a 3D landscape view. Huddles often become catalysts for immediate fixes and changes, such as when a team member brings a question back that gets instantaneously answered or resolved in the team and is then transferred seamlessly into practice.

It is remarkable how well the team members perform in what amounts to a dual role of co-ethnographer and insider-informant, as they help review and debrief our interviews and observations. Often, a team member will have found a useful way of asking about something of particular relevance to the topic, or will learn of someone else with whom we should talk, and then many new points for investigation arise. In this way, the sense of a collective, participatory engagement develops as we go along the multi-day Discovery work. This is an example of what we mean by *participatory ethnography:* members of the host community are pulled explicitly into the frame of the ethnographer vis-à-vis a community of others in the host organization.

Three Puzzler's Perspectives

We present three different characteristic positions and perspectives to be representative of the developments that Water Cooler Logic helps effect: that of the bed control nurse, of pharmacy, and of the chief of staff, a top-level manager as well as an MD. These three perspectives give a taste of the different operational and social faces of the problem and the situatedness of the individual experiences. Putting together these three "views-from-somewhere" can demonstrate the complexity of the problem and why no single person is capable of tackling it.

Of course, there were many more perspectives included in the project: those of the nurses and other clinical practitioners on the wards and in specialty clinics, the head nurse who organizes patient care throughout the hospital, and the social worker who arranges the discharge with the family. As the team actually absorbs all the important facts and features of the different angles, it begins to operate and conceptualize at higher and higher levels of competence and complexity.

Perspective 1: Bed Control Nurse

The person formally in charge of tracking and handling all routine bed assignments in this medical center is the bed control nurse. The bed control nurse's job centers on three main functions: keeping a running inventory of all beds that are available throughout the day, negotiating with the different parties that request a bed for a patient, and mediating the actual assignment of beds to both new patients and current in-patients (who are subjects for internal transfers).

What complicates the picture is that the staffed beds that are available are not all alike. The hospital, like any other, has different categories of beds, and different numbers of beds in those categories. The difference among beds lies mainly in the degree of support they demand from the nursing staff. The "monitored bed" is a class higher than the normal bed and reserved for more severely ill patients or patients in unstable condition. Beds in the emergency room receive the highest degree of attention from staff (that is, highest ratio of nursing staff to bed) and are reserved for patients in critical condition.

Whoever is in charge of bed control finds him- or herself in the middle of the contention for available beds that is all but non-stop. The bed control nurse in this medical center was a woman with years' of experience in several different areas of nursing, including work on the general wards. She starts each day by walking the units to find out who came in overnight, the tally of open beds, and the potential discharges.

Interestingly, she spoke of distrusting the newer, nifty computerized reports, as it makes it that much easier for staff to "hide beds," that is, describe a situation such that a bed will not become officially open quite so soon. Perhaps it is being saved for some patient on some doctor's request. We learn it is widely understood that some of the hardest administrative work in a hospital congregates around admissions and discharges. So hiding a bed may arise because the ward staff is trying to push work to a shift that is more highly staffed, or simply onto the next shift. And so the bed control nurse likes to see for herself the existing state of bed availability on the floors. She looks for overflows and evaluates the appropriateness of bed assignments, which can get out of control due to contingencies such as emergency admissions, sudden changes in a patient's status, shifts in nursing staff assignments, and so on. She looks at the requests for changes from all sources inside and outside the medical center.

One of this bed control nurse's points of frustration, shared by many others, is the time lag between initial identification of a patient who is ready to go home and the actual follow-through: patients are often identified as likely to go home "the next day," but by the time the official discharge orders are written, it may be too late in the day to coordinate and implement the discharge. By then the day-shift support staff has gone home, including most of housekeeping, who would "turn around" the room for a new patient. The smaller evening-shift staff is confronted with an overload of both patient discharges and admissions, which is why the evening shift calls the time from 4:00 to 7:00 PM "the insane hours," or the "insane time." And there is no guarantee that the same problem will not develop for the same patient the following day.

The bed control nurse developed her daily routine and ways of working as a means of doing things reasonably well under tense circumstances. She learned to distrust reports from interested parties about available or urgently needed beds. She relies on people only for accurate accounts of where things stand: which doctor or nurse is saying what about the patient? Is the patient really waiting outside the door for his bed? Is the patient ready to leave, with a place to go to and a treatment plan and medications in place? How long until the bed will be empty and cleaned and available for the next patient?

Pressure for new admissions and internal transfers impact the bed control situation. The bed control nurse regularly fields a barrage of requests to locate or open up a bed for a patient needing to come in. The trick is to ride the fine line between being too eager or demanding in pressing for the transfer or discharge of a patient or allowing the "docs" to call the shots. Too often they are "looking out for" a particular patient of theirs and his/her family, not wanting to concede that this patient should be transferred to a lower care–level unit. To demonstrate how complicated it gets, she noted that one surgeon was frequently opposed to moving his patients out of intensive care, post-surgery, because he was convinced that inferior care on a step-down ward "might" increase the rate of noted complications or even deaths prior to the thirty-day mark, on which his high performance rating was based. Much of this was built, she thought, on the general prejudice toward the nursing staff on the general medicine floors. From others we heard that this prejudice was rooted in a perception that the predominantly immigrant nursing staff on those floors was relatively incompetent and, well, "lazy." The bed control nurse's point was that regardless of the validity of these types of claims, they contributed to the difficulty of determining and negotiating bed availability.

What if there is no bed for a patient who really needs to come into the facility, we asked? It is very rare that a patient suffers any care deficit directly related to bed unavailability. In case of emergency, the patient is referred to a community hospital or another VA. The problem is this scenario costs the VA a large sum. Emergency patients are virtually always accommodated; indeed, accommodating them is one of the hooks that regularly snarls a careful plan for bringing someone in a non-emergent condition from another VA or from a community hospital to the VA facility.

For the bed control nurse the work of puzzling is made the more difficult because the rules, agreements, staffing, and resources are themselves not only in flux over the weeks and months but also subject to deeper, strategic-level change, changes rooted in decisions that she is not generally privy to until some time later. For example, high-level executives may strike new deals, or key physicians and administrations in different VA hospitals may make new arrangements about accepting one another's patients.

If she is too conservative, beds stay open and money is lost, practice gets lax. If she is too optimistic, agreeing to admit "too many patients" she feels herself contributing to the confusion, if not chaos, that ensues: patients stranded in the corridors on gurneys waiting for room assignments, emergency cases being diverted to other hospitals. Then fresh complaints rain down upon her and the administration.

The bed control nurse welcomed the chance to be part of the team because, for one, this meant that her issues would be addressed collectively by the different functions that she routinely tried to coordinate. If discharge could be made more transparent and predictable, it would make her life a lot easier. The WCL project allowed her to explain in depth her situation to the whole team. It also allowed her to appreciate the story of others who are part of this contest for beds.[13]

Perspective 2: Pharmacy

No one from the pharmacy was part of the core team. They stated that they simply could not spare staff to participate in the Discovery work. But they were happy enough to have the team visit and hear their version of the situation and later they participated in the integration of findings and Co-Design interventions. The head of pharmacy knew, of course, that she and her operation were seen as contributing to the problems of untimely discharge of patients. How so?

Only very few VA patients get discharged without having to take medications along. The routine is for doctors to write orders for "discharge medications," pharmacy to fill those orders, and, in many cases, have a conference with the patient about how to take his medications before leaving. The problem is, again, one of timing. A patient can be all ready to go, discharge order written and communicated, taxi waiting, so to speak. Yet the whole process stops cold, while every one waits for the "discharge meds." The head of pharmacy explained that the only way to have the "discharge meds" ready in the morning is to get the orders from the docs before 2:00 PM the day before. But, as everyone recognizes, and as the head of pharmacy confirms, this requirement is unworkable. At 2:00 PM the docs are unlikely to have made a decision about discharge, written discharge orders, or the orders for discharge medications. "Well," pharmacy says, "that is not our problem."

With regard to what *are* pharmacy's problems she relates that there are not enough staff in the evening and night shifts to ready prescriptions for 7:00 AM, or even for 10:00 AM in many cases. She explains that pharmacists have multiple roles: they must not only fill, but also verify all prescriptions; several of them go on rounds in the morning and cannot fill prescriptions during that time. Laws prevent them from using pharmacy techs for much of this regulated work. Lastly, they have a very hard time hiring and keeping staff because, "our pharmacists can work for us for one year then leave for a 40 percent pay increase the day after in the private sector."

Besides, she remarks, even if someone were available to do the work overnight, the doctors almost never get their orders for discharge meds written by evening time anyway. And when they finally do, the list of discharge meds they produce looks too often like a list of every medication ever used by this patient during his stay, the result—pharmacy suspects—of a cut-and-paste operation from the patient notes. Then pharmacy spends unnecessary time filling a long list of medications, many of which are not needed by the patient.

By the Co-Design, the head of pharmacy was willing to work toward a solution. For pharmacy this would mean bringing more pharmacy techs onto the night shift to work under supervision of a pharmacist for safety and legal reasons. Then pharmacy could probably ready all prescriptions turned in by 9:00 PM the evening before for the next day. She secured everyone's patience by making it known that she had first to work through the complicated business of closing down a pharmacy in one larger clinic, formerly a medical center itself, transfer the staff to this one, and angle for a new head count. Everyone in the bureaucracy knew what a hassle that would present but also knew that securing pharmacy's help in reconfiguring patient discharge was critical to success.

With pharmacy on board, the team turned its attention to the other key players, the "docs," or more formally, the "providers [of medical care]." Could it be arranged that docs on the house staff get the discharge medication orders readied the evening before? "It always comes back to us docs; we're always the ones who have to do one more thing to help everyone else out. What's another half hour in the evening writing up meds? It's another half hour less sleep, that's what it is," said a resident during a candid moment in the interview.

Perspective 3: Chief of Staff for Clinical Affairs (The "Chief Puzzler")

In his formal role the chief of staff is, among other things, a guardian of the overall quality of care provided by a hospital's medical staff. He is also concerned with overall policy, programs, and practice, including the education of interns and residents, and the relations with affiliated hospitals.

On the other hand, the chief of staff is not formally responsible for the overall patient-discharge process. In fact, no one is, at least not in a prescribed way. The difficulties concerning patient discharge arise and take the form they do largely because "patient discharge" is one of those intergroup work practices that is not any one's or any office's responsibility. The discharge process sits at the intersection of many different professional, administrative, and clerical units, and requires functions and routines from everywhere to gel, which is one reason why it is such an intractable problem to tackle.

This situation is not unusual in terms of how organizations "organize" themselves, and the organizational lacunae that result. Researchers at IRL in the early 1990s discovered a classic example of a critically important organizational lacuna in the Xerox Corporation. No one had noticed that there was no formal unit or department of "paper handlers" in the organization. The knowledge(s) about how to accomplish the critically important paper-handling feat was distributed informally among a fairly broad community of practice of Xerox engineers, designers, and repair people. The company only discovered this community of practice when a well-intentioned "re-org" sent half of its members packing to several new locations and new models started jamming much more frequently. Patients are not paper but it is not without basis that this entire cycle of admission to the hospital, assignment to a service and ward, coordination and delivery of care, and, lastly, discharge, is often referred to as "patient flow."

Given the importance of patient discharge and the intractability of the issue, the chief of staff elects to take up this work. He may, in fact, be expected to do so. Implicit in such an expectation is the recognition that the chief of staff, who is also a doctor, is in several ways ideally positioned to see the interconnections and be able to intervene.

This VA, like a number of others, is a teaching and research hospital. Its mode of operation depends extensively on its affiliations with physicians from a nearby, prestigious, private university medical school. Indeed, the approximately forty attending physicians at the top of the tightly graded, clinical educational ladder were "affiliated" MDs, which is to say, *not* VA staff physicians. Also, many of the VA "house staff," comprised of doctors in those graded ranks which the attendings educate clinically and supervise in delivery of care (chief, third-, second-, first-year *residents;* and second-, first-year *interns*), are only temporary VA staff, or non-VA staff "on rotation" in the medical specialty services in the VA. This situation is the norm throughout most of the VA system. It is one of the reasons why, in many medical centers, the nurses, who are often long-term VA employees, feel they run the hospitals—for in practice, they do run important aspects of them.

Suffice to say that affiliated physicians hold considerable power in any VA medical center. The system is heavily dependent on them for their knowledge, experience, and dedication to the work of both caring for the veteran patients and educating young physicians. One area they usually try to reserve to their discretion is how and when they spend time providing clinical education and overseeing delivery of care.

Much of the attendings' time in the VA is devoted to conducting medical and teaching rounds, which serve as the chief pedagogical tool for the clinical education of newly minted MDs into their specialties. Patient discharge is one event in this care-delivery process, but it is not one that many attendings regard as high priority. Attendings are however responsible for overseeing the discharge of a patient. The final step in this process is checking with the residents on the morning of the planned discharge to see if the patient's condition is still the same. This check-in would typically happen after the morning rounds and thus set a time for when, at the earliest, discharge orders could be finalized and written.

Initial success on this project would be to move the discharges from an indeterminate, mid-to-late afternoon time frame to an earlier time. The chief of staff approached the affiliated attendings with the request to make their medical rounds earlier in the morning, perhaps shorten them a bit, and to give more consideration to discharge planning. Some attendings treated this as another incremental assault on their traditional way of being physicians and clinical educators. Because of their status as affiliated non-VA physicians, the chief of staff did not have a lot of power over them.

At this point the chief of staff made a strong case that the current system that depended on so many affiliated attendings was contributing not only to the confusions and inefficiencies surrounding discharge, but perhaps also impacting quality and continuity of care. In his view and that of others, this situation often left too many residents with inadequate supervision. To compensate for lack of supervision, residents often worked harder, but not necessarily wiser: they order batteries of tests and procedures for unlikely circumstances just to protect themselves. This excess of medical procedures and tests burdens the system, adds confusion and potential errors, wastes money and effort, and postpones the moment when the patient could go home.

The chief of staff proposed to resolve this issue by going in a new direction: hire a small number of staff doctors to serve the role of attendings—often called "hospitalists"—and reduce the number of affiliated attendings. Hospitalists would be better positioned to ensure the continuity of care by working closely with the house staff and provide ongoing guidance to interns and residents. They would also help implement a more orderly pattern of patient discharge as part of care provision.[14]

Part of the reason why the chief of staff chose to invite Water Cooler Logic into the discharge work was because it promised to help him generate the kind of comprehensive view of the situation around which a consensus for action could be forged. He also understood the importance of demonstrating to all affected groups that an effort had been made to look into everything and that no easier, simpler, less-costly solution was to be had.

Bringing Agendas and Solutions Together

By the time of the Co-Design meeting (usually a two-day workshop attended by the full team and additional invited experts) partial solutions had emerged already (like the one described for pharmacy) as well as a tacit consensus that the final solution hinged on a distinct discharge time in the late morning or noon. (Obviously, we are gliding over a robust account of our Co-Design meeting as the other situated context of our work. In briefest summary: it starts as the end-phase of the ethnographic Discovery work, during which we analyze and model our findings, then, the meeting moves into the quite distinct modality of participatory design. Our approach to this design work is highly congruent with the approach of the Danish and European schools of participatory design [e.g. Ehn 1988]).

At Co-Design the team selected 11:00 AM as the best discharge time. This hour gives nurses the time to get the patient out of the bed, pharmacy time to teach the patient the medication regime and still leaves room for housekeeping to get the bed ready for afternoon admissions, thus providing bed control with beds to assign.

The new time forces a dramatic transformation of all the processes up- and downstream of discharge. The functions connected with discharge, such as social work, pharmacy, and patient education, had adjusted themselves to the absence of a specific time and had relaxed their standards since everyone else did, too. All of these interlocking processes now needed to be brought to the point where they could accommodate the new target discharge time. Other processes and events, which stood in the way of these adjustments, needed to be shifted to make room for them.

Part of the transformation had to do with introducing a structure of supervision to keep the process of moving the hospital practice steadily toward the desired goal on track over the intervening months.

The central points of the transformation were:

1. Morning teaching rounds were moved up one hour—from 10:00 AM to 9:00 AM—to free doctors for final discharge evaluation and paperwork.

2. Pharmacy made major staff and shift changes in order to accommodate discharge medication orders that were written late in the day and to fill discharge orders over night.

3. The chief of staff hired two hospitalists to help manage care planning and delivery and work with residents and medical students on a more consistent basis.

4. The bed control nurse created a discharge orientation class for all interns. Together with a second nurse she started tracking the times when a patient was first slotted for discharge up to the point when the patient was released in order to track and document the impact on discharge time and the efficiency of the new discharge process.

5. The hospital established a "Bed Flow" cross-functional committee, chaired by the head nurse, which meets monthly to review changes and address emerging problems related to discharge.

The changes took time to take hold in the practice of the hospital but after six months, average discharge time had been moved up significantly to approximately 1:00 PM. Fifty to seventy percent of patients are discharged significantly earlier, which constitutes a much greater availability of beds. The new discharge time means that the discharge-related tasks can be handled by the daytime shift, which has a higher number of nursing staff per bed. Other positive outcomes included changes in attitude and awareness that lead to new strategies of communication and knowledge sharing. The chief of staff himself declared, "I work differently now; I talk to different people; now I talk with the social worker, not just the supervisor."

The Water Cooler Logic process also helped the team members (a) devise new quantitative measuring protocols for tracking discharges (very close to practice), (b) compile story-laden scenes—a range of anecdotes—

that could answer practically any question aimed at parrying the need to act, and (c) achieve significantly greater conversational acumen about the issues in their broader contexts: conversations that could lead to devising practical solutions and agreements.

The team was grateful to the WCL outsiders for having facilitated bringing people together from many departments and units and establishing a climate in which everyone was listening to everybody else on the team. They especially liked the atmosphere in which for the duration of the project, at least, everyone was more or less on an equal footing. They also realized how important it was to go out into the organization and find out what really was happening. It also gave several of the members a major boost in how they thought about the organization and how they might act more effectively within it over the longer haul. It made them all much better puzzlers.

An Opposable Thumb

The chief of staff summarized the experience with WCL by saying that "Water Cooler [Logic] gave us an *opposable thumb*." He went on to say that until the project took place it was not clear how they should or could effectively take on these issues of discharge planning, bed control, hospitalists, and so on. The approach not only helped them to see things more clearly (the puzzling element), it gave them a process and a practical, organizational-political *forum* to take on these changes. He noted that things were now set up and in motion that would help assure progress or at least continued diligent prosecution of the issues for some time to come—including, for example, the monthly meeting with the head nurse and others on discharge planning, the dedicated training segment for new interns and residents, and so on.

The Value of Ethnography

"Discovery," also called a "fact-finding mission" or "needs assessment" and the like, is seen as the initial phase for a number of consulting processes. Its role is usually that of gathering information, which is then used in some further work. Our team recruits expect similar things from our Discovery and sometimes express early on that they see little difference between what we are asking them to do and what they have done on other task forces or process-improvement teams.

Participants gradually begin to detect a difference when we insist that we not overly formalize the Discovery work: usually we set out a range of topics to bring up, from which they are free to derive questions and format, as they see fit. Working without survey-like "instruments" unsettles some participants in the early going but once everyone has done a few interviews, it is far easier to discuss what ethnography is about. For most team members, the shift in the tenor of the engagement from information-gathering to joint meaning–making occurs by the end of the first day. Usually by that time everyone recognizes the value of a method geared toward opening conversations about otherwise taken-for-granted notions and patterns of action in a friendly, non-threatening, non-evaluative climate sensitive to the actual circumstance and person.

On numerous occasions, members of teams have expressed how the process sets people at ease, encourages them to talk about things that, if not quite taboo, are surely topics or perspectives that are typically to be avoided. The frame and tenor of the effort appears to invoke a revelatory mindset in the host-community members whom we interview, a moment in which the "natives" are free to reflect broadly, insightfully, and intimately on their work and the organization, without fear of saying the wrong thing or having what they say taken the wrong way. Over the experience of many projects we have come to think that it is the tenor of the interaction, born of the friendly, informal, non-evaluative frame in which the interactions are cast, that sets this kind of ethnography-styled engagement apart from other more formal interventions.

The approach induces trust that the space of these interactions is safe and that filters will indeed be placed on what gets seen and said and reported and how it will be said. The ethnographer's discretion is surely a part of this, something we remind everyone of regularly.

In most instances, team members acquire newfound respect for just how complicated everyone else's work (besides their own) actually is, how hard people are working, and how much puzzling everyone is constantly performing.

It is often argued that ethnography is good for generating superior data along certain lines of consideration, data that better reflect the realities on the ground in the contemporary scene; data that better represent the way the people under study parse their "world" or work; more accurate, up-to-date data, and so on. It is suggested that ethnography helps formulate what additional data should be collected through formalized survey methods or data extraction. These claims about ethnography are all true. On this project, during the Co-Design, we were able, just by using ethnographic insights, to develop a means to track patient discharge in the center.

Yet this data-generation feature is only part of what makes ethnographic-styled Discovery compelling. Ethnography is not simply about generating better data or data of a certain kind, generated out of qualitative methods as distinct from quantitative ones. Instead, ethnography done well is also about growing relations among people who share their view of things with one another; and from this exchange generate a refreshed model of that conjoint "reality," which can be reflected and acted upon. Ethnography is as much about assembling—through negotiated instances of shared frames—a new or revised model of system-like complexity as a basis for joint action, as it is about collecting or even constructing pieces of data.[15]

By the end of our Discovery work, we were in a position to remodel patient discharge to a degree of specificity that no one on the team was previously able to do. Most of this understanding is not explicitly expressed, but informs the actions and decisions in a tacit manner. Even where the "new" model contains elements that are generally known or supposed (especially by persons such as the chief puzzler), the Discovery work serves as a highly reliable means of validating those suppositions, thus raising the confidence level in what the team proposes as a solution. It is also a means of "democratizing the model" among staff at many different stations and levels in the organization.

Puzzling Is a Social Enterprise

The puzzling we orchestrate cannot be said to result in any one grand "totalizing" 3D picture of the world: it is not a puzzle with a million pieces solved and on display. Instead, the puzzling itself is piecemeal in what it accomplishes; things come into partial view better than they did before. The gaps are still there and people act and continue puzzling in and around our efforts to display the results of our collective work. It helps to think of these puzzle pieces as alive or at least elastic and responsive to handling in a mode of deliberated uncertainty.

There is a time of disengagement from immediacy that the ethnographic rounds provide, a time of analysis and modeling. This phase corresponds with the "writing ethnography" phase of traditional fieldwork. But in Water Cooler Logic it does not go on long before the outcomes of that analysis are returned to the reality of practice in the medical centers. In many ways, these ethnographies are prepared, cooked, and consumed on the spot, as it were, with little by way of shelf life or preservatives to keep them around. Our final reports are short, capturing only the turning points in the project, and incomplete by choice. The key accomplishment of the approach lies in the change in the collective understanding and attitudes of the participants, which is rarely if ever represented exhaustively in written form, but begins straightaway to translate into decisions and actions and forms a basis for future joint decision making and dialogue.

The puzzling should be recognized as taking place *socially* and *dialogically*; it is not a phenomenon solely or mainly of "a" or "the" lone puzzler, and is a far cry from the image and motif of the lone ethnographer. Some of the key moments in a WCL project are indeed the "ah-ha" moments that individual para-ethnographers report after a particularly insightful interview. But overall the puzzling that Water Cooler Logic instigates and shapes is geared to helping people enunciate and draw out into the open for collective interpretation their considerations of what is going on. This work of public or social enunciation is, in our view, quintessentially *cultural* work. Cultural enunciation is about a local, societal group's strategies and practices for "finding the right expression" to identify for themselves and others what is going on, what has gone on, and what is going to happen at any given time.

Participatory Ethnography at Work and the Proliferation of "Othered" Selves

Ethnography itself is a form of basic cultural work, and, as such it is both co-extensive with these goings-on in the host community and reflectively dependent on them. Johannes Fabian's work on the ethnographer's "other," "othering," and the relation to a "self" that is formed in the dialogic process of ethnography brings in a relevant reflective dimension. In 2006 he reviewed the history of the idea of "the other" in contemporary anthropology and summarizes things in a way that characterizes what we try to heed in Water Cooler Logic. It's also a synopsis of what we argue our host organizations could benefit by doing: "As far as anthropology is concerned, the short answer [concerning alterity's continued place and relevance in ethnography] is: Speaking about others needs to be backed up by speaking with others. We will do this as long as we do ethnography." (2007: 321).

In organizations like the VA, speaking *about* "others" is common enough. Speaking *with* "others" in that certain way that recognizes them as people and recognizes also the social forces at work beyond the everyday interactions of people at work does not occur as often and usually calls for a more deliberate approach. A fully nuanced reflection on what goes on and into the whole issue of ethnographic selves being hatched out of the deliberate work of "othering" one's workplace colleagues is beyond what we can attempt here. But we can say this much regarding further considerations along these lines: in many of our organizations, people and functional units are not only persistently silo-ed, as the common term puts it, the members in these silos are regularly solo-ed even as they are cogged and homogenized. They are routinely solo-ed and cogged, and they are systematically deprived of the occasions and permission to engage in ways that allow each to grow into themselves out of their relations with others, especially those who are not one's immediate co-workers or who are higher or lower in hierarchy. Of course, people at work do so anyway, and complex social forms rise up everywhere distinct from the systems/process designs of the organization, key to the work of communities of practice. But to have such conversations about common work is much less common than one might suppose.

Ethnographers working in organizations know this and build practices around it. But why should the professional ethnographer have all the fun and carry all the weight? What are the professionals to do with what they learn, more or less on their own, if not then to turn around and re-present it, more or less on their own, to the powers that be? Participatory ethnography invites people at work to engage "ethnographically" not simply with ethnographers but with each other. Staffs get to engage with their co-workers as consociates farther away from their local scene and in a way that is just different enough from their typical patterns to encourage this mutual co-development of themselves beyond business as usual. Looking, seeing with fresh eyes, yes; and asking questions of others, they participate with us in the ethnographic mode of relating to their colleagues and consociates.

Acknowledgments

We wish to thank the US Department of Veterans Affairs for its support and funding of our work in the VA and acknowledge our collaboration with Dr. Robert Means, National Director of Research Design and Dissemination of Innovations (RDDI) in the VA's Employee Education System, and Genna Gallegly, Project Manager, RDDI. We are also very grateful for the collaborations with literally hundreds of VA staff across the country. A large portion of the model we have been using derives from our time at the Institute for Research on Learning (IRL) from 1994–2000. Many with whom we worked had an influence on our thinking, especially Meredith Aronson, Libby Bishop, August Carbonella, Melissa Cefkin, Brigitte Jordan, Charlotte Linde, Patricia Sachs, Susan Stuckey, Lindy Sullivan, and Etienne Wenger.

Notes

1. This very general definition of discourse is taken from *Discourse Theory and Practice*, by Margaret Wetherell, Stephanie Taylor, and Simeon J. Yates (2001).
2. Paul Plsek (2003: 5) demonstrates the difficulty by listing the regions of actions and decision-making in a healthcare organization.
3. In chapter 6, "The Anthropologist as Ontological Choreographer," Francoise Brun-Cottan also draws attention to the importance of this orienting concept of "sociality."
4. A good deal of the work on complexity has surfaced in the popular scientific press and discourse under the rubrics of "complex dynamic" or "complex adaptive systems," "chaos," and "dissipative structures." The groundbreaking mathematical and philosophical work on complex dynamic systems is associated with Ilya Prigogine and Isabelle Stenghers (1988) and Stuart Kauffmann (1993) and others at the Santa Fe Institute. A widely read book in management literature, Malcolm Gladwell's *The Tipping Point: How Little Things Can Make a Big Difference* (2000), has its roots in concepts of complexity.
5. Ralph Stacey (1996) dedicates a whole book to making the connection between complexity and creativity in organizations.
6. "Passive" in the sense given to it by Stefano Franchi, Helga Wild, and Niklas Damiris in *Passion of Life* (chapter 4; forthcoming 2009).
7. See, for example, Mosko and Damon (2005), which uses concepts from chaos theory—nonlinearity, fractals—to describe anthropological phenomena. There is an inherent danger, which the book is not able to completely avoid, that in doing so one ends up using ethnographic data as mere illustration for complexity science.
8. There is one important distinction to make between the extended case study school and how we conceptualize our work as ethnographic anthropological praxis: a written full-length, detailed case study text (article or book) is not the form our analysis takes; our interventions are the case studies, and the team of analysts, including our para-ethnographers, supplants "the analyst" called out in Kapferer's view.
9. See Paul Plsek (2003). The description of the VA as a complex healthcare organization might also draw on the complexity that arises from the concept of health in general. See also David Byrne (1998).
10. What complicates the situation further is that VA is mandated to (try to) provide a wide and deep range of health care services to what is essentially a moving target of migrating, resettling veterans. To simply determine where the veteran populations are congregating in any decade is daunting, affecting decisions about where to locate facilities; as vets move about, they often leave behind perfectly functional and substantial (and very expensive) facilities and settle where there are few facilities. As the cost of construction continues to rise, the decision of where and when to build a major facility is a necessarily delicate one. Las Vegas, NV, for example, is just getting its first major tertiary care hospital. Trying to keep up with veterans' residential roving is a bit like the task facing Woody Allen's character in *Take the Money and Run* where he must keep planting his folding chair on the ground on which to sit and play his cello, all while the band marches on.
11. The key persons among many within the VA championing and collaborating with us in the development of the WCL method are, most notably, Dr. Robert Means, National Director of Research Development and Diffusion of Innovation (RDDI) in the VA's Employee Education System, and Genna Gallegly, Project Manager, RDDI.
12. For example, a WCL project in one medical center discovered how inadequate the workplace environment was for intake and eligibility clerks. The project was not tasked

to look into this issue, but the team decided that this was an important discovery. With members of the team, we co-designed a new layout and six months later the area was remodeled largely along the lines of our team's design. Staff and patients report that the setup is much better than before. Patient satisfaction jumped to 93 percent from below 60 percent on questions about convenience and service quality.

13. The hospital had already completed some work addressing this alleged inferior care on at least one of the general wards. With improvements underway, doctors and nurses closest to the issue said they'd seen genuine improvement. In fact, the WCL meetings served as sites for discussion of these actions already taken, helping to alleviate some of the concerns; this reminded them all of the need to communicate good things that were happening, lest justifiable complaints and prejudices hang around past their time.

14. This matter is another aspect of the particularity of the VA: unlike the pool of patients in many general hospitals, the VA patient population includes a large number of patients with higher morbidity ratings and multiple problems. Admissions and discharges tend to be nodes along a string of care; what happens to the patient as an outpatient becomes as critical to the overall continuity of care as their care in the hospital. Viewed in this way, patient discharge is truly another part of the care regime. This solution requiring hospitalists would amount to a significant, though not fundamental, re-negotiation of the relationship with the prestigious medical school. It would mean a small but noticeable strike against the traditional clinical educational model and habitus. This entire "episode" featuring "patient discharge" can be seen as part of the contemporary deconstruction of the customary patterns of the teaching hospital. Many of the physicians and high-level administrators in the VA recognized this. At a higher scale, the economics of teaching hospitals and the research angle that typically accompanies the teaching mission are also undergoing substantial changes after decades of relative stability. No one organizational participant in this grand scheme for providing clinical education feels in a position to bear the enormous cost of the effort.

15. For some theorists of culture and ethnography it is not too far-fetched to say that in the interactional exchanges that constitute ethnographic activity, the ethnographer and her subjects construct or invent the "culture" pronominally said to be under examination; it is a highly representational, negotiated entity, rather than an essential one operating in just those terms arrived at through the ethnographic work, ready-at-hand to be discovered.

References

Byrne, David. 1998. *Complexity Theory and the Social Sciences: An Introduction*. London: Routledge.

Ehn, P. 1988. *Work Oriented Design of Computer Artifacts*. Stockholm: Arbetslivscentrum.

Evens, T. M. S., and Don Handleman, eds. 2006. *The Manchester School: Practice and Ethnographic Praxis in Anthropology*. New York: Berghahn Books.

Fabian, Johannes, 2007. "The Other Revisiting." Unpublished draft of paper.

Franchi, Stefano, Helga Wild, and Niklas Damiris. Forthcoming 2009. *Passion of Life: Immanence, Efficacy and Non-Action*. Lexington, MA: Lexington Press.

Gellner, David N., and Declan Quigley, eds. 1995. *Contested Hierarchies: A Collaborative Ethnography of Cast Among the Newars of the Kathmandu Valley, Nepal*. Oxford/New York: Oxford University Press/Clarendon.

Gharajedaghi, Jamshid. 1999. *Systems Thinking: Managing Chaos and Complexity: A Platform for Business Architecture*. Cambridge: Cambridge University Press.

Gladwell, Malcolm. 2000. *The Tipping Point: How Little Things Can Make a Big Difference*. Boston: Little, Brown and Company.

Kapferer, Bruce. 2006. "Situations, Crisis, and the Anthropology of the Concrete: the Contributions of Max Gluckman." In *The Manchester School: Practice and Ethnographic Praxis in Anthropology*, Evens and Handleman, eds. New York: Berghahn Books.

Kauffmann, Stuart A. 1993. *The Origins of Order: Self Organization and Selection in Evolution*. Oxford: Oxford University Press.

Lassiter, Luke Eric. 1998. *The Power of Kiowa Song: A Collaborative Ethnography*. Tucson: University of Arizona Press.

———. 2005. *The Chicago Guide to Collaborative Ethnography*. Chicago, IL: University of Chicago Press.

Marcus, George E. 2006. "The Allure of Paraethnography: Care of the Data, With (Deep) Respect to Malinowski/Boas et al." Conference paper, Center for Ethnography. Irvine, CA: University of California, Irvine.

Marcus, George E., and Michael M. J. Fischer. 1999. *Anthropology as Cultural Critique: An Experimental Moment in the Human Sciences*. Chicago, IL: University of Chicago Press.

Mosko, Mark S., and Frederick H. Damon, eds. 2005. *On the Order of Chaos: Social Anthropology and the Science of Chaos*. New York: Berghahn Books.

Plsek, Paul. 2003. "Complexity and the Adoption of Innovation in Healthcare." Conference paper, National Institute for Health Care Management Foundation and National Committee for Health Care Quality. Washington, D.C.

Prigogine, Ilya, and Isabelle Stenghers. 1988. *Order Out of Chaos: Man's New Dialogue with Nature*. London: Flamingo.

Rofel, Lisa, and Sylvia Yanagisako. 2008. "The Twenty-First Century Silk Road: Reconceptualizing the Middle Ground." Conference paper, Center for Ethnography. Irvine, CA: University of California, Irvine.

Stacey, Ralph D. 1996. *Complexity and Creativity in Organizations*. San Francisco: Berrett-Koehler Publishers.

———. 2003. *Complexity and Group Processes: A Radically Social Understanding of Individuals*. New York: Brunner-Routledge.

Wenger, Etienne, 1998. *Communities of Practice: Learning, Meaning, and Identity*. Cambridge: Cambridge University Press.

Wetherell, Margaret, Stephanie Taylor, and Simeon J. Yates. 2001. *Discourse Theory and Practice: A Reader*. New York: Sage Publications.

Chapter 4

WORKING IN CORPORATE JUNGLES
Reflections on Ethnographic Praxis in Industry

Brigitte Jordan with Monique Lambert

Introduction

Though anthropologists and ethnographers have been working in global companies for a long time, they have recently attained an unaccustomed prominence. "Corporate ethnography," "industrial ethnography," and "business ethnography" have become buzz words in corporate circles and among business journalists. Even the American Anthropological Association, long based in and beholden to theoretically oriented academic anthropology, has begun to pay attention to this trend. Professional associations have begun to feature corporate ethnography in their official meeting programs. "Shadowing" (an offspring of anthropological participant observation) has become a fashionable household word in corporate research organizations.

At the same time, among anthropologists and the many ethnographers from other disciplines who work in corporate settings there is a new recognition that major changes are occurring in the investigative methods we employ, the representations with which we convey what we see and hear, the relationships we maintain with funders, how we position our projects and ourselves—all these have a somewhat different ring. Representational forms and tools, such as experience models (Jones 2006; Blomberg, Burrell, and Guest 2003; Beers and Whitney 2006), opportunity maps, or representations of economic ecosystems (Thomas and Salvador 2006) are clearly a step beyond conventional ethnography; digital ethnography (both in the sense of the digital representations of ethnography and of the ethnography of the cyber-world) is now widespread (Hine 2000, 2005; Moore, Ducheneaut, and Nickell 2007; Jordan forthcoming, 2009); tools and technologies for collaborative research—based on video and digital technology—have appeared that go far beyond paper and pencil methods and their successors. Developments of this sort lead me to propose that we are witnessing the appearance of a fresh, hybrid discipline, emerging from a foundation that was forged almost a hundred years ago by anthropologists who studied indigenous tribes and communities in exotic locations. Now it is shaped in major ways by the needs of far-flung, high-tech companies and other global organizations that need to understand how they, their stakeholders, suppliers, and customers function in a fast-moving globalizing world.

In this chapter, we invite you to appreciate the fact that something new and different is coming out of the last three decades of ethnographic research and practical experience (Jordan 1997). Some of this work will feed back to the sister disciplines that continue to participate in corporate ethnography, just as the methods and theories of these disciplines will continue to nourish and shape it. There are many creative ways in which ethnographers have changed conventional approaches, evidenced in the work of hundreds if not thousands of investigators from many disciplines—including those represented in this book, those cited by Melissa Cefkin in the introduction to this volume, and maybe especially by the wild and woolly collection of papers in the proceedings of the Ethnographic Praxis in Industry Conferences (EPIC).[1] It is that body of work within which our own investigations are located.

But what does twenty-first-century corporate ethnography look like? What changes in outlook, positioning, and methods are forced upon us, or are happily invented by us in this transition? What has changed in the migration from academia to industry? How have theory and method adapted to their new situation? What have they had to give up and what have they had to acquire, what languages, what customs? What can they become in their new home (Cohen 2005)? Drawing on what I see in the work of my colleagues and in my own experience in major and minor companies I propose to examine some of the issues that arise around this emergence.

For the sake of providing some way-posts in this chaotic terrain, I will draw many of my examples from one particular project, a project that I carried out for Intel Corporation together with my collaborator Monique Lambert. I draw on this project to provide a coherent set of examples which I intend to use to give some idea of what (one version of) those changes looks like in a project that in many ways is typical (and in others not) for the approaches and venues in which corporate ethnography now plays. This, I hope, will provide at least a "way in" to the messy, exciting, still-undisciplined terrain that I and many of my colleagues have been exploring.

Reflections on a Complex Project: Corporate Ethnography in Practice

> The bottom line is a learning curve.
>
> —anonymous

In the summer and fall of 2003, we had the opportunity to do a couple of field studies in Intel's chip-manufacturing factories—one in San Jose, Costa Rica, the other in Penang, Malaysia. These studies involved looking at the flow of product and knowledge on the production floors of two high-volume Assembly Test Manufacturing (ATM) plants where silicon wafers are processed into computer chips.[2] The first, in Costa Rica—where I live part of the year—I carried out as a solitary investigator, an outside consultant with little or no prior knowledge of chip manufacturing or Intel business culture. For the second, in Malaysia, I was joined by Monique Lambert, an experienced Intel employee with degrees in engineering and substantial ethnographic experience.

The Settings

Both ATM factories operate on two floors with most production happening on the warehouse-like ground floor. The production floors operate year-round on a work week of two twelve-hour shifts a day. Shift change ("pass-down") comes at 7:00 AM and 7:00 PM, at which point a new contingent of the operators who process wafers into chips, along with their supervisors and the technicians who maintain the machines, come on. The engineering and administrative staff on the second floor have a regular eight-hour work day.

The two factories are in many aspects the same. As a matter of fact, Intel prides itself on the interchangeability of machinery, work processes, and people between its factories, expressed by the ubiquitous slogan "Copy Exactly!" This fundamental principle allows the standardization of manufacturing facilities and processes through which the company is able to extend its effective manufacturing capacity beyond that of any individual factory. Semi-processed chips, for example, can be shipped overnight from Costa Rica to a factory in China if that factory experiences a critical shortage.

Figure 4.1. The ATM factory floor. All photos by the authors.

Figure 4.2. The second floor houses the cubicles of engineers, planners, and administrative staff.

Engagement with the Corporation: First Steps

It doesn't begin when it starts and it isn't over when it ends.

—Bob Wilks, video ethnographer

In contrast to academic research projects which are most often driven by an investigator who makes a proposal to a funding agency, corporate projects are typically initiated by a corporate decision maker—often high up in the hierarchy—who for reasons that may not be clear believes that an ethnographic investigation could help them achieve certain goals. This imposes particular restrictions on topic, focus, methods, timespan, and funding that the ethnographer has to come to grips with. Though our corporate counterparts tend to speak in terms of specific goals and unambiguous outcomes that need to be achieved ("a 20 percent increase in productivity"), it is often the case that at least in the beginning what they really need from us is less than clear. This is one of many unacknowledged issues that materialize in corporate work.

This was certainly the case when I was first contacted by my funders (a research organization within Intel) for the factory floor study.[3] They told me that they had already carried out a variety of investigations from an industrial engineering point of view that had resulted in lots of information on machine performance and the characteristics of particular work processes, but they felt that a more holistic look at the factory might provide people- and work practice–centered data regarding the flow of information and materials. They said they know a lot about machines and how to run them, but nobody knows how the pieces fit together (for similar complaints in another high-tech company, see Obata et al. 2007). They mentioned that they needed to go "from point optimization to understanding the dynamics of the system." They wanted to improve "operational efficiency." And they believed they needed "the people stuff" for that. I thought, they want their factories to run better? That's a tractable problem. Any ethnographic study should suggest many ways to move toward that goal.

When I expressed concerns that I did not have enough technical knowledge for this project, my sponsors said, "Don't worry about the technology; don't concern yourself about the machines. We already know all about that. Get us the people stuff, the knowledge flow, communication problems and, you know, that sort of thing." Potential further automation of the production line was mentioned occasionally, as well as Radio Frequency Identification (RFID) as one way to get there, but those topics were in no way central.

They also told me not to worry about Return on Investment (ROI), emphasizing that this was a research project and as such didn't have to be concerned immediately about financial payback. If I hadn't encountered that situation before, I might have believed it. During later "read-outs" (debriefing sessions), of course, the first question was always: "How does that impact our bottom line?" So the smart consultant had better think about that ahead of time.

In academic research, you are done negotiating with your funders once your project is approved. In corporate research, the situation is a bit more complex. Ethnographic consultants know that these early communications are really negotiations about who we are, what the sponsors want, and what we can deliver. They are extremely delicate. Neither party quite knows what they need, or desire, what they would be thrilled about or extremely disappointed with. This is the time when the two sides only begin to figure out what they could actually do together and what that might come to, what it might mean, how useful it might be, what would count as success and what would be deemed a failure in the end. Often this is a time of major revelations and disclosures, but also a time of major papering over of issues that all parties hope will work themselves out. We believe this is a common aspect of corporate work that is grounded in an implicit acknowledgment of a lack of shared understanding and an equally implicit belief that, over time, greater understanding will emerge. One would want to make sure that sufficient feedback channels exist to allow that mutual adjustment to take place. In the Intel project, there was powerful communication after the Costa Rica phase. It led to substantial modification in expectations and methods for the second phase in Malaysia.

In retrospect it seems quite clear that I was hearing "operational efficiency" as the main concern, a common issue for other companies I had been working with. I felt my charge was to figure out how to increase that, by looking not at machine improvement but at the details of the daily work in the factories. I thought this was an ideal situation and, based on experience in other similar projects, I thought that I would certainly be able to produce significant findings along those lines.

To anticipate, I did. But by that time what the company needed had changed.

While I was thinking about operational efficiency, corporate was playing with the idea of "people stuff." They had some vague notions that they were missing something in their current research approach, but didn't quite know what that would be. I suspect now that that was one of the reasons why they gave me rather vague instructions and left me a free hand within the constraints of company policy, Intellectual Property (IP) protection, security, and many other constraints to decide what I would actually look at.

During that time, I made a rather common mistake: given that Intel has had successful, highly regarded in-house anthropologists for a long time and since those early phone conversations contained words like "communities of practice," "work-practice analysis," "tacit knowledge," and the like, I assumed that my sponsors had a good idea of what an ethnographic investigation would involve and what to expect. That was not the case.

There may have been several factors at work: one was the high standing that ethnography had achieved within corporate circles at Intel, based on the remarkable successes of in-house anthropologists. A second factor, almost certainly, was the growing reputation of ethnography in the corporate world as an important research methodology that can achieve unique insights (chapter 1, this volume). What became clear to me only much later was that my sponsors were pursuing a strategy based on linkages with a variety of laboratories, research institutions, universities, famous researchers, and innovators, and were exploring a variety of interests that also included artificial intelligence and nanotechnology. Ethnography had now joined this illustrious circle.

As the fieldwork in Costa Rica progressed over a span of several weeks, the details of my on-the-ground engagement with the company became clearer. As is typical in such situations, my sponsors had arranged access to the fieldsite. I was assigned an official "buddy" in the factory, an amiable engineer who was following a management career. He would set up connections for me, arrange for an escort for my excursions to the production floor, answer my many questions, and give me the official inside story while keeping a close eye on me. I found that for reasons of security and to protect company secrets (a concern that is entirely reasonable) the scope of my research activities was restricted. The most implicative of those restrictions were that

- I could not go to the production floor (where wafers are made into chips) unless accompanied by an official escort.
- I had no access to machine-based data—important not only for such mundane things as meeting agendas but, most importantly, regarding the role existing automation played in the work of the factory.
- Any document in my possession had to be noted on a list and approved by my official buddy, a tedious process that ensured that I never got documents in a timely manner.
- I was not allowed to use a camera on the floor to take photographs or videotapes of the work—a restriction that was finally relaxed to allow my escort to take still pictures for me. He, of course, tended

to take pictures of machines and not of people, which is what I was interested in.

Those pictures were screened and purged before I left the premises at the end of the fieldwork period. I'd like to stress again that I find it totally reasonable that a company needs to protect itself from unauthorized disclosure of the details of how they operate. The problematic issue that consulting ethnographers have to face is that some of those restrictions hamper our best work, a trade-off that companies generally are not aware of because they are unfamiliar with ethnographic methods.

Obviously, some limitations on access, topics, and documentation are common in all types of ethnographic work. In university-based investigations they may be defined by Institutional Review Boards, the target population itself, ethical concerns, or culturally based restrictions on who can observe what kinds of events and ask what kinds of questions. But in corporate work there is an important difference: these kinds of constraints are bureaucratically embedded. They are also driven by competitive concerns about intellectual property, privacy, and image. What that means is that there is little negotiation possible at the local level once their negative effects become evident. In my case there were too many layers of the company that had to follow procedure in managing my presence, from the security at the factory gate through various levels of the administration, all the way up to the factory manager who was himself bound by company policy.

What is the anthropologist to do in such situations (other than her proverbial best)? I knew if there was to be a follow-up study—which had become a possibility by the end of Phase One—major changes had to be made. Refocusing a project and repositioning ethnographic work are issues that need to be elevated beyond the local level. If that does not happen, it is likely that the project gets ditched.

During the read-outs with my sponsors at the end of Phase One, I framed my positive recommendations with the limitations that were caused by those restrictions. When I explained that the information you get when you ask a worker a question with a company representative standing by, when you observe workers only when they are on their best, company-sanctioned behavior, when all you know about work processes is what fits into the short periods of time that your escort can take out from his regular work, they began to understand what kinds of data I was *not* getting, what kinds of observations I was *not* able to make, and what connections I was *not* able to see. At the same time, they also had become much clearer that they needed this study to contribute to the hot initiative on pushing factory automation ahead. Both sides had repositioned themselves. What remained was to work out what this could mean during Phase Two.

My funders solved the problem by teaming me up with Monique Lambert. Monique's entry, apart from providing all-important company-specific cultural and process knowledge that was unavailable to me in Costa Rica, was also a great solution to the access problem because, as a company employee, she could act as my escort and could be in charge of screening the information we collected. As we will show in subsequent sections, this generated a different approach, different methods, and a different conceptualization of the project and how it might be positioned.

For me personally the transformation from a solitary investigator to a "team" was a joy and a relief. I had been intellectually lonely during Phase One, much as I was excited by all the new things I learned. Before this one, almost all of my corporate projects had been done as part of a team, sometimes as team leader, sometimes as member, and I felt thrown back to graduate-student days when, jettisoned into a foreign world alone, we were told to "sink or swim." Now I again had a colleague, a partner, a friend who spoke the same language as I. Out of the intense collaboration of those weeks, the shared exhaustion and excitement, the problems jointly encountered and often solved, grew a deep, strong relationship that kept us going through the entire project and beyond.

By the time we began to talk about Phase Two, the goals of corporate research had also become much clearer. For one thing, operational efficiency became a minor concern while RFID-supported automation of the flow of wafers and chips became the focus and center of our ethnographic work. For this, Monique's ability to access machine-based information was crucial. It allowed us to characterize the complex ways in which the flow of computer-based information interdigitates with the information embedded in the work environment and worker's experientially based expertise. We were thus able to compare the physical flow of product and information, as observed, with the digital representation of that flow. These comparisons were a way to triangulate our observations and build a richer understanding of what was actually happening.

Doing Ethnography in the Corporation

> Process is king in the corporation, but practice rules the day.
>
> —shift supervisor

A special twist to research in corporate settings is that the goals that appear ironclad in early negotiations have a way of chameleonizing into something else. We have learned to speak the language of corporate project management that, for example, sets a goal of "increased operational efficiency," but we are not at all surprised when it turns out that in the end something else has become relevant (Jordan and Dalal 2006). One of the reasons for this lies in the nature of corporate-funded research.

In academic research, once you have been awarded, say, a project funded by the National Science Foundation, the funder has effectively signed off on your goals. You have the green light to proceed. In corporate projects, the light is never green. It is always shades of yellow—blinking into red every so often. Corporate ethnographers regularly find themselves in a position of having to (and wanting to) revise and re-negotiate what the project is all about. While we are always working toward the goals identified by the company, what exactly those goals are, and to what uses our findings might be put may not be clear at the beginning, though that is a fact that neither we nor they acknowledge. Working this out is part of the corporate dance, the micro-political work that has to be managed in every corporate project. The smart researcher is alert to that and keeps an ear to the company grapevine in order not to be broadsided by new demands. Interestingly, this problem, known as "requirements creep," is a well-known phenomenon feared by software engineers, for whom it is a notorious source of cost overruns and failed projects. It is rarely acknowledged by ethnographic researchers and their corporate funders.

Because of the zigzagging goals, much potentially useful information is collected but never acted upon. It simply falls into a black hole. For example, in the Intel project, after the switch to investigate RFID automation during Phase Two, there was no longer any serious consideration given to the findings from Phase One, though those remained crucial for us, the researchers, because they were the foundation for understanding how to manage Phase Two. At the end of Phase One there were two pages of bulleted observations and recommendations that, as far as I know, had no effect on operational efficiency. Many of these results could have been useful for other parts of the company, but there was no mechanism in place that would have ensured that distribution.

For example, during Phase One

- I dissected the learning issues faced by new workers. An already overloaded Human Resources (HR) department was trying to deal with increasingly bloated technical specifications ("the specs"), which in turn led to having to rely on e-learning and taxing lower-level workers with buddy responsibilities for on-the-job training (these developments were euphemistically called "maturing the training process");
- I pointed out the surprisingly low effectiveness of the communication technologies employed within the plant that introduced significant time lags in communication between floor workers and engineers;

- I shone a spotlight on meeting overload. People had as many as four meetings scheduled simultaneously. Many meetings had to be canceled. People often had to leave early or arrive late, in order to catch more than one important meeting;
- I drew attention to the unappreciated, largely invisible ways in which employees were relying on face-to-face communication, personal networks, and "the favor economy" to get things done, explaining that interpersonal relationships are of paramount importance for managing operational problems. For example, for the sense-making that has to go on twice a day at shift changes, reconciling discrepancies between machine data and on-the-ground data often had to be accomplished by informal communication.

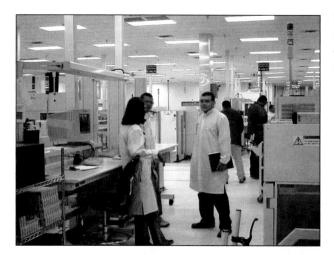

Figure 4.3a. Face-to-face information exchange is vital on the floor

Figure 4.3b. . . . and around the engineers' cubicles.

There were, of course, procedures for solving problems of a routine kind but, as I observed again and again, when a contingency was not covered by procedure, employees had to fall back on interpersonal relationships. This is an interesting phenomenon, quite common in corporate work, which leads to workarounds and bears directly on corporate-knowledge management. Making new knowledge available to people in the company who can use it should be a high priority.[4]

There are also particular constraints on participant observation and what we might call "deep ethnography." Chief among them are the time available for fieldwork and the nature of accountability. There are rare cases when a project allows for intensive fieldwork over a period of months or even a year, but the reality for most corporate projects is that actual fieldwork is limited to weeks or even days, generating a pressing need to adapt our methods to the contingencies of the situation. In the Intel project, for example, our fieldwork was restricted to two weeks at each site,[5] hardly comparable to the twelve years of on-and-off fieldwork I carried out when years ago I was doing academically based traditional research with village midwives in Mexico (Jordan 1993 [1978], 1989).

Another feature of corporate ethnography has to do with positioning and accountability. In university-based research, the relevant audience is the academic community and, usually in second place, the people and communities we study. In corporate research, accountability is first and foremost (if not exclusively) directed toward our corporate funders. They are the ones who will construct stories of success or failure, they are the ones who will decide what, in the work that was done in the field, is relevant to their enterprise and their interests. The construction of this story, of what ethnographic work comes to for them (as well as for us), is a dynamic process that has as much to do with company politics and the interpersonal relationships we are able to establish as with any objective evaluation.

If one were to paint a picture of the typical course of corporate work, one might say that it is characterized by some short stretches of activity where (you think) you know what they want, you may even think you know what they need, and you are doing good work to find out what needs to be found out. And then, sporadically but quite predictably, a hiccup occurs, and reality changes. This may happen because the CEO went to a conference and now the slogan has changed from "Process Engineering" to "Participatory Design," or from "Total Quality Management" to "Ecological Excellence." Or it may happen because the company has changed its product line and is now worried about what customers might think about the new gadget or service. For example, in a different project, one that was concerned with transforming a customer service center into a "Learning Organization," an order came down from headquarters that new facilities had to be designed for the center immediately. So we reoriented our ethnographic investigations toward providing recommendations that would be helpful for that (Jordan and Dalal 2006). When such a hiccup happens, it is important to figure out what caused it and renegotiate what "we" are up to. To be sure, this causes untold frustration, cynicism, and sleepless nights, but in some way it is also part of the excitement of doing corporate work. You need to be politically alert to what is going on in the company, build your channels of communication, educate yourself about the larger set of issues (both market issues and personnel issues) that the company is struggling with, and always be prepared to act on options. No straight-line thinking in this world!

Another set of issues significant in corporate work revolves around insider vs. outsider status of the ethnographer. An increasing number of companies now have in-house ethnographers who, by virtue of their employee status, have access to all the formal information and informal know-how that comes with insider status. They are a part of the context, they understand the local culture, they know about the speakables and the unspeakables in the company—precisely the kinds of things that hamper the outside consultant. On the other hand, coming from the outside, with experience in similar companies' problems and issues, the outside consultant can often see patterns and connections that for the insider are "invisible in plain sight."[6]

These differences are thrown into high relief in the Intel project. Monique's entry in Phase Two, the Malaysian part of the project, changed things dramatically. Monique had been working in Intel Manufacturing for seven years but had done ethnographic work for her PhD at the Jet Propulsion Laboratories in Pasadena (Lambert 2005). As an engineer, she brought with her a wealth of technical knowledge and a deep understanding of the chip-manufacturing world, but a major part of her contributions arose from her status as an insider, her insider's cultural knowledge, and her expertise in interpreting and speaking Intel's corporate language.

Speaking company language, and knowing what the company-relevant issues were, Monique was invaluable in interpreting some of my more opaque observations, and in helping me to identify my own cultural preconceptions. For example, in Penang I saw the Malaysian women's teamwork as positive. Monique, however, pointed out that while teamwork is an espoused Intel value, it can conflict with Intel's culture of meritocracy, which rewards employees for work that "showcases" individual responsibility and ownership on key projects and initiatives. In Phase One, I had identified "anti-values," attitudes deeply rooted in Costa Rican culture, ubiquitous but largely invisible, that challenge Euro-American assumptions about work. Monique helped me understand how some of the culturally preferred ways of acting and interacting in Malaysia also ran counter to Intel business culture. It was also Monique who in the end crafted our company-intelligible PowerPoint presentations that convinced corporate research that attaching RFID chips to "lots" of product would not be the way to implement factory automation.

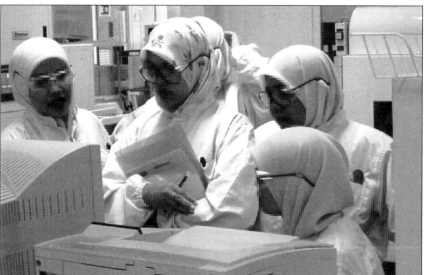

Figures 4.4a and 4.4b. Malaysian operators tend to work in groups.

Adapting Our Methods: Challenges and Opportunities

Workers know more than managers know that they know.

—Paul Allaire, former CEO of Xerox Corporation

But one might ask: Why has ethnography become so popular in the corporate world? The allure of ethnographic methods undoubtedly is a major reason why the popular press has seized every opportunity to publish stories about how ethnographers work. The business world has become enamored with the idea that ethnographers actually go out into kitchens and factories, print shops and sweatshops, that they "hang out" on tuna boats and in hospital emergency rooms, that they ride in the trucks of service technicians and put on a hard hat to follow construction workers. This is what the stories in the business press are made up of. These are the stories that company executives tell each other at their meetings. At the same time, corporate ethnography is surrounded by a mystique that draws on romantic ideas of traditional ethnography, the time when anthropologists ventured out to live with undiscovered tribes in the jungles of South America and New Guinea. Corporate decision makers readily see the parallels between understanding the culture of "the natives" and understanding the culture of their customers. And while earlier ethnographies may have served the interests of colonial administrations, corporate ethnography clearly serves the interests of its industrial funders. Yet, both do more than that.

As we will argue, methods bear the brunt of the workload for taking advantage of new opportunities. Ethnography's expansion into new niches provides welcome challenges to our established procedures and our opportunities for being creative, for forging new paths, for thinking about how to accomplish the fundamental objectives of an anthropologically grounded ethnography in a new territory. It also makes visible the tremendous variety of adaptations that corporate practitioners have invented to deal with the contingencies of new situations. Of course some degree of methods modification has always been the case, but with the move into new domains and the availability of new technologies this process of revision, invention, and reinvention has accelerated. The two phases of the Intel project provide some examples of the ways in which ethnographic methods for data collection, analysis, and representation can be fitted to the requirements of the situation.

What immediately emerged as a major issue in the Intel work was a challenge to what has traditionally been the mainstay of anthropological data collection: participant observation. In the pages that follow I describe in some detail our methodological adaptations in the Intel chip-manufacturing plants where, in one case, observation was limited, while in the other, question asking was restricted. What do you do if you are unable to do conventional participant observation? How do you get beyond the official rhetoric of what is going on and begin to understand the situation from the point of view of factory workers, shift leaders, engineers, and HR personnel? What do you do when you cannot observe people in their workspace and follow them around in their workday? When you cannot build the kinds of relationships that allow you to ask in-situ, on-the-spot questions?

In both factories, the kind of live-in, participatory sharing of people's work and home life we normally would engage in was impossible because of access limitations (in Costa Rica) and time compression (at both sites). A major amount of the necessary information could not be obtained directly. However, in Costa Rica I spoke enough Spanish to be able to draw on semantic data from interviews and in-situ question asking which constituted my best source of information. In Malaysia, on the other hand, since neither Monique nor I speak either Malay (spoken by the Malay women who constitute the majority of floor workers) or Chinese (spoken by the majority of the engineering and administrative staff) we relied primarily on observational data. The underlying issue is always: what are the questions that need to be answered, and then, not what is the best *possible* method, but rather the best method *under the given conditions*. In this case, as is true for practically all but run-of-the-mill projects, we had to adapt standard ethnographic methods to the particular requirements of our sponsors and to the limiting possibilities of our situation.

In Costa Rica, with limited access to the factory floor, my solution was to look for occasions where I could talk with people informally, without having a representative from management standing by. I felt that being escorted made me look like I was working for "them" and that I was carrying out some kind of evaluation of employees' activities and competence. This is an issue that is always under the surface in corporate settings, and defusing it is part of the micro-political positioning work we need to do if we hope to get useful data (see chapter 6 of this volume for Brun-Cottan's insightful consideration of this concern).

I compensated for the deficiencies generated because of limited interactions on the factory floor by taking advantage of every opportunity that offered itself (and creatively constructing a few myself) for initiating conversations. I always took my meals in the company cafeteria. Visibly a foreigner and an outsider in the chow line, I often started by asking the people next to me for culinary recommendations. It was easy to start up a conversation by then asking if I could join them at their table. They were always delighted to have me sit with them. They usually asked what I was doing at the factory, and that provided a welcome opportunity to undermine the ubiquitous fear of evaluation. People often think that a researcher is a kind of spy from management, but we need to make clear that we have an iron-clad commitment of not communicating information that could be personally damaging if it goes up the corporate ladder (Jordan and Dalal 2006). So I would say something like: "I'm interested in what kinds of tasks operators like you find easy to learn and what you find hard, or what difficulties you see in the training process, but I will never tell anybody that you thought a trainer was incompetent or things like that." That way I got opportunities to talk to a fairly broad cross-section of people working in the factory, ranging from engineers, technicians, and manufacturing specialists to administrators, contract workers, and students doing internships.

Figure 4.5. Cafeteria conversations.

On the upstairs engineering/administrative floor, much of the daily activities could be sampled through the acoustic overflow from behind the low partitions. I made it a habit of dropping in on discussions in and around the ubiquitous cubicles, sometimes joining the conversation when two or three engineers were standing in the hallway, and sometimes just listening to what kinds of issues they discussed (yes, I suppose one could call that "eavesdropping," but in cubicle land everybody knows that conversations are overhearable).

Figure 4.6. Engineers trouble shooting in their cubicles.

I saw this as the best possible approximation of what I was rarely able to do, that is, observe problems as they arose on the factory floor. At least I could get direct information on how the engineers saw those problems and what they thought should be done about them. I felt that this was still vastly more useful than asking about generic troubles during a cold interview (in Malaysia the language barrier largely prevented such overhearing).

Figure 4.7. Overhearing is easy and commonplace.

I also invited people to a meal offsite or for a drink at my hotel, often in return for some kind of favor they had done for me. Other times, I would simply say to a potential source of information that I know they do this interesting work and I'd like to know more about it. Would they have time to talk with me maybe after work? I admit that I also joined the smokers' group outside the factory doors. I listened to what they talked about and asked them questions when that was possible.

As a general strategy, I took advantage of whatever opportunities arose for informal interaction with employees. As I saw issues emerging, I tried to crosscheck what I heard with people on different levels of the company, always aware of the fact that there are multiple truths to be discovered. Those strands eventually congealed into what I began to think of as "findings." For example, it became quite clear that there was a deep rift between the upstairs world of the engineers, planners, and administrators and the downstairs world of the operators and technicians; that training was seen as in need of improvement not only by new workers but also by HR trainers and the designers of training courses. As time went by, I was able to conceptualize ways in which these obstacles might be overcome and formulate recommendations that would improve operational efficiency. With comprehensive floor observations not possible, I needed to devise alternative ways of compensating for lack of access to the crucial venue by drawing on other methods in the ethnographic toolkit. In that sense, the approach was a reconfiguration of methods rather than a radical change or invention of new ones.

In Malaysia, a more radical adaptation of methods had to occur. While the focus in Phase One had been on operational efficiency, with automation emerging only vaguely in discussions during late stages of the fieldwork, once we got to Malaysia we knew that we had to focus squarely on potential RFID automation. The key question when trying to apply RFID to track the movement of objects within an existing process is "What precisely *is* the unit (or entity) to be tracked?" It was clear that while our sponsors had detailed engineering information on the basic chip-manufacturing process, precise details were needed about the flow of knowledge and materials through the factory. This understanding of the problem, driven by the sponsors' interest in demonstrating the application of RFID to automate a supply chain, led to the research methodology we employed in Phase Two: we decided to attach ourselves to a lot of wafers and document, in detail, what happened to it in the course of its journey through the factory. (We refer to this special focal lot as the "LOT" [capitalized] from now on.) We intended to capture any tacit, hidden factors that the automation engineers were not aware of, but that might have an impact on the success of the technology changes that were already being planned. With lot following as given, we invented lot shadowing (taking a cue from people shadowing) and combined that with the new resources available to us in machine-based data that were accessible to us now because of Monique's status as an employee.

Figure 4.8. Lambert tracing our LOT on a work station.

The pace in Malaysia was frantic. Those were grueling days quite different from the leisurely pace in Costa Rica. In traditional research, there is usually time to write up notes, do preliminary analysis, get feedback, make a plan for what to focus on for the next day or the next week. While that was quite possible in Costa Rica, where I generally spent a couple of days at the factory and then retreated to my own house for the rest of the week, the more typical situation in corporate research is the one we encountered in Malaysia.

Figure 4.9. Jordan writing up field-notes offsite in Costa Rica.

Since there were now two of us, we discussed various divisions of labor, but decided in the end to work as a closely connected team rather than capitalizing on a division of responsibilities that could have assigned different parts of the process to each of us. (Another reason for this decision, of course, was that I could not be on the factory floor alone.) The advantages of operating "joined at the hip" (as one of our sponsors put it) were many: in a foreign environment that is dense with machines, people, noises, sights, requirements, exceptions, and languages, a partner is of great value for everything from a simple hearing check ("Did he really say that?") to noticing some of those things that are "invisible in plain sight." On occasion, however, we split up for more effective coverage. When it became apparent at one point that lots spawn sublots, Monique could be found haunting the stacks, obsessed with finding all of our child LOTs, while I might be documenting how a machine is loaded, or interviewing an English-speaking technician about the process. So we did specialize to some extent, but we were almost always in the same physical location.

The way we actually investigated what we came to call "the lot of the LOT" was to pick a specific LOT at the beginning of its course and track it in all its incarnations as it moved through the factory. We did observe and ask questions about other lots whenever the opportunity arose, but we

Figure 4.10. Lambert looking for child LOTs in inventory.

Figure 4.11a and 4.11b. Jordan asking questions in situ.

doggedly pursued the single LOT that we had chosen. This proved to be a most fortunate decision since it made us pay attention precisely to what was "invisible in plain sight"—crucial features of the production process that were not documented and not readily talked about. It got us over the ubiquitous problems of getting "the party line" on processes and events from people we might interview. It allowed us to document in detail—with notes, audio tapes, and photographs—what was actually happening. Using our LOT as a thread through the chip-manufacturing process, we could then ask specific questions pertaining to generalizability (How typical is this LOT compared to other lots?), exceptions (How do you know when something is wrong with a lot, and what do you do when that happens?), differences between day and night shifts, and so on. Interestingly, as we put our LOT under the microscope, the very notion of "a lot" became more and more complicated and eventually problematic.[7]

As soon as we got into actually doing observations, we realized that to understand what our LOT was up to we needed to track not only the LOT in the narrow sense (that is, the wafers, die, chips, substrate, and so on that make up a lot physically), but also the transport medium (the vehicle on which it gets moved from work station to work station), how it is identified, what paper documentation and what electronic records accompany it, and so forth. It became clear almost immediately that those characteristics do not remain stable during the journey but are in constant flux. As a matter of fact, the compound changes of those features could be seen as constituting and reconstituting the LOT at various stages of the process.

What drove our data collection were two issues that had emerged from what we had learned in Phase One and in the discussions we had had with our corporate partners: the first was to investigate discrepancies between process and practice; the second was to investigate the stability of the LOT.

For the first issue, we needed to collect data that would allow us to understand the official engineering view about workflow. We knew by then, from the results of Phase One as well as from anthropological theory, that we were likely to find inconsistencies between the engineering view of workflow and the ways in which knowledge and materials actually move through the factory. We also thought that such a discrepancy, if it existed, might constitute a significant obstacle to RFID-based automation.

To shed light on this issue, we collected every representation of workflow we could get our hands on: we took pictures of wall charts, diagrams, and display boards on the factory floor and in pass-down rooms and collected sketches that engineers made for us, ending up with different official representations showing tool views, operational views, and electronic-process views of the workflow. We also drew on the information I had collected in interviews with engineers in Costa Rica.[8] Not unexpectedly, all of these official representations were deficient in one way or another. For example, one work area was simply represented as inventory; the representation said nothing about the major changes that occurred there in the form and identity of lots. If we had relied on official representations, even if augmented by interviewing based on such documentation, we would have missed precisely what we were charged to find out about. A key conclusion was that there exists a major discrepancy between the official documentation of work processes and what actually happens in the factory.

By investigating "the lot of our LOT" we were able to identify in detail the many instances where documentation simply glossed over important processes, relying for its efficacy on operators' embodied, tacit, localized knowledge. Automating such tacit knowledge and expertise would be highly problematic for any straightforward implementation of RFID. That documentation leaves things out is, of course, one of those things that "everybody knows." What our study demonstrated to our funders, however, was the massive prevalence of this phenomenon in every nook and cranny of the operation.

For the second issue, the question of what actually is the fate of the lots that come in as wafers and go out as chips, we drew on shadowing techniques. Shadowing is generally used for following persons through their daily routines, but we decided to shadow a specific lot, to investigate "the lot of the LOT" by following it from the time it entered the factory until we had enough information to answer our question. The process we followed produced what I have described as an Object-Oriented Record (Jordan 1996; see also Blomberg, Burrell, and Guest 2003). By observing what happens to an object (our LOT in this case) we learn something about the process that moves it from one physical location to the next, and transforms it from one manifestation into another. Thus the LOT served as our "guiding thread" through the manufacturing process. It provided us with a "way in" to seeing the process from the point of view of the lot. A concern with objects, artifacts, gadgets, and technologies has long been a standard feature in anthropology and in ethnographic work (cf. Appadurai 1986; Hoskins 1998; Fine and Leopold 1993), but systematically focusing on an object may be particularly appropriate for situations like the one we encountered in Malaysia where asking questions was possible only occasionally, when floor workers happened to speak enough English so we could communicate with them. Though we did as much observation and in-situ question asking as was possible, under the circumstances we encountered in the factories traditional participant observation was simply not feasible.

While it certainly would have been desirable to study the production process in its entirety, we knew that doing so would not allow us to produce the kind of close-up detail that we needed in the short period of time available to us. Drawing on Monique's knowledge of chip produc-

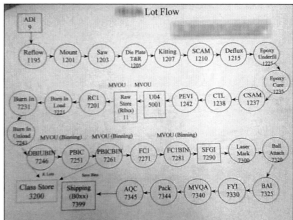

Figure 4.12 a, 4.12b, and 4.12c. Some of the official process representations we encountered.

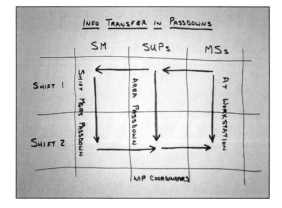

tion and my prior experience in Costa Rica, we carved out a piece of the manufacturing process that we thought would provide us with enough information for our purposes. The piece we studied intensively in the end comprised about one third of a lot's journey, from the holding area where incoming lots of wafers from the waver fabs are stored through the point where "dies" and "substrates" are joined to form "chips." We had yet to empirically demonstrate the practicality and efficacy of our methodological approach, but we felt that this was a sufficiently large piece of the whole so that we would be able to determine if ethnography could identify some of the unknown and undocumented aspects of the production process necessary for RFID implementation.

Of the various electronic data streams in use in the factory, the most significant proved to be an electronic workflow application called "Workstream" that was used to track and manage the flow of lots. Machine operators used Workstream to implement various processing commands (for example, "select the current lot from a list of lot numbers" or "move a lot out of an operation after processing is complete") and to record certain engineering data about the lot relevant to a particular operation. The idea was that operators entered these data when they received a particular lot at their station and when it left.

Workstream was designed to log every transaction that occurs on a lot's journey from workstation to workstation. But as one supervisor told us (transcript slightly edited):

> The Workstream system only tells you that the lot was moved from one work station to another; so, by inference, the lot should be [physically] there. The computer might tell you that all of these lots are in front of this equipment, but when you go there it isn't there. And that happens because the movement [of lots] is by hand [in carts] and that would be one way in which you could lose a lot. Or there was a quality concern with this lot and somebody moved it to a lab to check it out. A lost lot might happen if somebody sees something wrong, takes the lot to be tested, and forgets to put that into the computer. Or a lot might be misplaced if it is moved between different parts of the factory because you need a tester that's not operational on one side and you have excess capacity on the other. So Workstream knows where the lot should be. Not necessarily where it is.

And he continues:

> So that's a big issue because we make a lot of decisions on downtimes, setup times, and so on based on Workstream and if the operator doesn't plug in the data appropriately or is not conscious of what state the machine is in, then our data is incorrect and our decisions could be incorrect. So we base our decisions on the Workstream data *plus* the pass-down data of what

really happened, so you match the verbal data with the Workstream data and see what makes sense.

These kinds of troubles invariably had to be resolved by face-to-face interaction, either by trouble shooting on the floor or by reconciliation during pass-down when shift supervisors came together around a conference table.

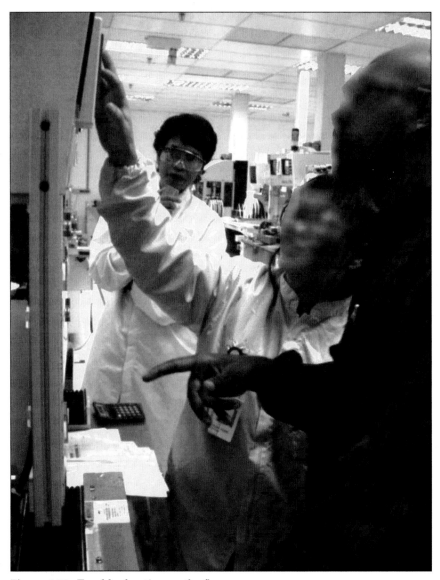

Figure 4.13. Trouble shooting on the floor.

So Workstream knows where any particular lot should be. Not necessarily where it is. Most of the time, of course, where it is and where it should be are the same. For example, when our LOT split into several child LOTs, and each of the child LOTs was assigned to a location in a temporary inventory, we indeed found those child LOTs where Workstream said they were.

Since the factories operate around the clock on two twelve-hour shifts per day, access to the Workstream application was crucial. By logging on to the factory computer, Monique could follow what happened to our LOT while we were eating or sleeping. Several times this showed that it was sitting in a temporary storage area, as in the example above. However, other times this "cyber view" of the LOT revealed location changes or changes in LOT identity, arising from mergers and splits. Armed with this information, we would then go back to the production floor to hunt down the physical LOT and its children.

Combining machine data and observational methods proved to be the most critical success factor in our study. Access to the Workstream data not only allowed us to keep tabs on our LOT twenty-four hours a day, but it also allowed us to study how the factory saw it as it moved through the manufacturing process. These data provided important information about where and how changes in LOT identity occurred, which in turn provided key evidence about the possible limitations of RFID for tracking lots within the flow of product. Since current automation still requires workers to physically enter information, there is always latency between the physical action and when that action is recorded. If the factory relies on the electronic version, then they are assuming a level of accuracy that may differ to a greater or lesser extent from what is really happening. The rigidness of technology does not accommodate the various contingencies that emerge in the context of routine work, and this leads to inaccuracies in the electronic data that, in turn, generate workarounds on the floor.

During the two weeks we were in Penang, we spent almost every day at the factory. The influx of data was torrential. We each took hundreds of photos, sheaves of scribbled notes, and a quantity of audio-tape recordings. We were on the floor on our feet almost every day, using our hotel rooms for writing up notes and planning the next day's activities. At night, Monique would be tracking our LOT on the computer in her room, giving us visibility into the "night life" of our LOT that would have been difficult to know about otherwise. That's also when we wrote up field notes, transferred and labeled our photographs, prepared for presentations we were required to give to factory senior staff, and typically fell into bed totally exhausted.

Though we spent almost all of our time at the factory together, we always had the feeling of not enough face-to-face time for discussing what we saw. We are sure we could have benefited tremendously from more analysis during data collection, both for really processing our notes and indexing pictures (after a while you don't remember what machine this was or why you even took the picture) and for more extensive mutual consultation about issues that emerged. Under such pressure it is truly difficult to heed Margaret Mead's warning that unanalyzed data are worse than no data.

In retrospect this lack of in-the-field processing time generated a double loss. Not only were we producing an incredible amount of data that we had no time to process, but we were also in danger of losing some of the benefits of teamwork: the mutual calibration of observations, the conversations that generate new hypotheses, the sense-making activities that are the first steps toward deeper analysis.

The value of conversations that are not motivated by needing to solve an immediate issue was brought home to us rather forcefully on the only occasion when we, after an exhausting day at the factory, decided to make a stop at our hotel bar for a few moments of relaxation, with the specific idea of not talking about the project. Of course we couldn't avoid it. We immediately fell into project talk. We began to ask questions: What kinds of objects are important for us to track beyond "the lot" (whatever that was)? What kinds of people are there that deal with those objects? What kinds of processes are there that affect them? Sitting at the bar, we began to build ontologies and determine where we were lacking information. This conversation was instrumental in focusing our data collection in the coming days: We determined that there are many different kinds of transport vehicles that move lots around the factory; there are different ID carriers, there is different software used in different parts of the factory.

Figure 4.14. A variety of vehicles is used to move lots around the factory.

We established ontologies based on lot nomenclature (for example, A-lots, M-lots), type of transport media (human-operated vehicles, trolleys, locked carts), type of unit carrier (wafer boxes, cassettes, frames); paper work (travel tickets); software systems (Workstream, Map View, SAP software); holding areas (inventories, WIP areas); materials (substrate, tape, reels); and many others. These emergent ontologies became a framework for documenting our observations and developing the observation-based classificatory schemes that in turn informed our reports back to the company.

Continuing the Conversation

> Practicality defeats relevant sociological analysis almost every time.
>
> —Howard Becker

In fields as diverse as design, applied anthropology, and industrial ethnography there has recently emerged a conversation about what ethnography is, what it can be and even what it should be (Baba 2005; Cefkin 2006; Dourish 2006; Hamada 2000; Hill and Baba 2000; Paiement 2007; Rylko-Bauer, Singer, and van Willigen 2006).[9] This is a wide-ranging discussion that revolves around the question of what ("really," "truly") is ethnography anyway? And who should be allowed to call herself an ethnographer?[10] Suffice it to point out that those disputes have to do with disciplinary and territorial claims regarding who is entitled to a hundred years of legacy.

At this time, new practice niches are opened up by globalization, and that, combined with novel data-collection technologies and the creeping approbation ethnography has gained in the business world, has generated an influx of new practitioners, many of whom, if the truth be told, are not particularly well trained. Nevertheless, given the terrific demand generated by the corporate market, countless consulting operations inside as well as outside of academia have sprung up that carry a version of "ethno-something" in their banner. In the worst case, they pass off anything as ethnography that isn't quantitative.

I believe it is important not to confuse shoddy ethnography with short-term, focused investigation. Short-term, highly focused projects have existed alongside long-term projects in anthropology for a long time, but it is in the corporate rather than the academic world that short-term ethnography has experienced a runaway career. At this time, it is expanding rapidly with the corporate pressure for quick, easily sellable results.

A varied, eclectic, and unruly way of tackling the issues that crop up in a globalizing world has emerged in the crucible of needing to combine short time spans and pressing demands for immediate results with the time-honored anthropological techniques derived from long-term fieldwork. I point here to an evolving constellation of practices, attitudes, methods, and goals that has arisen as trained (and untrained) ethnographers respond to the demands of corporations to help them understand the details of their customers', their clients', and their workers' needs. The attendant pressures have often led to shortcuts, workarounds, making do with insufficient sample sizes, and then unjustified claims based on those.

As a consequence some of this, work has been branded as "light" or "quick" ethnography, or even as "quick and dirty," "impoverished," "anemic," "pseudo-," and "quick-fix" ethnography. What all of these terms have in common is their derogatory nature. As a matter of fact, they implicate not only the credentials of the ethnographers to whom they are applied but also the quality of the work they produce. Though "light" is not a negative for many people, like those who can see the benefits of Pepsi Light, most hear it as light-weight, insufficient, without methodological rigor.

I would suggest, however, that it may be productive to consider that new contingencies have arisen in our work, and that, in turn, might lead us to think less of long-term, deep methods, and rather of economical, tightly focused tactics that produce the results the situation requires (and no more). This applies when a limited set of issues is at stake, as, for example, when a prototype of a new product or application needs to be evaluated and the traditional data collection in an ergonomics lab or a survey of users is replaced by a set of observations of customers as they employ the tool in their accustomed home or work environment. These kinds of studies are valuable because the way people behave in a bona fide use environment is demonstrably different from how they act in artificial laboratory situations. There are many variations here; for example, the study might be done in a simulated naturalistic environment (living labs, smart houses) rather than in users' actual home or work situations.

In many cases short-term approaches provide exactly the data a company needs to resolve its issues. Especially when the investigator already knows what to look for, when the relevant questions, variables, and categories are already defined, short-term ethnography can flesh out the details and validate corporate hunches, but it will take deep ethnography to discover unknown patterns, relationships, and connections.

Short-term ethnography has been characterized as relying on ethnographic techniques, with the distinct possibility of missing some of the fundamentals of deep ethnographic research (Rea-Holloway et al. 2006).

Not surprisingly, it often requires the use of methods that are conducive to rapid, structured data collection, such as focus groups, structured interviewing rather than asking questions in-situ, or shallow versions of shadowing rather than deep participant observation.

Deep participant observation (Bell 2006), on the other hand, involves a complex intellectual/psychological stance where the researcher participates to the greatest extent possible in the events of interest, while at the same time maintaining the stance of observer and recorder. Traditionally, this has involved "living with the natives," that is to say, long-term immersion in the life of a community, that provides an intimate understanding of members' worldview. Here the investigator comes not as the expert with clipboard, camera, and interview schedule in hand, but as a learner, a student, a novice, and often as an apprentice, actually learning to live the life and do the work. Several of my colleagues at PARC, for example, became proficient at taking orders in a copy shop they studied (Vinkhuyzen and Szymanski 2004), Jack Whalen trained to become a call taker in a 911 call center (Whalen 1995), and I became an apprentice to a traditional Maya village midwife (a *"partera"*) when I studied childbirth and indigenous obstetric practices in the Yucatan (Jordan 1993).[11]

Deep participant observation requires sophisticated parallel processing, the ethnographer becoming aware not only of what is going on around her, but also of her own reactions and feelings, and how those are progressively molded by exposure to the events in which she participates. It means experiencing the boredom as well as the drama of mundane work and everyday life firsthand, and giving each its due in attention, reflection, and analysis. It means progressively absorbing the knowledge and practices of the people whose lives we are involved in.[12] Achieving this balance requires long training, a commitment to self-reflection, ongoing, sustained discussions with mentors, painstaking note taking, and more—the kind of experience and experiences that can be acquired in years of graduate training and ethnographic practice, but not in a quick exposure to ethnographic practice. The end result is a deep understanding of culturally and organizationally embedded events from the point of view of the participants, while retaining a version of one's own point of view. This allows contrasting those views and identifying areas of concurrence or conflict. In the ideal case, participant observation will lead to understanding a situation simultaneously "from the inside out and the outside in," and "from the bottom up and the top down."

Beyond a particular methodological attitude toward data collection, deep ethnography also brings some special expertise to data analysis, to making sense of what is going on and drawing useful conclusions. One of the particular skills trained ethnographers have developed is the ability to look for known patterns (sometimes based on sociocultural theory, sometimes on prior experience), while at the same time remaining alert to interesting observations that might herald a new pattern or simply an important local idiosyncrasy. Other investigators have also considered the pattern analysis stage the most difficult.

For us, it also includes a profound, reflective conviction, inherited from our roots in academic anthropology, that in any situation there are multiple truths and multiple kinds of knowledge that it is our business to investigate. This then means specifically not to take the sponsoring company's ideas at face value, but always see them as one (goal-oriented) reflection of what is going on, and especially one that does certain kinds of "work." This is why we prefer not to start with a fixed interview schedule or a list of predefined variables to investigate.

Like many corporate projects, our venture at Intel struggled throughout with the tension between what we would have done under ideal circumstances and what was possible. Constrained by a corporate agenda that squeezed field time into two weeks at each site and imposed a number of serious restrictions, it seemed destined for a heavy emphasis on quick techniques.

Interestingly, there were significant differences in the effects of these restrictions between Phase One, which I managed in Costa Rica as a solitary outside consultant, and Phase Two in Malaysia, when I was joined by Monique. In Costa Rica, the main problem was lack of access to the physical field site, the factory floor, which I could enter only escorted by a company employee. But apart from that, I was able to fairly closely approximate conventional ethnographic fieldwork, the kind that is typical in situations where observation and interviewing (though not active hands-on participation) is possible. In Malaysia, this kind of learning by doing was equally impossible and, in addition, interviewing was limited because of language restrictions. On the other hand, the removal of access restrictions to the site and to computerized data made possible very detailed observation as we compiled an in-depth record of the "the lot of the LOT," the trajectory of a lot of wafers and chips as it moved through the factory.

In contrast to the Malaysian phase, Phase One allowed a careful study of local cultural values that were operating within this global company (for similar issues embedded in another high-tech company, see Obata et al. 2007). Only because I had time to discuss my onsite observations with Costa Rican professionals and was able to carry out follow-up observations and offsite interviews that I began to realize that there existed cultural values and "anti-values" that conflict on a deep level with Intel business culture.[13] Having lived in Costa Rica for extended periods of time I had come to realize that effective teamwork as we understand it in American and European business culture runs up against what I have come to call "the favor economy" and a cultural preference for taking care of one's friends. On the factory floor as well as in the engineers' cubicles the commitment is not so much to the work but to one's associates. I also began to appreciate that the idea of "accountability," basic in Euro-American business culture, has no immediate linguistic, conceptual, or behavioral equivalent for the workers on the floor in San Jose, Costa Rica. To get to this level of understanding was possible during Phase One because, living in the country, I had some appreciation for local work and lifestyles and patterns of behavior. In Malaysia, without that context, we had no way of uncovering similar discrepancies though we are sure they exist and could be articulated in a more extensive investigation. In both phases, we managed to incorporate some aspects of deep ethnography, most significantly probably in our insistence on not taking the official version of how work gets done as the basis of our investigations, but rather looking for what people actually did as they carried out their daily work.

I would suggest that when an issue arises around how to approach a particular project, we need to ask: What does the problem at hand require in terms of data that would solve it (or at least illuminate the issue)? This, and this alone, should determine the value of whatever combination of methods and approaches should be used. It is always the nature of the question under investigation that should determine which way to go.

When the project involves a team, data collection can often be carried out by trained assistants as long as there is an experienced team leader who can do the micro-political communication work I mentioned earlier and who can take the lead in data analysis. This is where the difference between a trained, experienced ethnographer and a short-term practitioner becomes apparent. It may be easy to collect masses of data. What is not easy is to figure out what the data mean. This requires pattern analysis and an ability to turn findings into actionable results.

Corporate ethnography is clearly shaped by practitioners of many disciplinary roots and many methodological approaches. Most of us have a leaning in one direction or the other, but for most of us the requirements of the corporate-driven projects that we take on determine how deep we can go. There is also great variability in the extent to which particular projects boast different mixtures and exhibit the consequent negotiations and tensions. Still, even in short-term projects, we generally look for ways in which (in the words of Rick Robinson) our work can generate new methods, concepts, approaches, and models that will move corporate ethnography "from a collection of cases to consensus and from particulars to generalizations, thereby contributing to emerging ideas of how praxis and theory relate to each other in the global analysis of organizations" (Robinson 2005). High-tech factory floors as a site for ethnographic work are still rather uncommon (for an early study, see Hull 1997), so we see our investigations at the chip factories as joining the many recent investigations that colonize new venues by taking on issues emanating from globalization.[14] But if theory is built by moving from specific cases to generalization, then the fact that corporate ethnography substantially expands our traditional domains of study holds the promise that it will also make significant contributions to anthropological theory.

Acknowledgments

The "with" in the author listing for this paper acknowledges the central role of Monique Lambert in the fieldwork and analysis that led to it as well as in its final production. Without her, as is clear on every page, this chapter would have looked very different. I also want to acknowledge the tremendously insightful remarks of the anonymous reviewer for this volume, which, together with the insistent comments of my co-authors, were instrumental in substantial revisions. Melissa Cefkin, the editor of this volume, has been a constant source of support and gentle, productive advice. As always, this is a collaborative effort and I thank Robert Irwin, Robert Moore, Michael Powell, Peggy Szymanski, Inga Treitler, Diane Schiano, Lee Ann Osbun, and Judy Tanur for their contributions.

Notes

1. So far four EPIC conferences have taken place with sponsorship from governmental as well as industry and professional organizations. Through papers, workshops, posters, and meal and hallway discussions these conferences are a major venue for constituting the ethnographic research community concerned with issues of ethnography in the corporation.
2. Glossary of acronyms used throughout this chapter:
ATM Assembly Test Manufacturing (Chip Factory)
EPIC Ethnographic Praxis in Industry Conference
HR Human Resources (Department)
IP Intellectual Property
PARC Palo Alto Research Center
RFID Radio Frequency Identification (attaches ID chip to an object in order to trace its course through a process)
ROI Return on Investment
WIP Work in Progress

3. There were antecedents to this, of course; for example, talks/walks with John Sherry, a prominent Intel anthropologist, a phone call from him inquiring about my availability, and others.

4. This is a parallel phenomenon to the one pointed out by Jim March who has shown that corporate decision makers tend to ask for way more information than they can use, that the decisions they make are not based on the information they have solicited, and that they keep seeking more information even when decisions are already made (1991).

5. In Costa Rica, the two weeks of fieldwork were distributed over eight weeks; in Malaysia, it was two weeks of continuous factory time.

6. As Bob Moore pointed out in a personal communication, the outside consultant often has a certain kind of credibility with management because of his or her neutral status. Frontline workers and other insiders often know what is broken in the process and have good ideas about how to fix it, but when they propose a change, they are often perceived by management as "whining" or being "lazy." However, if the consultant learns about these problems and the proposed solutions from insiders, checks them against his or her own observations, and then presents them to management, they tend to be taken much more seriously.

7. I was struck by the similarity of this development with what I had encountered in Costa Rica when I tried to map out a "production line" by following its course. It quickly had become apparent that while people in the factory talked about "a line" as if it were a river rushing to the sea (the warehouse in this case), the reality was more like an estuary with many splits, cross-channels, and multiple arms, meandering through the countryside.

8. Here is where "Copy Exactly" was very useful to us since those documents were intended to represent workflow as it was implemented in all chip factories of the company.

9. The best way to get a feeling for the flavor of these discussions and the wide variety of practitioners who have strong feelings about the issues, is to listen in to the discussions on the Anthrodesign distribution list and follow up on the various blogs that are mentioned there. Not surprisingly, though it is now widely accepted that formal training as an anthropologist is not required in order to work as an ethnographer, we are now seeing attempts to institute certifications of ethnographic competence.

10. See also the lively, if also occasionally vituperative, discussions during the EPIC conferences and on the Anthrodesign list serve.

11. Over the twelve years during which I spent several months each year in a rural Maya community in the Yucatan, my mentor saw to it that I learned both practical skills, such as performing an external cephalic version (turning a mal-positioned baby around before birth), and theoretical and spiritual concepts, such as the connection between the functioning of the body and the universe.

12. Among inexperienced ethnographers, a common misunderstanding is that participant observation means the researcher observes the participants. In deep ethnography it means that the researcher *becomes* a participant while at the same time maintaining an observational stance.

13. I am particularly indebted to Gilbert Aubert, a Costa Rican management consultant, for long discussions that helped me verbalize my observations in terms of *"valores"* and "anti-*valores*" (values and anti-values). However, revealing such company-relevant cultural issues has remained a delicate issue for me. I knew, for example, that theft and robbery are quite common in Costa Rica, not only the notorious thefts from tourists but also break-ins in the houses of locals as well as foreigners. In a telling example, the president of the Bank of Costa Rica had his laptop stolen from his top-floor office, in

spite of security guards. People would dismiss this—"Well, that's Costa Rica for you"—and sometimes there is a hint of gloating in that. I have trouble discussing this (and a number of other such problems) in the corporate environment because it throws such a negative light on my host country. On the other hand, these cultural undercurrents clearly influence all kinds of corporate issues, especially when they blatantly affect the bottom line, as in the theft of easily concealed chips and electronic assemblies. One week after I left Costa Rica on this particular trip, *La Nacion* reported that one million dollars worth of chips had walked out of the plant. This would be unthinkable in Malaysia, a country that is governed by different *valores* and *anti-valores*.

14. One aspect of recent corporate ethnography that I am not able to discuss in detail here is the work that looks at the relationships that globalization produces between corporations from developed countries and the economic structures they generate in recipient countries. See, for example, Theodor Bestor's (2004) work on the worldwide tuna trade, Carmen Bueno Castellanos (2001) on Mexican auto-parts factories, and Robert Alvarez (2006) on the global mango and lime trade. In such cases the scope of investigations expands to trace multiple connections and investigate multiple spaces in which the relevant actions take place, becoming truly global, multidisciplinary, and multi-sited (Marcus and Fischer 1986; Marcus 1995). One result of this expansion in scope is that the number of anthropologists working for multilateral development agencies and bilaterals has increased sharply. Thus the World Bank's in-house corps of professional anthropologists and sociologists increased from one in 1974 to over fifty by the mid 1990s (Cernea 1995, as cited by Paiement 2007).

References

Alvarez, Robert R. 2006. "The Transnational State and Empire: U.S. Certification in the Mexican Mango and Persian Lime Industries." *Human Organization* 65(1): 35–45.

Appadurai, Arjun. 1986. *The Social Life of Things: Commodities in Cultural Perspective.* New York: Cambridge University Press.

Baba, Marietta. 2005. "To the End of Theory-Practice Apartheid: Encountering the World." In *Ethnographic Praxis in Industry Conference Proceedings,* 167–68. American Anthropological Association.

Becker, Howard S. 2003. *Making Sociology Relevant to Society.* Paper given at the meeting of The European Sociological Association in Murcia, Spain. http://home.earthlink.net/~hsbecker/relevant.htm.

Beers, Robin, and Pamela Whitney. 2006. "From Ethnographic Insight to User-centered Design Tool." In *Ethnographic Praxis in Industry Conference Proceedings,* 144–54. American Anthropological Association.

Bell, Genevieve. 2006. "No More SMS from Jesus: Ubicomp, Religion and Techno-spiritual Practices." In *Proceedings of Ubicomp 2006,* Dourish and Friday, eds., 141–58. Berlin: Springer-Verlag.

Bestor, Theodor C. 2004. *Tsukiji: The Fish Market at the Center of the World.* Berkeley, CA: University of California Press.

Blomberg, Jeanette, Mark Burrell, and Greg Guest. 2003. "An Ethnographic Approach to Design." In *The Human-Computer Interaction Handbook: Fundamentals, Evolving Technologies and Emerging Applications,* Jacko and Sears, eds., 964–85. Mahwah, NJ/London: Lawrence Erlbaum Associates.

Bueno Castellanos, Carmen. 2001. "The 'Glocalization' of Global Quality." *Practicing Anthropology* 23(4): 14–17.

Cernea, Michael M. 1995. *Social Organization and Development Anthropology*. Environmentally Sustainable Studies and Development Monographs Series, no. 6. Washington, DC: World Bank.

Cohen, Kris. 2005. "Who We Talk About When We Talk About Users." In *Ethnographic Praxis in Industry Conference Proceeding*, 218–23. American Anthropological Association.

Dourish, Paul. 2006. "Implications." *Proceedings of CHI 2006*, 22–27 April 2006, Montréal, Québec.

Fine, Ben, and Ellen Leopold. 1993. *The World of Consumption*. London: Routledge.

Hamada, Tomoko. 2000. "Anthropological Praxis: Theory of Business Organization. In *The Unity of Theory and Practice in Anthropology: Rebuilding a Fractured Synthesis*, Napa Bulletin #18, Hill and Baba, eds., 79–103.

Hill, Carole E., and Marietta L. Baba, eds. 2000. *The Unity of Theory and Practice in Anthropology: Rebuilding a Fractured Synthesis*, Napa Bulletin #18. National Association for the Practice of Anthropology.

Hine, Christine. 2000. *Virtual Ethnography*. London: Sage.

———. 2005. *Virtual Methods: Issues in Social Research on the Internet*. Oxford: Berg.

Hoskins, Janet. 1998. *Biographical Objects: How Things Tell the Stories of People's Lives*. New York: Routledge.

Hull, Glynda. 1997. "Manufacturing the New Worker: Literate Activities and Working Identities in a High-Performance Versus a Traditionally Organized Workplace." In *Transitions in Work and Learning: Implications for Assessment*, Papers and Proceedings, Board of Testing and Assessment, National Research Council, Lesgold, Feuer and Black, eds., 89–135. Washington, DC: National Academy Press.

Jones, Rachel. 2006. "Experience Models: Where Ethnography and Design Meet." In *Ethnographic Praxis in Industry Conference Proceeding*, 82–93. American Anthropological Association.

Jordan, Brigitte. 1989. "Cosmopolitical Obstetrics: Some Insights from the Training of Traditional Midwives." *Social Science and Medicine* 28(9): 925–44.

———. 1993 [1978]. *Birth in Four Cultures: A Crosscultural Investigation of Childbirth in Yucatan, Holland, Sweden and the United States*. 4th edition. Revised and expanded by Robbie Davis-Floyd. Long Grove, IL: Waveland Press.

———. 1996. "Ethnographic Workplace Studies and Computer Supported Cooperative Work." In *The Design of Computer-Supported Cooperative Work and Groupware Systems*, Shapiro, Tauber, and Traunmüller, eds., 17–42. Amsterdam: North Holland/Elsevier Science.

———. 1997. "Transforming Ethnography—Reinventing Research." *Cultural Anthropology Methods Journal (CAM)* 9(3): 12–17. Also in, 1996, *Groupware—Software für die Teamarbeit der Zukunft: Grundlegende Konzepte und Fallstudien*, Schiestl and Schelle, eds., 200–12. Marburg, Germany: Tectum Verlag.

———. Forthcoming 2009. "Blurring Boundaries: The 'Real' and the 'Virtual' in Hybrid Spaces." In *Knowledge Flow in Online and Offline Spaces*, Special Section for *Human Organization*, 68(2), Jordan, ed. http://www.lifescapes.org/Papers/blurring_boundaries_-_hybrid_spaces.htm

Jordan, Brigitte, and Brinda Dalal. 2006. "Persuasive Encounters: Ethnography in the Corporation." *Field Methods* 18(4): 359–81.

Lambert, Monique. 2005. "Greater-than, Equal-to, or Less-than the Sum of the Parts: A Study of Collective Information Processing and Information Distribution in Real-Time Cross-Functional Design." PhD dissertation Stanford University.

March, James G. 1991. "How Decisions Happen in Organizations." *Human-Computer Interaction* 6: 95–117.

Marcus, George E. 1995. "Ethnography in/of the World System: The Emergence of Multi-Sited Ethnography." In *Ethnography Through Thick and Thin*, Marcus, 79–104. Princeton, NJ: Princeton University Press.

Marcus, George E., and Michael M. J. Fischer. 1986. *Anthropology as Cultural Critique: An Experimental Moment in the Human Sciences*. Chicago, IL: University of Chicago Press.

Moore, Robert J., Nicolas Ducheneaut, and Eric Nickell. 2007. "Doing Virtually Nothing: Awareness and Accountability in Massively Multiplayer Online Worlds." In *Computer Supported Cooperative Work* 16(3): 265–305.

Obata, Akihiko, et al. 2007. "Ethnographic Inspection Identifying Project Risks." In *Ethnographic Praxis in Industry Conference Proceedings*, 151–61. American Anthropological Association.

Paiement, Jason Jacques. 2007. "Anthropology and Development." In *Applied Research and Practice from the Next Generation: The NAPA Student Achievement Award-Winning Papers, 2001–5*, NAPA Bulletin #27, Wallace, et al., eds., 196–223.

Rea-Holloway, Melinda, et al. 2006. "Getting over the Hump of Ethnography 'Lite': Ethnographic Techniques vs. Ethnography." In *Ethnographic Praxis in Industry Conference Proceedings*, 283. American Anthropological Association.

Robinson, Rick. 2005. "Let's Have a Conversation: Theory Session Introductory Remarks." In *Ethnographic Praxis in Industry Conference Proceedings*, 1–8. American Anthropological Association.

Rylko-Bauer, Barbara, Merrill Singer, and John van Willigen. 2006. "Reclaiming Applied Anthropology: Its Past, Present, and Future." *American Anthropologist* 108(1): 178–90.

Thomas, Suzanne, and Tony Salvador. 2006. "Skillful Strategy, Artful Navigation and Necessary Wrangling." In *Ethnographic Praxis in Industry Conference Proceedings*, 109–24. American Anthropological Association.

Vinkhuyzen, Erik, and Margaret H. Szymanski. 2004. "Would You like to do it Yourself? Service Requests and their Non-Granting Responses." In *Applying Conversation Analysis*, Richards and Seedhouse, eds., 91–106. Basingstoke, UK: Palgrave Macmillan.

Whalen, Jack. 1995. "A Technology of Order Production: Computer-Aided Dispatch in 9-1-1 Communications." In *Situated Order: Studies in the Social Organization of Talk and Embodied Activities*, Psathas and ten Have, eds., 187–230. Washington, DC: University Press of America.

REFRACTIONS OF ANTHROPOLOGICAL WAYS OF BEING AND KNOWING

Chapter 5

WRITING ON WALLS
The Materiality of Social Memory in Corporate Research

Dawn Nafus and ken anderson

Introduction

This chapter explores the materiality of ethnographic practice within a large technology firm. As with the other chapters in this volume, it seeks to articulate a ground that is neither prescriptive of "best practices" in uses of ethnography, nor, as Cefkin (chapter 1) describes it, "one of angst-ridden hand-wringing about researchers' moral and political complicity." This chapter will reflect on the use of project rooms—a physical, three-dimensional space to write, display artifacts and media, and draw. Though used differently in different places, the practice of writing on the walls has become an everyday part of life as an anthropologist in industrial contexts. Walls have become materials to think with, think through, and perform what it is researchers are thinking about. Our main claim is that these are not just simple mnemonic devices, a record of what happened while doing fieldwork or while thinking through business problems, but that these materials make a certain social configuration possible. Social relations happen in the process of people moving between text, visual material, and orality. It is possible to see these project rooms as a microcosm of one way that social memory plays a role in capitalist organizations. Capitalist organizations are usually seen as destroyers of the past rather than holders of it. Farms are bulldozed to build factories; traditional craft knowledge is replaced with assembly line labor. Yet these materials hold together everyday acts of both remembering and forgetting within the day to day life of capitalist organizations, which makes product "innovation" just as reliant on the past as the present.

By writing about these spaces, we are in effect writing about a very different form of "writing" (a theme echoed by Cefkin [chapter 1], Darrouzet, Wild, and Wilkinson [chapter 3], Blomberg [chapter 8], and Fischer [chapter 9] in this volume). This gives us pause to reflect on how anthropologists have thought about writing, and how anthropologists represent the people who participate in research. In the 1980s anthropology underwent a crisis of representation, which rethought the politics of writing about non-Western people. There was much about this crisis that assumed one uniform anthropology and a shared model of knowledge production. An assumed "we" write monographs and journal articles of a certain length, with a certain font and regimented layout. The monograph and the journal article were the unmarked starting point, as if people had equal ways into an anthropological text, and for that matter cared in equal quantities. It was as if representations of the Other could be interrogated independent of the form those representations took. The debate took place as if everyone equally could just read it and judge for themselves what was orientalizing and what was not. A recent move from an academic environment to an industrial one, however, revealed to one of us (Nafus) just how much anthropological knowledge goes unmarked as a neutral kind of knowledge practice. In corporate settings there is no commitment to a particular kind of text, visual, or oral form. While the central issues in the writing-culture debate—such as power, neocolonialism, and representation of the Other—permeate all aspects of anthropological research outside academic institutions, the issue of the material form that knowledge takes, and therefore the various ways into the work, is not a stable given.

In fact, quite to the contrary, it is highly unstable. There is little in the way of expectation about how an argument should flow, which in academic anthropology is policed to some extent through material form. While there are some experiments in anthropological fiction (McClard 2005; Jackson 1986; Schmidt 1984), and interesting developments in museology (Moutu 2006), on the whole this is the far more difficult route to tenure. It is still the case that an abstract, introduction, and analysis should look and sound a certain way. This in turn is constituted by a naturalized material aesthetic. The black and white starkness, page size and length, and placement of institutional affiliations next to authors inscribed right on the front are all enrolled in the processes of making legitimacy.

Particularly in large, post-Fordist organizations, knowledge is situated by and through multiple milieus. Reorganizations occur frequently, cross-team collaborations happen regularly, new specialisms crop up, and one never knows exactly who has the ear of whom. One outcome of the transformation into a knowledge/network economy (Castells 1996) is that as these milieus expand and fragment, legitimacy is increasingly contested.

Often the one known quantity is that people are differently situated to a body of knowledge, yet all claim one sort of expertise or another (as Flynn's exploration of the political economy of design, chapter 2, illuminates). It makes a certain sense in that there is no one way to produce knowledge and no one form to legitimate it. Initially moving into industry, Nafus imagined that the central challenge would to state, in the simplest possible terms, what was happening out there in the world with products. Eventually she came to understand that the problem was not one of simplicity, but heterogeneity. She found herself engaged in a long-term dialogue with the technology industry with many moments when people were nominally engaging in the "same thing" but on very different and forever-shifting terms.

Just as the actors shift, so do the props. It is never clear what ethnographic knowledge is speaking to—sometimes it shapes physical technologies, sometimes business strategy, but also occasionally social science itself. Although participatory design advocates often talk about design processes as a set of translations from researchers to designers (for example, Hansen 2006), in our experience, this notion of point-to-point translation elides the instabilities that happen along its course. Ethnography, at least at Intel, instead resembles more of a sustained dialogue through which multiple knowledges flow. This in turn means producing, sustaining, and destroying many boundary objects—that is, things in which people have shared stakes but on radically different terms and often to different ends.

Because of this instability, boundary objects like project rooms are particularly good places to start to understand how this heterogeneity and instability of knowledge practices within late capitalist organizations happens. Project rooms are places where people who have different levels of engagement and different disciplinary commitments dip in and out of a research effort. This instability usually seems to lead in a certain direction. It has a theme of sorts. Knowledge does not just circulate, but is consistently made to appear as if it were new, regardless of its origins. Capitalist firms, after all, "innovate." Project rooms can reveal how this occurs.

In a different paper it would be possible, in a more direct way, to interrogate materiality as itself an issue. While there is a recent push to theorize materiality in academic circles (see, for example, the debate in Ingold 2007), we approach it here simply as a way *into* understanding how things are made to become perpetually new. If we were to follow Tim Ingold (2007), we might say we are addressing materials, as opposed to materiality, which he argued has been so over-theorized as to have little bearing on actual physical artifacts. In a tongue-in-cheek sort of way, we stick with the term *materiality* because we suspect there is a similarity here between what may happen to create over-theorization, and how these corporate processes escalate similar self-induced, politicized complexity, with multiple knowledge producers all attempting to position themselves as experts by mixing the pot. At least in the corporate setting, this abundance of knowledge production does indeed create a distance between what is at stake in the discussion (politics and prestige) and anything that ends up in the hands of consumers (stuff).

In what follows we will present the story of one project and the artifacts it produced as it went from field research to brainstorming session with key stakeholders. It is worth taking some time to explain what sort of story this is. We expressly do not consider ourselves expert users or inhabitants of project rooms. Indeed, in speaking with colleagues elsewhere as part of the background research to the paper, there were many people eager to convince us of the *worth* of having such space. Our colleagues, who are the real experts in this case, steered conversations in the direction of what a dedicated space for such practices was good for. While there are normative stories among ethnographers about the value of these artifacts, our story is not one of them. Nor is the present story intended to signal what we have done at Intel as either "best practice" or a tradition of sorts that is set to go on indefinitely. Instead, we tell the story of one project room as a way of thinking through the much longer–standing phenomenon of memory in enterprises, which exists beyond talk of what project rooms are supposed to be good for. For our purposes, then, whether or not the artifacts succeeded in building consensus, or representing an ethnographic point effectively or ineffectively, matters less than what they reveal about the paradox of memory in institutions that seek to create novelty.

The second note on our story, then, has to do with how we intend to treat social memory. There has been extensive anthropological and historiographical thought on the relationship between memory, material artifacts, and the body (Nora 1996; Stewart 1996; Connerton 1989; Bourdieu 1977; Battaglia 1992; Forty and Kuchler 1999; Buchli and Lucas 2001). This line of thought has, interestingly enough, not intersected with the design and human-computer interaction (HCI) research on collaborative space for knowledge work. The research on project rooms, for example (Barthelmess et al. 2006; Cohen and McGee 2004) and on "corporate memory," and knowledge management more generally, takes memory as an a priori fact on the way to designing systems to encourage even more collaboration. Collaboration is an assumed end to itself (a self-legitimating ethos becoming somewhat of a wider trend [Strathern 2003]), and as a result, the authors working in these paradigms simply call out the importance of shared artifacts as a way of sustaining collaboration across time. This type of work does not problematize memory, but assumes it away as a brute psychological capacity.

Both Pierre Nora (1996) and Paul Connerton (1989) address the social life of memory, though not in the context of "collaboration" as an explicit form of social relations. Connerton famously made a distinction between incorporation, where bodily habit lives and is transmitted as a kind of memory (think cooking traditions learned from elders), and inscription, the manipulation of the physical world into building monuments, memorials, and texts that outlive people (think recipes). In doing so, he privileges one model of memory (inscription) as the exclusive property of "modern," and literate, societies, while others are left with embodied tradition. This bears some similarities to Nora's treatment of memory at first glance. In his view, history, in the sense of professional re-accounting of events, is meaningful only when some rupture in memory occurs, which is modernization. Memory for him is "life, always embodied in living societies and as such in permanent evolution." Embodied in social habits, and transmuted across time, Nora finds a gulf between memory and "history, which is how modern societies organize a past they are condemned to forget because they are driven by change. ... At the heart of history is a criticism destructive of spontaneous memory. Memory is always suspect in the eyes of history, whose true mission is to demolish it, to repress it" (3). Returning to the cooking example, Nora might draw attention to the violence done to practices of cooking by the historian's account of it, devoid of human attachments. In what he calls *lieux de memoire*, both inscription and incorporation take place. *Lieux de memoire* are places of remembrance that exist in a social world that constantly seeks to get ahead of itself, to "innovate." These can be literal places, such as museums and archives, but also, more broadly, festivals, calendar rituals, and indeed canonical historical accounts. These are places that refuse to give the disenchantments of History the final word. "*Lieux de memoire* are fundamentally vestiges, the ultimate embodiments of a commemorative consciousness that survives in a history which, having renounced memory, cries out for it" (5, emphasis added).

Deborah Battaglia (1992) has written against these distinctions between history and memory, inscription and incorporation. They are not just ethnocentric, where "modern" people have one and "traditional" people the other, but hide from view the importance of active forgetting, obscuring, and erasure. She argues that in these theories of social memory, forgetting can only be a way of eliminating dissent, as power comes as a function of who can remember what. She sees forgetting not just as an aspect of repression but as a constructive aspect of sociality that makes it possible to reframe and reconstruct. This anticipates later work by Victor Buchli and Gavin Lucas (2001) who describe the relation between remembrance and forgetfulness as a struggle.

Nora's work seems to work fairly well with this idea of forgetting and remembering as a kind of politics or struggle. Like Nora's modernizing France, in corporate environments people *set out* to achieve the sense of rupture so central to Nora's work. The pressure to create disruption is enormous. Particularly in technology firms, but also among designers of many persuasions, remembrance is thought of as a sort of constraint. The job is perceived to be one of improving and making new rather than remaining content with the old. Ethnographic research is caught up in this project, too. It is there to see something "new" among consumers. Yet to do this one must do lots of remembering. Project rooms remember field sites, they remember the interests of those sitting around the table, and in a wider sense they "remind" firms that a social relation exists with the people who buy their products. For these reasons, when we discuss memory, we pay attention to the embodied nature of what is being transmitted across time, and we include in the notion a hefty dose of forgetting.

A Brighton Street in Seattle

One way to describe project rooms is as a container that extends the shelf life of intermediary research artifacts. Both academic and non-academic anthropologists produce much more than publications. Videos, photos, notes from discussions, quotes from research participants, and diagrams representing either social relations or design ideas rarely see publication in academic work. But in project rooms they are debated and reworked with various insiders and semi-insiders. Just how long these artifacts "live" varies from firm to firm, but on the whole their extended life reflects the betwixt and between position of ethnography in firms. Their physical display invites people who did not perform the field research into the production of knowledge. These can be other members of the company, colleagues, and research managers. It is tempting to say that heterogeneity is "managed" in project rooms, as if these artifacts were somehow framed, disciplined even, by the interiority of the walls. In post-Fordist models of production heterogeneity is not necessarily a problem to be contained. Instead, the most important feature of the "container" is its open doors, built to invite interjection and interception from various parties.

Switching back to the comparison with academic writing, working through project rooms, rather than individually authored texts, de-centers the self as the technology of knowledge production. Historically, anthropologists have always dealt with stakeholders of various kinds, and have worked to take seriously others' voices in our accounts. The extensive de-centering of project rooms does, however, push the boundaries of anthropological knowledge production. As Sherry Ortner has it, "minimally [ethnography] has always meant the attempt to understand another life world using the self—or as much of it as possible—as the instrument of Knowing" (2006). Here though, this interpreting self as the *instrument* of knowing is acutely problematized. Other people and objects, along with the self, partially traverse sites of knowledge from field to "home" at various moments. This means that moments of anthropological shock, those disjuncts between "our" world and "theirs" that are the engine of interpretation, proliferate in these contexts. The interjections are as multiple as they are constant. What will they read into things? What do they want to know? Project rooms provide good grounds to question what happens to anthropological interpretation, indeed ways of claiming anthropological expertise, in these circumstances where the technology of interpretation (the self) is so radically de-centered.

At some companies the display of researcherly artifacts is de rigueur, and there are even local languages that describe and classify these intermediary artifacts, which is a common practice in interdisciplinary contexts (Galison 1996). At Intel, there are practices that happen with varying degrees of consistency. Sometimes posters and displays hang on in the office for weeks, as if there were an extended midstream thought. At other times there is a dedicated session in which stakeholders are invited and writings take place on large whiteboards with post-it notes attached. The artifacts left tend to variously reflect designerly, managerialist, anthropological, or engineering commitments. For example, as we write this we are sitting among diagrams describing usage scenarios for mobile technologies, complete with pictures of people and artifacts accompanied by short scenarios. This is a layout that would be recognizable in any human-computer interaction (HCI) or design context. These sit next to a hastily drawn 2x2 square for a project to show how social perceptions of time influence technology adoption. This is hugely ironic. The project was an attempt to revisit David Harvey's (1989) critique of global acceleration, yet to do it the researchers use a drawing that owes aesthetic debt to managerialist techniques used to *quicken* decision making in businesses. While project rooms do hold together strange bedfellows like these, there are also expectations that do narrow the field of possibilities. PowerPoint and whiteboards are expected, interpretive dance is a non-starter. They in theory should contain artifacts from various moments of inspiration. If your inspiration happened to come from "suspect" sources, such as religious texts, this can be smuggled in only through disguise.

Figure 5.1. Brainstorming in a corporate project room for the Smart Streets project. Photo courtesy of Smart Streets Project.

The above picture was taken from a meeting in our Seattle lab that we held for a project called Smart Streets. The research, led by Wendy March (standing at back), was to explore the technological possibilities for shared public infrastructure at the street level. Taking the street as the unit of analysis, the ethnographic question was to identify which kinds of social interactions within mixed-use streets one could design technologies around. This led us to consider the interstices between neighborly, stranger, business, and kin and state interactions.

When this photograph was taken, we had begun the first leg of this three-part project. The other two were set to take place in mixed use streets in Brazil and China. This was also, unusually, a joint project with Nokia, the mobile-phone manufacturer. The project took place in the context of this broader corporate partnership. The goal for both firms was to identify and open up design opportunities. Historically the two companies have tended to do this differently. Intel researchers had focused on publishing alongside internal presentation, whereas for the Nokia team recognition and reward was more linked to writing patents. Both sides were also using it as an opportunity to exchange methodological knowledge. In the end, the project did all of these things, with both companies participating in equal measure.

In this picture, four researchers had recently returned from fieldwork in Brighton, UK, and had invited other Intel staff to a session that conveyed something of the results, and involved them in the brainstorming process for drawing up concepts for new technologies. Up to and including the day before, the materials visible in the picture—the street reconstructed along the walls with photographs, the lists on large white pieces of paper—were enrolled in a somewhat different process, which was to create the themes presented that day. This is when the project room artifacts began linking people together.

Creating themes meant identifying and selecting the dynamics of social relationships we found of potential interest. For example, some themes centered on deconstructing what does and does not count as "infrastructure," or the ways in which identity plays out in geographic space. These themes were in midstream at the time of the brainstorm. *Midstream* here meant stable enough to easily articulate and form the basis of comparison for the other field sites, but not stable enough to discuss publicly. Working among four researchers, these themes did not arise "naturally" as if research participants had simply reported them to us, nor did they arise through the anthropological way of extensive note taking followed by extensive reading. With four researchers from two different companies there was a high emphasis on externalization of knowledge early on in the process, even in the field. Historically at Intel we have relied on the traditional separation of fieldwork and ethnography writing, but for our partners the opposite was the case, doing all the analysis in-field. This project did a bit a both.

During fieldwork, researchers held daily discussions of research events. Track was kept by taking notes of conversations on large white papers that could be viewed by everyone in the room. The writings were mostly headline-style words or phrases, around which one person might orally relate the idea behind it ("trading," "visibility," "garbage," and so forth). Each day we could return to these as emergent sites of knowledge, to either confirm, refute, or otherwise redirect depending on the experiences the researchers had on the street. The walls did the work of threading together a conversation. They were three-dimensional hypertext. In part, the headlines cut off conversations, in that we did not have to repeatedly trace our steps starting from nil. "Visibility," "garbage," and so on, were constantly present, no longer in need of assertion. This is the central premise behind oft-used brainstorming strategies: if one writes it down so everyone can see it, in theory it need not be restated. There are people who struggle to get their agendas taken seriously and will repeat themselves in any available forum, especially brainstorms. These people are seen as a threat to progress, and the wall can be used to make complete consensus unnecessary. To prevent repeated returning to (marginal) issues, meeting leaders will write these pet agendas on walls to provide acknowledgment of these voices that struggle to find a home. This was one of the things it was widely said to be "good for."

This appeasement strategy assumes ideas are a stable, "done" thing. However, just because something is written does not make it meaningful. The writing of headlines on walls cuts off further discussion, but will just as likely ensure repetition. With headlines it is not possible to remember the origins, inflections, and tones, particularly when working in a group that shares little in terms of conceptual models and sensibilities. There is much oral work that has to be done to make these writings conceptually meaningful. Talk around these categories continued right through the life of the project until they more or less did signify consensus: "This was the idea that ... and I think it came from you," until who was speaking became arbitrary. Writing on walls meant that people became "good at" enacting one another's discourse. In this sense, the seeming neutrality of "capturing" what is said is entirely false. Each headline was an occasion to enroll one another in a point of view.

In the course of all of this the team had assembled a photo montage of the street studied. While the team pasted together the street they also papered over epistemological difference. The slowed pace of arranging and taping allowed a brief acknowledgment of epistemic differences. One member of our team worked in ways similar to photojournalism; for him, knowledge was produced in the hundreds of photos he took each day. At such volumes photos become not just mnemonic traces, but a way of knowing the world. He literally had a lens through which he saw things, and this made his experience of that street radically different from Dawn's. For her, the street was interesting only in as much as it forced her to grapple with anthropological concepts in new ways. Whether or how this could be done meaningfully photographically was not obvious. The thought of getting behind the camera felt distracting at best. The researchers were mutually suspicious of one another. What could be gotten with all those photos? Or all that theory?

The awkward conversation about these issues revealed just how poorly language grapples with epistemic difference. Our brief acknowledgments of the different perspectives ended up becoming banal statements of working from "bottom-up" observations or "top-down" theory, expediency, and institutional expectations, and so on and so on. It was a respectful enough conversation, but nonetheless one disconcertingly suffused with identity making, culture, and affect (Knorr Cetina 1999; Ratto 2005). These things, however, are never socially legitimate accounts of why we are committed to seeing the world in the way that we do. "Because that's what my kind of anthropologist does" is the accurate, but wrong, account. Project rooms present the opportunity to *not* make this account. Difference could be glossed by focusing on the street seemingly "out there," which can be photographed and reassembled as a shared referent, out of which we could get different things. Dawn could read into it an imagination of social relations, and our photographer could read into it a visual instantiation of phenomena on the street. The pictures of the street made debate unnecessary and allowed us to both remain equally enchanted with it.

Remembering

The photographed street kept present the multiple conversations researchers had with residents up and down the street. The potter could be shown to have something to do with the restaurant up the road. The collage and the writings that held our discussions are two different devices. The pictures were displayed to bring viewers back to the street, and the writings were there to move beyond it. Still, when they came together in a project room they gained a sociological equivalence. We illustrate their equivalence by way of a third object, canoe prows in Papua New Guinea. All three could be considered technologies of enchantment (Gell 1992, 1998). Alfred Gell argues that art should not be addressed according to its aesthetic qualities, but rather as technologies of social engagement. It works by enchanting the viewer, dazzling and seducing him into doing things he would not necessarily do on his own accord. Canoe prows exert the agency of their makers, because trading partners become dazzled by them as they arrive on shore, which changes the power relationship between partners. Similarly, both the photographs and the writings exerted some power over their viewers. They returned people to a "site" of a memory that they otherwise would not have revisited.

It is worth probing into how this enchantment is achieved, and why these objects enchant so much. They do not, as in Gell's example, enchant through the technical skill of the assembler. There is nothing remarkable about the particular arrangements of notes and photographs. Jane Bennett describes enchantment as "a mood of fullness, plenitude, or liveliness, a sense of having had one's nerves or circulation or concentration powers turned up or recharged—a shot in the arm, a fleeting return to childlike excitement about life" (2001: 5). This rapturous version may be a bit too strong here, though fullness is definitely key. In fact, to one of the strategic planners present in the brainstorm, "fullness" is the whole point of ethnographic photographs. He in turn brings these pictures to his meetings as a way of creating "a-ha" moments, to persuade and inspire senior management to take action. To him some technical artistic skill certainly helps, but the photographs' ability to instantly assemble the dots together in new ways is the real treat. Pictures make it easier to argue, for example, that the street infrastructure has an effect on the technologies people carry, if they can show devices intermingling with their environment.

It is the speed of this transportation, both conceptually and out of the drab office into the "real world," that is so enthralling. To people who spend the majority of their waking hours in uniformly sized gray cubicles, the photographs also entrance in roughly the same way as fleeting glimpses out the window to the outside world do. Viewing them is not so much a replication of some experience "out there" as the promise of new possibilities "in here." The "facts" that they capture, such as the presence of commerce on the street or the practices of putting out the trash, are in a sense less important than how they perform the "outsideness" of the world. As photographs, they made an empiricist move by performing a commitment to a world separable from the researcher (for more on this, see Nafus and anderson 2006). Drawings of trash or the street would be suboptimal. Too much interpretation and not enough "facts." It needed to be made clear that researchers were "really" there, and that we had talked to "real people" in a "real place."

The allusion to "out there" is necessary to the engagement for reasons beyond empiricist legitimacy. It brings forth more immediate concerns of what to do with the information. This nod to empiricist epistemology—the conceit that an "out there" exists—suggests to people sitting in the room that something ought to be done to intervene in it. They are not accounts of events as much as signifiers of the question "What's next?" In this way, photographs and writings call the viewer to his or her own agency. The question recharges excitement. Pictures that cause the "a-ha" moments give people attachments to multiple strands of thought at once—a penny appears to drop. The question appears answerable because of the remnants of modernism involved. Even in this unstable, heterogeneous post-Fordist world, a contained world is still seen as a knowable world, and therefore can be managed. The cast and characters of corporate politics may be shifting ground, but the photographed outside world can be made to appear as if it is less shifting and complex. Photographs smuggle in the Enlightenment idea that external(ized) facts are apprehensible, and this fuels the charge. Collaging a single street stabilizes it, yet involves enough components to contribute to a feeling of fullness. These combined make it a thing to act upon. The photographs and notes enchanted people into questions about the future, and once this dazzle set in, the researchers began working very hard to steer conversation back to the field site in some meaningful way. This is the moment where the demand for whatever pet technological aspirations people have gets suddenly remembered. Jet packs are demanded. The researchers repeatedly drew the technology developers back to the pictures to force them to not "forget" the street, and to remind them that they are not the only relevant agents. The intention of the researchers was to entice people to not design for themselves, or for individuals, but for this particular street. Bennett's dazzle plays a role, but it is the Gellian aspect of enchantment as an agent of memory that gives it a more sustained power. As the phenomenological immediacy wanes, these objects become *lieux de memoire*—sites to which one might return. Having already been taken in by the artifact, the question of "What next?" *returns* people to it.

As James Leach (2006) points out, Gell's notion of agency is underwritten by the idea that single person is the agent. Individuals make art objects, not collectives. He goes on to point out that art-science collaborations similarly hold this assumption, such that people positioned themselves to be seen as the authors of objects. In his case, artists sought to author gallery works and the scientists worked toward publications and patents. Here, the question of skill was negotiated differently. It was possible to *not* seek to author any particular object in the room, as they required no skill to produce them. The question of who was the creative agent could be put on hold, momentarily. These artifacts can never constitute the final, authoritative say, in part because there were simply too many threads which would make no sense to authoritatively assemble as some final end. These threads do have an ultimate endpoint, either in intellectual property or in writings or conference papers. But for now talk of the street was in a holding pattern, which made the institutional heterogeneity seem okay for a time.

The holding pattern has certain advantages, particularly in technology companies. The very fact of repetition does the work of longer-term enrollment. While the inscriptions on walls endured as a kind of social memory from session to session, it was the speech, embodied in speakers and practiced over time like so many gestures made while cooking a staple dish, which outlived the physical materials in the end. To bring people back to the street, the *lieux de memoire*, meant not just pointing to pictures but inspiring them to repeat themselves in the street's terms. Researchers could only hope that whatever changed in that reframing was carried forth in their future conversations. Though written to transcend (fleeting) conversation, over the long term the written account of the research is actually the more ephemeral of the two. It fades into the background as discourse takes hold. It is eventually destroyed physically. Papers and photographs on walls have a shelf life of a couple of months at most. Success of ethnographic research at Intel is talked about explicitly in terms of the durability of the discourse produced. The goal is to "change the conversation," that is, change the terms of discourse about technologies and their value to people.

Yet the phrase "changing the conversation" betrays a wider undercurrent of repetition. Conversations are in fact repeated until they are changed. One way to do this is to stabilize conversation on one's own terms. When the strategic planner quoted earlier uses these pictures in subsequent venues, researchers' agency is exercised. The conceptual work done in drawing out the connections in the photograph—that streets are an interconnected web, and that technologies can work through those connections—has a chance of being remembered when the picture gets repeated through other venues. Just as researchers get good at one another's talk, so do others in the organization.

However, owning the wall does not mean owning the conversation. The powerful can fill the wall with different aspects of the same agenda, essentially shouting people down visually. Similarly, people interjected one comment to set up an ally to put his or her idea onto a wall. This volume can make pictures become "really" about some technical trajectory none of the researchers cared about, though this did not happen in the Brighton meetings. At its most power-suffused, post-it notes become tokens in a marketplace, currency for trading and negotiating, where an agenda is not emergent from an open dialogue but already set by the social relations within the room. Among the initial four researchers, the shared headlines meant practicing each other's ways of talking, but the rapid drawing of connections among project-room materials can create a pyrrhic consensus that legitimates offstage social relations by creating the fiction that ideas generated emerged through egalitarian talk.

This account has shown how returns *to lieux de memoire* emerge as important, agenda-changing things, and how this memory operates within processes of forgetting. Forgetfulness about disciplinary concerns is primary, as epistemological differences get glossed over by the shared assembly and viewing of photos and other artifacts. To the extent pet agendas succeed, the group has to forget them as someone's pet project. Contexts similarly get forgotten in order for memory to succeed. To stay on the street, or in the project room, would be a failure to move on to what's next. The materials in project rooms navigate, enroll, and seduce through these remembrances and forgettings. They do not hold memory as a kind of elaborate mnemonic device, but act as an engine of the present, initiating a discursive site that outlives any one material form.

Making Things New by Forgetting That They Are Old

The stakeholders within the company were at the brainstorm to hear something new about the world, so that they in turn might create something novel with technologies. The mental model of this, to the minds of nearly everyone sitting in the room, was that of a funnel. Many nascent possibilities, concepts, and material ingredients populated the wide end, which grew ever narrower up until the moment of production. Images of these funnels circulate within the company, and have a social life well beyond it in management studies departments and business punditry (for example, Hank Chesbrough's *Open Innovation* [2003]).

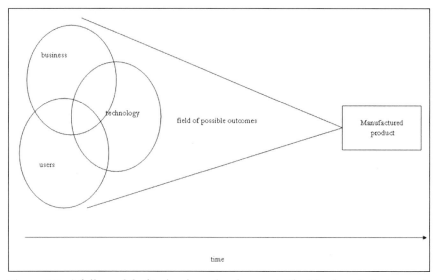

Figure 5.2. A folk model of technology development. The idea here is that a product must work technologically, on business grounds, and fit in users' everyday lives. Many product concepts fill the beginning of the funnel, and are eliminated as their failures in one or more areas become clear, ever tightening the three fields of knowledge until the product is manufactured.

In this project room, a visual analogy was taking place. If we were at the beginning of a funnel, the widest part, then it must be "filled" over time. One good idea simply would not do, particularly if people hear stories of research precisely to have their point of view disrupted. Tales of the unexpected in turn demand an unexpected response, and the only way to do that is through a volume of ideas, assumed to be discrete and independent, but nevertheless emergent through dialogue. The first three ideas shouted out to the room are always predictable, but still are perceived to need to be said. They begin populating the funnel's edge. The technology flavor of the day can always be counted on to start things off. Sure enough in our Brighton session the first ideas brainstormed had to do with tricks drawn from ubiquitous computing, a trendy technology paradigm. Other contributions then fill the space, each given their own distinct spatial frame by sitting on their own post-it note, making each separable from the other. If imaginary arrows could be drawn between notes, there was a convincing visual argument that multiple possible trajectories were present. The notes made it seem as if knowledge could be recombined at any moment and different arrows could be drawn. We were drawing and filling out in a rather visceral way to traverse the widest part of the funnel. The Brighton project room had this kind of volume by the end of the day. The participants had a very clear marker that they had achieved something new by being immersed in this visual analogy of the product-development funnel. The sheer volume of words on walls made it matter less what the words actually meant. The long-term enrollment work that happened earlier in the project, with long discussions about what head-line-style phrases meant, in the brainstorm took a back seat to the feel-ing of fullness in having completed the space. While there was indeed a dynamic of returning to sites of memory, the sense of having returned to something, having undergone an act of memory, was obliterated in the service of seeing oneself as making something new. The mental model of the funnel suggests that if there are lots of notes, something new probably happened.

When we spoke to colleagues, particularly those from design disci-plines, writing on walls was seen as a technique good for circumventing convention. The claim was that volume, indeed occasionally explicit de-mands for ever-greater volume from session organizers, thwarted repro-duction of "old" ideas, not just those persistently marginal ones that held meetings hostage. In this context the blank wall came to be seen as a threat of sorts. They were rendered incomplete by the impetus to write on it. This threat was said to "push" people to think outside their own conventions. Post-it notes are the technology of choice for the reason that they can be moved around. Again there is an analogy being made here. Discourse can be seemingly repositioned by moving around words on notes. Perhaps, too, so can people be repositioned in relation to that discourse. By seeing your thoughts among many, the idea is that participants detach their com-mitments to any particular one.

In this sense, the post-it notes frame orality as an almost tedious, and at the same time uncontrolled, building on each other's speech. Indeed, Dawn was part of another workshop that involved mostly academics and a designer who suffered a good deal of frustration, not with the tone of the conversation, but with what seemed to him to be the conversation's circularity. By circular, he meant that "the conversation wasn't being re-corded." The statement is interesting in that the workshop had two people visibly taking detailed notes as well as an audio recorder on the desk. But for him these technologies of keeping account were no account at all. They were not embodied in a way that pushed along the funnel. The physical memory (or Connerton's incorporation) of going up to the wall and doing the writing, makes the "brainstorm" a meaningful, socially coded activity for him.

Roy Wagner (1973) argues that all social acts are simultaneously conventional as well as an invention of sorts. There is always something new in traditional acts, and something old in seemingly inventive activities. What matters is where people attribute creativity. Here the cards were stacked decidedly in one direction. Making something seem to be new is where participants attributed creativity. Many technologies sit on the shelf, as it were, until the marketplace is ready for them. With good timing money can be made. But if the ethos is "innovation," then it is not legitimate for them to be seen as old technologies which have sat around; they must be constituted as new in order to find their way into secured discourse and eventually the marketplace. Faced with new information about the social life of the street, people responded by constituting their notions of what technologies should do as similarly new, or made new by this new context. Many of the "ideas" discussed in the brainstorm were in fact twists on technology fads, wrangled into a form appropriate for the street. Old ubiquitous computing scenarios became newly meaningful in Brighton. The tantalizing originality posed by the brainstorming fantasy, where the volume of post-it notes loosens up people's dispositions and attachments, seems an impossible version of novelty that is never really achieved—and perhaps should not be. If memories weren't constructive, why hold on to intermediary documents for so long?

At the same time, however, the fact of a shared referent occasionally affords genuinely surprising conversations. Happily one never really knows who the project room is actually speaking to. In a different project room researchers had printed out four Russian words associated with "usefulness," and attached pictures of artifacts that people associate with those words. One Monday morning five new post-it notes had appeared, commenting on those artifacts in Russian. The researchers wrote back, asking who they were from. A whole week passed and the following Monday they learned students from Russia were doing a work abroad program as an extended holiday, and were cleaning the offices. This then drew in other ex-pats around the office, and took the research in a new direction. This was a totally different sense of "out-of-the-box" thinking. It startlingly shifted the field "site" away from a far-flung locale and brought it home, not as a collection of artifacts for display but as a set of ongoing relations. For these researchers, this project room almost felt like the fieldwork of traditional anthropology.

Conclusion: The Cost of Institutionalization

Deep in the belly of capitalist systems, we have traced the ways in which the past is not a scarce resource (Appadurai 1981) but a fecund one, in which reframings and reconstructions proliferate amidst radical heterogeneity. The ethos of newness allows people to mine the past with great plasticity, as long as it is made new again. The social life of ethnographic research materials in corporate settings shows how rupture, in Nora's sense of breaking away from the past in the course of "modernization," is something achieved through memory, not despite it. In the resurrecting of past fieldwork experiences in project rooms, and re-articulation of past technological paradigms alongside fieldwork documents, knowledge practices are made eerily "traditional." Not unlike "traditional" craft knowledge, "innovation" knowledge is embodied in physical gestures and speech that endures over time. They fit rather well into the anthropological descriptions of memory.

The struggles of remembering and forgetting involve efforts to make enchantments with past intellectual or technical trajectories take place alongside their eventual destruction. It is as if the modernist impulse to codify and systematize does not drive out lived, embodied memory, but rather the very promise of systematicity, the smoothed contours of a social world rendered miniature inside four walls of a project room, invites an embodied, lived experience of creative satisfaction. The funnel is filled! Actions will happen! Each headline and photograph ultimately yields to those oral patters that strive to configure some sort of agenda.

The simultaneous stabilization and destabilization that happens with these artifacts betrays something about a context with proliferating boundaries. Like Nora's modernity in the institution of History, "rupture" takes place at multiple points, and yet itself is becoming institutionalized. There is a wider context that sets up this paradox. The notion of disruption as a theory of markets (Christensen 1997) has been widely embraced in technology industries. This is the notion that market-changing technologies struggle to come out of large incumbent businesses, and are most likely to be produced by lone, marginal mavericks. The imagination of a marketplace suffused by disruptors and disruptees could be seen as a continuation of a social imagination that is interested in the apparent shifts rather than the continuities of techno-social life (see Woolgar 2003).

Yet to call a large incumbent a fixed entity is a fiction, as they are themselves crosscut internally and in their relations with smaller businesses, think tanks, consultants, consumers, and universities. Project rooms are a field in which to enact those crosscuttings. It cannot be coincidence that "disruption" became such an assumed model of markets around the same time that brainstorming-type events in project rooms, such as the one in Seattle, started becoming institutionalized. The enforced forgetting of brainstorming sessions is becoming an explicit social form. People now know what they are getting when attending a brainstorm, and what to do with all those post-it notes. The notion of markets as "disruption" enforces a forgetting that small players are a part of the market as well as large ones, and creates an imagined nowhere from which technologies are thought to emerge.

The danger of this, however, is that what starts out as a "model of" quickly turns into a "model for" (Geertz 1973). Project rooms emerged as a way to engage with these institutional complexities, and grew, implicitly, as a model of them. Some colleagues, however, have told us that it can give the appearance that qualitative research is essentially some sort of algorithm with inputs and outputs. Input field data into a certain configuration and out pops the answer to a research question. This renders invisible the critical-thinking work that goes on within the space. Similarly, the designer colleague who grew nervous about a workshop going "unrecorded" also acknowledged the problems of such thorough institutionalization. As much as his post-it notes asked people to push the boundaries of their own knowledge, it also delegitimized knowledge which did not come in the form of bold, sweeping statements required of "out-of-the-box" performances. The specific social configurations, designed to avoid prejudgment, in fact required a prejudgment of sorts.

Ethnography has been popularly touted as a method(ology) that helps companies see beyond their own assumptions and gain deeper insights about their customers and markets. Where there is consistent pressure to make something new, social conventions develop as a way to be seen to be forgetting the old ways of doing things. Ethnography continues to have an uncomfortable relationship with more routinized models of producing knowledge. It is one of the few research techniques that seek the radically unexpected by directly challenging researchers' personal worldviews. Ethnography was created to destabilize, but it is entirely possible that a routinized form could emerge. We wonder whether the enchantments that ethnographic practices deliver will survive as the institutionalization of corporate ethnography itself becomes greater, and descriptions of whatever this job is becomes clearer. If the work is routine, no one is disrupted.

Acknowledgments

The authors would like to thank the many colleagues who shared with us their perspectives on project rooms—colleagues who we will not implicate by naming here. We would also like to thank Melissa Cefkin, Maria Bezaitis, Rick Robinson, and Brigitte Jordan for helpful commentary on earlier drafts.

References

Appadurai, Arjun. 1981. "The Past as a Scarce Resource." *Man* 16(2): 201–19.

Barthelmess, Paulo, et al. 2006. "Human Centered Collaborative Interaction." *Proceedings of the First ACM International Workshop on Human Centered Multimedia,* 1–8. Santa Barbara, CA: ACM Press.

Battaglia, Deborah. 1992. "The Body in the Gift: Memory and Forgetting in Sabari Mortuary Exchange." *American Ethnologist* 19(1): 3–18.

Bennett, Jane. 2001. *The Enchantment of Modern Life.* Princeton, NJ: Princeton University Press.

Bourdieu, Pierre. 1977. *Outline of a Theory of Practice.* Cambridge: Cambridge University Press.

Buchli, Victor, and Gavin Lucas. 2001. *Archaeologies of the Contemporary Past.* London: Routledge.

Castells, Manuel. 1996. *The Rise of the Network Society, The Information Age: Economy, Society and Culture,* vol. I. Oxford: Blackwell.

Chesbrough, Hank. 2003. *Open Innovation the New Imperative for Creating and Profiting From Technology.* Cambridge, MA: Harvard Business School.

Christensen, Clayton. 1997. *The Innovator's Dilemma.* Cambridge, MA: Harvard University Press.

Cohen, Phillip, and David McGee. 2004. "Tangible Multimodal Interfaces for Safety-Critical Applications." *Communications of the ACM* 7(1): 41–46.

Connerton, Paul. 1989. *How Societies Remember.* Cambridge: Cambridge University Press.

Forty, Adrian, and Susanne Kucher, eds. 1999. *The Art of Forgetting.* Oxford: Berg.

Galison, Peter 1996. "Computer Simulation and Trading Zones." In *The Disunity of Sciences: Boundaries, Contexts and Power,* Galison and Stump, 118–157. Stanford, CA: Stanford University Press.

Geertz, Clifford. 1973. *Interpretation of Cultures.* New York: Basic Books.

Gell, Alfred. 1998. *Art and Agency: An Anthropological Theory.* Oxford: Clarendon.

———.1992. "The Technology of Enchantment and the Enchantment of Technology." In *Anthropology, Art and Aesthetics,* Coote and Shelton, eds., 40–66. Oxford: Clarendon.

Hansen, Thomas. 2006. "Strings of Experiments: Looking at the Design Process as a Set of Socio-Technical Experiments." *Participatory Design Conference Proceedings,* 1–10. ACM Press.

Harvey, David. 1989. *The Condition of Postmodernity.* Oxford: Blackwell.

Ingold, Tim. 2007. "Materials Against Materiality." *Archaeological Dialogues* 14(1): 1–16.

Jackson, Michael. 1986. *Barawa and the Ways Birds Fly in the Sky.* Smithsonian Series in Ethnographic Inquiry. Washington, DC: Smithsonian Institution Press.

Knorr-Cetina, Karin. 1999. *Epistemic Cultures.* Cambridge, MA: Harvard University Press.

Leach, James. 2006. "Differentiation and Encompassment." In *Thinking Through Things,* Henare, Holbraad, and Wastell, eds., 167–188. London: UCL Press.

McClard, Anne Page. 2005. "Nested Tales: Gendered Representations of an Azorean Festival Cycle." PhD Dissertation, Brown University. Providence, RI.

Moutu, Andrew. 2006. "Collecting as a Way of Being." In *Thinking Through Things.* 93–112. London: UCL Press.

Nafus, Dawn and ken anderson. 2006. "The Real Problem: Rhetorics of Knowing in Corporate Research." *Ethnographic Praxis in Industry Conference Proceedings,* 244–258. American Anthropological Association.

Nøra, Pierre. 1996. *Realms of Memory.* New York: Columbia University Press.

Ortner, Sherry 2006. *Anthropology and Social Theory: Culture, Power, and the Acting Subject.* Charlotte, NC: Duke University Press.

Ratto, Matt. 2005. "'Don't Fear the Penguin': Negotiating the Trans-Local Space of Linux Development." *Current Anthropology* 26(5): 827–34.

Schmidt, Nancy. 1984. "Ethnographic Fiction: Anthropology's Hidden Literary Style." *Anthropology and Humanism Quarterly* 9: 11–14.

Stewart, Kathleen. 1996. *A Place on the Side of the Road.* Princeton, NJ: Princeton University Press.

Strathern, Marilyn. 2003. *Commons and Borderlands: Working Papers on Interdisciplinarity, Accountability, and the Flow of Knowledge.* London: Sean Kingston Publishing.

Wagner, Roy. 1973. *The Invention of Culture.* Englewood Cliffs, NJ: Prentice-Hall.

Woolgar, Steve, ed. 2003. *Virtual Society? Technology, Cyberbole, Reality.* Oxford: Oxford University Press.

Chapter 6

THE ANTHROPOLOGIST AS
ONTOLOGICAL CHOREOGRAPHER

Françoise Brun-Cottan

> Thus the Theory of Description matters most.
> It is the theory of the word for those
> For whom the word is the making of the world.
> The buzzing world and lisping firmament.
> It is a world of words to the end of it
> In which nothing is its solid self.
> It matters because everything we say
> Of the past is description without a place
> A cast of the imagination, made in sound.
>
> —Wallace Stevens, *Description without Place*

Ethnographers—anthropologists, sociologists, social scientists, and others trained in using ethnographic techniques—encounter a myriad of difficulties when they go into the "field"[1] and attempt to understand and then describe the behaviors of the people they are studying in terms both meaningful to the people studied and relevant to other people interested in the understandings gleaned. In this chapter several problematic elements intrinsic to conducting and reporting about activities studied in anthropological fieldwork will be considered and some of their most trenchant causes noted.

For current purposes, I am concerned with situations in which anthropologists are hired, as employees or consultants, to observe and analyze the activities of third parties (in collaboration with other people from other

---

disciplines, or not) with the objective of informing issues the employer has stipulated: designs, product development, marketing strategies, and so on. Difficulties arise around questions concerning: Who gets told what and why? Who has a stake in the method and findings in the ethnographic enterprise? What obligations do anthropologists have to study participants and informants? How does what gets shown or said get selected and what relationship does it have to what is being depicted?

These are classic concerns. But ethnographic work in industrial contexts, especially, has made these questions even more complicated as the number of stakeholders in outcomes increases. The stakeholders are the people — engineers, designers, technicians, sales personnel — who will have to deal with, or develop, or sell, or in some way accommodate the findings and insights — the "outcomes" — of our studies. We ethnographers have promoted and characterized ourselves as positioned to deliver a commonality of understanding across a complex "multiplicity of interests" (Fischer 2003: 15) and aspirations. Unfortunately, the implications and consequences of our studies may not be of immediate or equal benefit across organizational divisions, many of whom harbor their own competing preferences.

There are several challenges inherent in our positioning. One set of complications arises from the combining of Recipient Design on the one hand and use of the same terms across different audiences on the other. Recipient Design describes speakers' use of terms whose referents they understand or assume will be understood by the recipients of their — the speakers' — utterances. Recipient Design is a fundamental and irremediable feature of interaction in conversation. Tailoring findings to maximize understandings across differing organizational perspectives is a common and sensible practice. Unhappily, the two in concert often act to fragmentize and de-contextualize the accounts in which our findings are embedded.

Converging with yet another classic anthropological concern, the implications and consequences of our reportage may not be much appreciated by the people we have studied whose expertise and means of livelihood may be undermined by the very innovations we specifically are meant to inform. If we are to embody and advance our own discipline's evolution, there is an imperative need for us to maintain mindful vigilance regarding our principled placement between informants and employers. There is a risk in helping industry commodify results of ethnographic studies into goods and services. That risk is the commoditization of anthropology such that only immediately expedient methods signify. Increasingly, the value of findings derived from fieldwork is acknowledged but there is a desire for us to leave the messiness of individuals and contexts — including the messiness of consequences for study participants and informants — in the field. I suggest that traveling further along those convenient oversights would be a loss for both industry and for anthropology. We will see how these two seemingly disparate sets of concerns come together when we consider their implications for how we work.

Losing the Personal

Let us begin with a story. It is 1993 and I am sitting with Dee,[2] a study informant, and feeling pretty good. The fieldwork part of the study is finished, but I've come back to ask Dee what she thinks about using an actual tool we might be developing. Actually, methodologically, it is wonderful to be talking with her as I am using this opportunity to see if she agrees with the way I have characterized some of her work activities. By this time, she knows that if she doesn't agree she can say so straightforwardly and, moreover, be thanked for it. And indeed she does say something, something that haunts me to this day.

The fieldwork took place in the home office of GrinderCom, a company that builds giant, one-off construction machines, and had branch offices in sixty countries. The study was to serve two sets of corporate interests. GrinderCom wanted to know how it might streamline its records-management practices and DocuGiant—my employer—wanted to know how GrinderCom managed its records. The latter had the additional aims of better understanding a nascent technology as well as of helping a good customer become more techno savvy.

Once the initial agreement to allow a study[3] had been made, the interdisciplinary team of five of which I was a part gave a presentation to GrinderCom's executives, the department managers, and the staff of the "records" department. We described how we worked, using real live anthropologists as well as industrial designers, and doing exotic anthropology techniques like interviewing, "shadowing," and videotaping people going about their daily work. We showed examples from prior fieldwork studies, and highlighted the sorts of unforeseen gems our "ethnographic" approach could uncover for them and for us alike. We promised and promised and promised that what we saw would be used only for research purposes.[4]

Like many of the records staff, Dee did not start out particularly thrilled at the prospect of being followed about, observed, and recorded on tape while working. She had, of course, the "option" to refuse. However, it was clear to her and the rest of the records staff that management wanted them to be cooperative. Some people grumbled, some tried being monosyllabic. One person did refuse, and we worked around her, studiously not complaining about her refusal. After a few weeks of visits, most came around, some begrudgingly, some eagerly. Dee did it with forbearance verging on amusement. Mainly, they just couldn't understand why we found the stuff they did everyday so very interesting. "Oh that, why do you want to know about that? We do that all the time." But it was clear we savored every little detail, which eventually added up to lots of little details and some notions.

At the conclusion of the fieldwork we gave GrinderCom management and staff a presentation of a few of the initial discoveries we were making. It should be noted that reflections about some of the managers' ignorance of how things got done, or some of the employees' preservation of fiefdoms were omitted. Exculpatory omissions? We were not there to report on the social glue; we wanted everyone to be open to hearing those things we thought important that addressed the stated aims of the project: issues, and opportunities in the records management department. Basically, and also not by coincidence, much was made of the complexity underlying the seeming simplicity of the day-to-day work. The complexity and the details of its construction would be of interest to both GrinderCom's understanding of changes they needed to consider and to our own company's understanding of the possible first applications of a functionality that was still in its infancy. We took familiar tasks and deconstructed them, revealing layer after layer of understandings required to accomplish apparently seamless operations. If recollection serves, we compared department personnel favorably to star athletes or dancers whose grace and agility make the most difficult moves look easy. (The unpacking of one of those forty seconds or so bits of tapes of Dee at work remains a favorite moment to this day; see Appendix A.) A choreographed ballet of exquisite steps executed in the face of the proverbial continual unforeseen contingencies.

All of the people we had taped were genuinely pleased with our presentation. Even those who had grumbled and were concerned about what we might report came up to us on their own afterward and thanked us. They felt that finally management had been given a clear way of seeing the knowledge and competence it took to deal with the details of the work. Indeed, this display to management of the skills required in seemingly simple tasks is one of the "gifts" we can offer informants in return for the enormous value of the time that they spent with us (Wall and Dalal 2005). The person who had refused to be taped came to us and said she wished she had let us do so and offered herself up for an interview.

So, that done, I'm sitting with Dee a few days later and feeling that, as these things go, this study went really well for everyone concerned. And she says she thinks maybe she's gotten some new respect for the work she does, though she doesn't expect that will translate to a better salary. She's also very impressed with what the new device might do. And then she says (and I'm quoting from the tape), "You're trying to get rid of people aren't you, heh he heh?"

Whoa! Stop the train.

Well, I try various tacks to change that impression and make her feel better (or was it to make me feel better?). "The technology will free people to accomplish the job with greater ease in less time (spates of work overload being one of the complaints we had heard); new jobs will come; in any case, progress is going to happen and new tools will be developed that will result in lost jobs but we might as well make those tools as helpful and easy to use as we can." Dee responds that while she can acknowledge all those things, she still mourns a lifetime of doing a job which will now be accomplished by a machine.

The replacement she fears will not be realized in "this" case—the nascent technology is years from general release, by which time Dee will have retired—though it is clearly the case for an increasing number of "office" jobs. Moreover, whatever device emerges, the "knowledge" work Dee performs will still require the sorts of company knowledge, intelligence, and problem-solving skills that make Dee the superb analyst that she is. Nevertheless, what I do come to understand is this: Dee has been working with us all along with this notion of her easy "replaceability" in her mind, this image of herself as expendable. And I, who have been so self-satisfied in representing her as she is manifest in her work, have been oblivious to all the other parts of her which make her who she is (Dee) and to the high degree of grace involved in her cooperation in the face of her belief.

And how does this little anecdote end? Dee notices *my* consternation and says, "Would you care to go out and have a cup of coffee?" She was consoling me.

Ontological Choreography

I was indeed derailed, for the little ontological ballet I had been choreographing and presenting—to study participants and employers and colleagues—and with which I had been so pleased, had come to a sudden halt and one of my chief dancers was out of step. And that is because I had been concentrating on the steps and overlooking the dancer. I should have known better! I do not mean just knowing that this might be a concern of hers. It is not such a far reach after all. The notion that technology replaces workers is older than Ford's assembly line and hardly a secret. And I might have at least addressed the issue with her early on. Rather, I mean I should have known—given my claimed expertise in bringing the human element into play—that having spent some forty hours with her over a period of weeks, having become friendly and somewhat trusted, did not give me access to the complexity of her being. I did not merit the easy complacency of my confident manner with her that in turn, and most egregiously, did not allow me to value the degree of generosity involved in her sharing of insights in the face of her belief that she could well be contributing not only to the loss of her job and but also to the devaluation of a lifetime of work.

If we hadn't had that conversation, would it matter to the description I would come to make of the *"work's* components" and what it takes to accomplish it? Perhaps not, but how could I know if it hadn't come to the surface? And is not the value of bringing an understanding of the "human" elements at play in the analysis of observing "work in context" one of the primary reasons that industry has turned to anthropological methods of inquiry and analysis? Yet, one of the first things we confront is having to take our understandings right out of the context in which they were derived in order to share them with others, in yet other contexts. What is certain is that this interaction with Dee drove home for me the ongoing continual possibility of layered alternate ontologies. And though it may be impossible to deal with all the layered bits that make up the wholeness of peoples' ontological structures, that should not prevent our continual consciousness of their "not-dealt-with" presence.

The descriptor *Ontological Choreographer* comes via Donna Haraway—who studies practically everything, but in this instance from her studies of cross-species nature cultures (2003: 8). She was enlarging the term as deployed by Charis Cussins—studying assisted in-vitro fertilization and reproductive practices (1998: 166–202). In both cases their emphasis is to reinsert agency and dynamism in consideration and accounts of "others'" selfhood and motivations. Among other things, this means not leaving Dee's concerns and gracious compliance in her perceived obsolescence out of the accounts of her work.

I want to use the descriptor to point to anthropology as, and ourselves as practitioners of, a discipline which offers artful and principled ways to observe and report on "the dance of being" going on everywhere around us. (I do not mean to imply that we invent the dance's steps.) It is an offer that as practitioners we must take up, both the artfulness and the principles, because that choreography is fundamental to the anthropological ethnographic enterprise. Our enterprise embraces the messiness of attempting generalization across the "then and there" of local contexts. We are embedded in the paradox of unitary human selfhoods whose constitutive elements are continually shifting and under construction. It is not an easy business. I concur with the proposition expressed by Clifford Geertz, himself agreeing with Max Weber "that Man is an animal suspended in webs of significance he himself has spun. ... I take culture to be those webs and the analysis of it to be therefore not an experimental science in search of law but an interpretive one in search of meaning" (1973: 5). A semiotic bias, to be sure.

I take that to mean that we have an obligation to try to present for interpretation not just the "ways and meanings" we uncover but also to convey—as much as possible, whatever that may come to mean—the contexts in which they were formed. Not just the rules, but also the understandings with and by which they are constituted. In the context of the work in industrial settings this is complicated by having to report to a multiplicity of sometimes-conflicting interests in which we ourselves are embedded.[5] That is to say: We owe the adequacy as well as accuracy of those representations to those we study, to those to whom we report findings, to those who hire us, to those with whom we work (designers, engineers, marketers, sales representatives, and so on), and to those who will be the consumers of "our work" itself (our colleagues, our discipline). Or, as Pat Sachs eloquently puts it, "There is an ongoing challenge in the work we do as practitioners in translating across boundaries and co-constructing frames that make mutual sense for clients and scholarly practitioners/consultants [and I would add for our study participants and informants, as well]. The clients with whom we work are often embedded in frames of reference and explanatory systems that we must address" (2005). See Nafus and anderson, chapter 5, for further elaboration of multiple knowledges and multiplicities of meaning.

And are we not the trustees acting on behalf of the informants—the users, participants, actors, and so on—whose behaviors populate our accounts? I mean here that we act as trustees of honest renditions of what they say and do and represent these as meaning. I do not mean that we stand for or bestow validation on their actions. As trustees, are we not laden with the punctilio of our own position vis-à-vis both the informants/participants in the studies and the recipients of our findings, corporate and/or academic?[6] Further, I would suggest that this "point of honor" may be not just another burden among the many we carry but also may be a lifeline through the interpenetrating strata of seeings, understandings, translations, ontologies, and representations we must negotiate.

In line with considering issues of translations and interpretations of boundaries organizational and ontological, I would point to a structure of basic interaction which informs the terms one—consciously or not—chooses to use with particular recipients on particular occasions of interaction: namely, Recipient Design. The ubiquity of the operation of Recipient Design in interaction does little to lighten our task but does clarify some of the problems inherent in the effort to establish and maintain intersubjectivity.

Different recipients of talk in interaction can and do require different terms of reference. This very fact can lead to difficulties in explaining understandings gleaned across different communities of practice and ontologies. Recipient Design operates from the interpersonal conversational level to the organizational and polity levels, and is unavoidable.

> Interaction is the primary, fundamental embodiment of sociality—what I have called elsewhere (1996a) "the primordial site of sociality." From this point of view, the "roots of human sociality" refers to those features of the organization of human interaction that provide the flexibility and robustness that allows it to supply the infrastructure that supports the overall or macro-structure of societies in the same sense that roads and railways serve as infrastructure for the economy and that grounds all of the traditionally recognized institutions of societies and the lives of their members.

> If one reflects on the concrete activities which make up these abstractly named institutions—the economy, the polity, the institutions for the reproduction of the society (courtship, marriage, family, socialization and education), the law, religion, etc., turns and talk in interaction—figure centrally in them. When the most powerful macro-structures of society fail and crumble (as, for example, after the demise of the communist regimes in Eastern Europe), the social structure that is left is interaction, in a largely unaffected state. People talk in turns, which compose orderly sequences through which courses of action are developed, they deal with transient problems of speaking, hearing or understanding the talk and re-set the interaction on its course; they organize themselves so as to allow stories to be told, they fill out occasions of interaction from approaches and greetings through to closure, and part in an orderly way. I mention this here to bring to the forefront of attention what rests on the back of interaction: the organization of interaction needs to be—and is—robust enough, flexible enough, and sufficiently self-maintaining to sustain social order at family dinners and in coal mining pits, around the surgical operating table and on skid row, in New York City and Montenegro and Rossel Island, etc., in every nook and cranny where human life is to be found. (Schegloff 2006)

Understanding of the structure and operation of Recipient Design comes to us from Conversation and Interaction Analysis, but Recipient Design's applicability to what and how we report our observations to various audiences is fundamental and its influence is problematical[7] in that the very terms we use reflect—whether we are engaging with study informants or reporting our work findings to corporate recipients—our understandings of what we think constitute their varied ontologies: their orientations, understandings, values, experiences, interests, and beliefs.

And although we might be pointing to a particular referent—for example, a work activity, a technical problem, a design feature—we often need to change our descriptors for different audiences: different departments in the same organizations, different management levels, colleagues with different methodological or theoretical orientations, and so on. The "tweaking" or rewording of material for different presentations surely is a familiar phenomenon. Just as our "observations themselves cannot be neutral" (Law 2004)—for we bring our own beliefs, understandings, and so forth, with us—neither are the terms we select in reporting what we have observed to our various audiences to suit their varied purposes.[8] Despite our best efforts, terms are not always equivalent in what they express about the things—objects, activities, people—being referred to. How we are to reconcile sensitivity to the particular frames of reference and explanatory systems of participants with the need to address all with fairness and accuracy is a formal issue and a vexing one by no means limited to the anthropological enterprise.[9]

It hardly seems possible to address any, much less all, of these interests wholly, but even "fragmented communication across irreducible differences, across the incommensurable tacit knowledges of diverse communities of practice, matters. ... Situated partial connection matters" (Haraway 2003: 49). I take the understanding that it matters to be anthropology's jewel in the crown as well as its thorn in the side. Our corporate employers, and fellow employees, may want just the golden nuggets we have discovered, but it would be a huge mistake for us to let go of the bedrock in which they formed and are found.

And yet, having spent years trying—and in some small way managing—to convince multinational widget producers or software makers, libraries, universities, and state governments of the unique insights that our discipline enables us to provide, I now wonder if success will come back and bite us. A success disaster, so to speak.

If in 2004, as *PC Magazine* claims, Intel corporation spent some five billion dollars on ethnographic research (Johnson 2006), then indeed there is some pressure to produce "actionable" deliverables, that is to say, findings which will get used to: inform design, create, or improve a tool or service; identify and eliminate obstacles to using a tool or service; and reveal or create a previously unperceived need. (Let me issue the caution that if the findings are indeed deemed immediately "actionable" there may be even less than there should be in the way of examining how they were derived.)

But, are we not hired to provide such insights in the service of our employers' interests and specifically to filter the useful—to them—bits of ore from the gross matter of our observations and produce it in such a way that it can be refined, retooled, and reused for their pursuit of serving their customers' needs, and perhaps—better yet—creating those needs? We have told them, assured them, and held out the promise to them that in using our training and observational and analytical skills we will assist them in achieving their goals. We tout being able to do just that (and more) when we recommend ourselves for hire. I myself have listed the following as outcomes of their investment: "Valuable outcomes of such an investment include: descriptions of users' current work practices, user based definitions of technology requirements, development team comprehension of the users' perspectives, technology impact evaluations, innovative solutions and insights for future product directions" (Brun-Cottan and Wall 1995: 61–71).

Or consider the following "marketing materials" proffered on behalf of ethnography—as an introductory list for companies who have not yet used it—in an email post seeking confirmation or criticism from a very active distribution list of anthropologists and designers:[10]

1. Showing what people say they do versus what they actually do;
2. Exploring cultural norms. For example, different cultures define beauty differently;
3. Identifying unmet needs and seeing what's missing;
4. Identifying product and service opportunities;
5. Showing how small things can have a large impact;
6. Explaining abstract beliefs.[11]

This proposed "marketing" list, seems to be quite good fit with the sorts of qualities being sought in an ad placed in May of 2006 for someone to " help drive the future of Yahoo" in the "User Experience and Design team" and have the following responsibilities:

- User research, including planning and running usability studies (including rapid iterative studies), ethnographic field studies, benchmark studies, competitive evaluations, participatory design sessions, user surveys, heuristic evaluations, and similar methods;
- Provide insight and vision for the team based on researching user needs. Convert research findings into actionable items;
- Work closely with interaction designers, visual designers, product managers, marketing, technologists, and other user-experience researchers to improve and define the user experience of Yahoo! Mail;
- Collaborate with other research organizations within Yahoo! (market researchers and data mining analysts) in order to create comprehensive coordinated research;
- Understand the business needs, while researching the needs of the

user, in order to create solutions and opportunities for the business unit.[12]

These would require us to mine our data to abstract what is apparently, or possibly, of interest and render it "sharable" to the various communities within the larger organization we serve. Problematic aspects inherent in this separation of the user/activity from the context of its occurrence have been dealt with extensively elsewhere, but how to avoid them while in the service of particular industrial or organizational ends and within generally short operational timeframes is hardly resolved. Given the fierce nature of market competitiveness and the rapidity of technology and product development for many of the companies in and for which we seek to do field work, the quest is indeed for "rapid iterative studies and converting research findings into actionable items," and they may feel they simply do not have a lot of time for much richness and depth, however much benefit we think it may provide them.

Personal experience and the accounts of peers indicate that we work under tight deadlines and generally do not have enough time to conduct studies and represent our findings as we would under ideal circumstances. We present our findings in bulleted highlights, charts, workflows, video clips, and frame grabs; in terms of "opportunities," and solutions in response to the familiar cries of "tell me what I need to know," "tell us what's broken," "how do we fix it," "what's our stake in the ground," "what can we do our competitors can't or haven't," "what would make it be better," and "what would trip us up." And we must always be mindful of Return On Investment (though the problem of how one proves a negative haunts us here; for example, how do we demonstrate that we earned our keep and saved the company by virtue of the mistake that was not made?). (See Jordan, chapter 4, this volume, for astute commentary about issues surrounding this topic.) And all the while, the persistent leitmotif of "Have you found 'it'?" the patentable thing that will get them lining up around the block with money in hand is always lurking in the background. Nevertheless, putting our own interests aside for the moment, delivering "just" what they want may not always involve giving either them or study participants their *just* due. Let us turn to an example that, unfortunately, may not only be illustrative but also symptomatic.

A Case Study

Around the turn of the twenty-first century, in upstate New York, several school districts employed a "public educational collaborative." The mission of the collaborative was and is to provide quality programs and services to several school districts more economically than the districts could do so individually. There are a number of collaboratives for different districts throughout the state. The claim is that sharing staff members, office space, equipment, and services reduces duplications in ways that save taxpayer money. The chief executive officer of a collaborative also serves as district superintendent of schools and works closely with local school districts as both liaison to and agent of the state commissioner of education. Hence local school districts receive a channel for input to higher government levels.

The collaborative in our example, Edutech, provided a great many valuable services for the community. High among these was to provide advice about, and assistance with, purchasing and setting up useful technologies. In some cases the technologies were intended to be useful to teachers as well as to service the needs of administrative staffs of both Edutech and its signatory schools.

The director of Eductech was a well-connected, enthusiastic, and visionary technophile. DocuGiant was a large manufacturer with whom he had formed a strong relationship and from whom he had already purchased equipment over the years. The director learned—it was revealed to him tantalizingly—that DocuGiant had a promising emergent technology that had not yet been installed in the educational sector. The new brochures described the device's easy installation as "plug and play." It was agreed that the device—the Document Machine—would be installed in several schools. Edutech would facilitate the corporation's ethnographic study of how the device was or might be used. DocuGiant would share work-practice understandings—of teachers' and administrators' activities—and possible applications with Edutech. Edutech's administrative staffs admittedly needed help negotiating their mountains of paper. If the technology could also help teachers enter more fully into the rapidly developing digital world then so very much the better. It would be a personal coup for the director as well, who would have his astuteness confirmed, thus according greater weight to his opinions.

The opportunity for DocuGiant was huge. There was a promise that student records, tests, homework, teachers' lectures, and much more could be made digital. Moreover, one of the really innovative features was an option to use a paper interface to the device. Teachers were typecast as notoriously resistant to migrating to the digital domain. It was hoped that being able to use a paper form to instruct the device rather than its digital user interface would help teachers bridge the digital divide. In some cases teachers didn't even need to originate material digitally, or even have a computer, in order to send documents to a database or an email address—

test scores to parents, for example—via the Document Machine installed in some school's hallway. If some instructors were familiar with computers, then again, so much the better.

DocuGiant had some clear understandings about what the device could do, and it had developed some very promising functionalities. But having developed the technology with the understanding that sometimes "you need to build it before consumers know they want it in order to be the product leader of the pack," it wanted to learn what sorts of things district teachers and administrators actually would want to do with it, and what would be needed to fulfill those needs. The study could perform a sort of triage on the first product-release possibilities for education use. The Document Machine could fax, copy, scan, connect to the internet, and email and archive documents in a database.

"Scan?" the teachers asked, "What's that?"

The devices were installed by DocuGiant in several schools in the district. Members of its sales organization oversaw the installation. It was put through the routine tasks of copying and printing and was pronounced functional. Unfortunately, the innovative paper interface could not be tested by sales personnel as internet connectivity did not fall within their bailiwick. It should be noted as well that the sales force received no reward for the time spent overseeing the installation as their compensation was based on device sales and not software enablement. Hence, time spent overseeing the installation meant time taken from actual sales activities.

Edutech's IT staff's instructions and the Document Machine's manuals centered on the devices' various connections and requirements and technical specifications. In the not unusual way that projects of this nature get a bit off schedule[13] despite best efforts (for example, late delivery of equipment, cancellations of meetings, routine emergencies), the IT staff had little time to test and debug the devices.

Several teachers were "volunteered" to take part in the pilot project, and agreed to be studied by an ethnographic team of two people: an anthropologist (myself) and a designer well steeped in ethnographic theory and practice. Fortunately, initially, and as it turned out subsequently, some computer scientists / software engineers were also on hand. Meetings were held in which the functionality and hookups of the devices were described to the Edutech information technologists, who indicated no comprehension difficulties. Two ethnographers sat in on these meetings, more so that we be would familiar with the Edutech staff than because we wanted to understand technical aspects of internet connectivity and wattages. From our various experiences in trying to understand teachers' and administrators' current work practices and observing them learn the new technology, I submit the following.

Although most of the teachers had received computers for their class-rooms, more than a few sat unused despite widely available after-school training. Perhaps they were wary that this experiment would go the way of numbers of others in which had put forth extra effort to no productive end. Maybe in their world of being constantly overworked there was just not enough time.

One of the volunteered teachers—the music teacher—was a computational neophyte whose students had organized the computer he had been given the year before. Nevertheless, after hearing some things the device could do, he came up with some wonderful ideas that he wanted to try. He thought he might host homework assignments online, record student performances so they could experience the improvement in their own playing over time, even let them compare their playing with that of professionals. He talked with fellow music teachers at other schools who expressed interest in collaborating with him. An inventive enthusiast, how great!

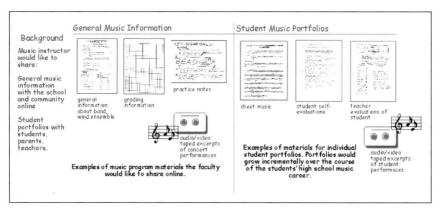

Figure 6.1. Example materials participants wish to share online. Image courtesy of Patricia Wall and Francoise Brun-Cottan.

We too were excited. Someone was eager to put the technology through its hoops. But after several interviews, when we gathered video and pens in hand to record him take the initial steps, we were surprised to discover that he didn't have the rights to download anything from the internet to his computer. Nor did he have permission to change his own computer's operating-system settings. Not so great.

This was especially problematic as the software files required to enable fundamental Document Machine capabilities, although free, needed to be downloaded from one of two companies' servers: either DocuGiant's or Adobe's. In other words, our teacher couldn't even begin to use the wonder device. Well, that was a glitch. There were others waiting in the wings, but they needn't be elaborated here. Let me just say that password-protection and permissions issues for hundreds of people at the dawn of the twenty-first century offered a multitude of "opportunities" for DocuGiant to address. While some of these opportunities—namely, in this case really monstrous problems—are being addressed by DocuGiant and others, the area of passwords, permissions, and privacy protection is particularly hydra-headed. Other equally fun opportunities present themselves in the areas of old code, obsolete devices, personal document archiving and retrieval, and encryption.

In our "project findings" presentation to our upper management, the inability to download was listed in the relatively "neutral" language of "obstacles to adoption," nevertheless in the end Edutech's IT staff took the brunt of the heat for that glitch. Yet there were actually valid reasons for the IT staff's internet blockage. Charged with keeping the district's servers functional, they had prevented teachers—known to be technological neophytes—from being able to download files that would choke the school's server. They had achieved this security by setting a high default security level, which prevented teachers from gaining any net access at all. A crude fix to be sure, but certainly effective.

That, as well as being beset by their own organization's conflicting preferences, the Edutech IT group also had little time, and were given barely any instruction by "us," were factors we knew and with which we sympathized. However, that the IT group had not been "consulted" about what the system would have to bear versus its current capacities, and the complications that could arise, was not emphasized in our high-level presentations. There were sensitivities on the part of the various managements and IT engineers in both organizations that overrode minute examination of some of these oversights. What sensitivities?

Let us consider some implications of the device's failure to be "plug and play." This is generally seen as a good quality for both the buyer/user of a piece of equipment and for its manufacturer. For the former it promises ease of installation and use. For the manufacturer it means that, overall, less time is spent by various company personnel, including sales people. At the time of this study, compensation for sales personnel was based on devices bought and placed, that is, on boxes sold. Extra time taken for installation and testing was not remunerated. If the news that the device was not plug and play was bad for the corporation it was equally unwelcome for sales. The Document Machines were critical for DocuGiant's survival, much less its dominance in the digital domain. They needed to get released to the public. Somewhat like the fax machine, the more of them that were placed, the more services they could perform, and the more they would be wanted. The sales team wanted the company to succeed—their livelihoods depended on it. That said, the news that they would have to babysit the installation of the devices meant hours not spent selling boxes and not being compensated. It is not just a case of what is bad for the company is bad for the organizations within it. It is a case where what is bad for the company is a world of hurt for this particular organization. That is not news you want to rub into the noses of upper management.

Or consider the following. There was the existing, mutually profitable, relationship between Edutech and DocuGiant. There was the desire that the relationship would extend into the future. Such an extension would mean that several of the people and groups involved in setting up the study—the Edutech IT staff and administrators, sales and marketing, and perhaps even the ethnographers—might well have to work together. In which case, pointing fingers and casting blame in official presentations would hardly smooth the way to re-engagement.

Within DocuGiant, the ethnographers certainly hoped to work again with members of the sales team. Sales personnel with long and direct histories with clients can hugely facilitate the introduction of ethnographers into clients' workplaces and contribute profound understandings they've gathered over years of involvement. As well, the ethnographers definitely wanted to maintain a good relationship with our own software engineers as we would need their expertise in future explorations of digitally driven functionalities. It behooved us to get that expertise given grudge free. We did, however, get to quietly convey some of the mitigating factors leading to the technical glitches to Edutech's director and we shared them internally with those more immediately connected to the device's development.

Interestingly enough—given notions expressed earlier about bringing human elements to play while considering technological innovations—the school district and Edutech came to understand that if they wanted teachers to "use" the system then a dedicated human mediator would be required for a year or so—technically required. A tangle of passwords, permissions, formats, applications, and access hurdles had to be cleared before the system could provide the benefits that were touted. That understanding was leveraged by the school district to create just such a position, a small investment for a large payoff.

So the bad news for sales, that the device was not plug and play and that its installation needed guidance and knowledge of the clients' information technology and organizational structure in order to function properly, was good news for the business services division of the DocuGiant. The fact that Edutech was willing to create a salaried position to help teachers and staff make the transition to using digital technology implied that there was a potential business case for customer service and support for DocuGiant. Here was yet another instance supporting the proposition that providing consulting services for various clients would not only facilitate their adoption of new technologies, but presented a business opportunity in its own right.

The complexity and difficulties of these—and other—issues had not been foreseen by either Edutech or DocuGiant and the early discovery of their existence and potential impact played a significant role in Edutech's commitment to make the Document Machine work in their environments. And for the ethnographers? Well, we showed we were still worth keeping around.

Reflection

Let's take a very high-level look at the tangled web of beings and relationships and stakes, each with their own obligations and world views. There is the director and his reputation as someone who provides visionary technology guidance to the school districts, as well as a renewal of his contract with them; and there are the district's obligations to students, parents, state officials, and teachers. There are the teachers, beleaguered by learning new "systems" every few years, and beholding to all of the above. There is the IT support staff whose job it is to enable teachers/students, but also to enable and advocate for—from a self-interested point of view—the investment of time and money and practices in information technology. There is the manufacturer, (developers, engineers, designers, marketers, sales, and on and on) who has an immediate stake in the success of the particular device and discovery of which directions to pursue first in its development; there is the manufacturer's principled stake in the general technology strategy to which it has committed, and there is its relationship with Edutech, who buys lots of its widgets for the school district.

For the anthropologist and the ethno-designer there is the absolute need to demonstrate that this ethnographic methodology provides useful and unique workplace understandings and actionable product insights. It also should be noted that passionate ideological conviction and job retention, here as well as with the IT staff, are not necessarily mutually exclusive. Especially fortunate ethnographic researchers also get to provide some of those insights back to the people into whose work life we have intruded. This aspect of our work should not be left to luck but rather should be understood as mandated.

Workflow charts, organizational maps, statistical methods, focus groups, questionnaire results, design scenarios, and so forth, have their value. But— to use a term familiar to our industrial employers—they are not differentiators, for us. One certainly does not need to be a trained anthropologist to be adept at them.

Stepping even further back a bit we can revisit the ethnographer's plight. At one level there is our desire to tell all, or at least all that we think we have discovered. This can conflict with our desire to play nicely with our corporate fellows—by not hanging them out to swing in the wind—for the greater good of our parent company and in enlightened self-interest. In this sense I agree with James Clifford's proposition that, "ethnographic truths are thus inherently partial—committed and incomplete." "Moreover, the maker (but why only one) of ethnographic texts cannot avoid expressive tropes, figures, and allegories that select and impose meaning as they translate it. In this view … all constructed truths are made possible by powerful 'lies' of exclusion and rhetoric. Even the best ethnographic texts—serious, true fictions—are systems, or economies, of truth" (1986: 7).

In our efforts to maximize communication and inter-subjectivity across communities of informants and recipient audiences it is likely that things get lost. Noticings, observations, and conjectures relevant to one population receiving our descriptions fall out in reports to another set of recipients. This phenomenon is reinforced at a different level through the sustaining structure of Recipient Design in interaction so that even if things—people, concepts, activities, meanings, values, and troubles—don't actually disappear, the terms in which they are conveyed across the recipient groups are likely not commensurate.

What a quandary! Having met the enemy and realized that it is inescapable, where does that leave us? Certainly not unaccountable, not free to say any old thing. The effort must be undertaken to make our omissions exculpatory. The looking, recording, reporting, representing, and projecting that we do must be subjected to rigorous methodologies, detailed and microscopic examination, continually re-examined in the light of the findings of others, and subjected to every analytic tool at our disposal.[14] One of the things we can do is acknowledge and address fundamental structures of interaction by and through which our communication is constituted. This is often grueling and dreary work, no matter the rewards of its successful completion.

Our accountability lies in our ability to reconstruct for ourselves and the recipients of our work—corporate or disciplinary—the grounded basis upon which we selected and arrived at the findings we postulate. For it is just this honorable negotiation, this punctilio, about how we engage and interpenetrate these ontological boundaries that provides the through line across the differing perspectives and conflicting preferences with which we are confronted and through which we construct choreographed accounts of how and why what we've observed to happen. It is unfortunate that these accounts tend not to conform to bulleted items and decision trees, because in order to display the deepest value of our work we really must convey to our employers more than just what they think they want to see, more than just what is merely accurate. And we must figure out how to transmit our findings to one another in ways that preserve more of the culture of the particular "social Petri dishes" with which we have been engaged.

I fear that if, under pressure and in the name of efficiency, we forgo our own discipline's ontological underpinnings—some of which explicitly have to do with the value of preserving subtleties and variances of experience and description—we undermine the very skills and ways of seeing that make us unique. Part of those skills have to do with identifying, describing, and representing the different communities (their practices and crafts, and their relationships to and understandings of each other and the technologies—that is, tools and artifacts—that are interwoven in the accounts about them) in ways that adequately reflect their various perspectives and the stated "realities" of the informants while also capturing the forces at play in their actual as opposed to "reported practices," and, moreover, doing that representation in ways that render the information and insights accessible to the different recipient parties. In promoting those skills we must agitate for the time and space that allow us to impart the sorts of matchless insights this discipline trains us to perceive. Our further challenge is to accomplish this while honoring a commitment to our informants or study participants to—at the very least—do no harm.

There are so many questions for our workplace practice. How are we to protect the users—as particular individuals—that we are studying, whose practices we are using to identify product opportunities and to inform the design of technologies that will in some instances eliminate their jobs? Can we? Should we? How do we reconcile "do no harm" with the "March of Progress for the greater good of society, and our company"? I don't mean this meanly, there is a march of progress (certainly away from the past at any rate), and many companies are trying to do good. As stated by Melissa Cefkin (chapter 1), "Questions of the nature of anthropological relations resulting from the corporate encounter and of the social functions performed by this work remain at the core of that questioning."

I believe that if we are to address these quandaries, and find the means to enforce our resolutions, we must keep not just the findings but also the processes, the rich detail, the thick description, the very analytic grounding of our work visible. Showing just the tip of the iceberg of our work, just the dance steps and not the dancers, if you will, allows acknowledgment of the nature and value of our contributions to remain tacit. Tacitly acknowledged we become undifferentiated from all the other sources of inputs. It may be all to the good to be a team player, but undifferentiated we risk becoming invisible. Invisible, we—and the value accorded to the contributions of our informants—risk disappearing.

Acknowledgments

The author wishes to thank Melissa Cefkin for her encouragement and tireless efforts, and Sara Bly, Patricia Wall, and Catherine Marshall for their readings, comments, and aid. The author is forever indebted to Emanuel Schegloff for any understandings she may have of the exquisite methods by and through which meaning is co-constructed and accomplished in social interaction.

Notes

1. This might be an isolated community of hunter-gatherers or air traffic–control operations at a large airport or shoppers getting snacks at an all-night gas station.
2. All names of informants and companies are pseudonyms.
3. The study arose from a negotiated agreement between the sales and marketing departments of our employer and the president and head of purchasing of their company.
4. By which we meant that their faces or identities would not show up in newspapers or on TV without their written permission. This did not mean, however, that they might not show up within the research organization of our company or in reports to other organizations across the company, if requested by our management. (Thank you to Brigitte Jordan who encouraged me to push on this.)
5. "The Ethnographer is an analytic object as much as informants are, therefore it is relevant to make available the ethnographer's meta-observations" (Traweek 2005).
6. "A trustee is held to something stricter than the morals of the market place. Not honesty alone, but the punctilio of an honor the most sensitive, is then the standard of behavior." Meinhard v. Salmon, 249 N.Y. 458, 464, 164 N.E. 545, 546 (1928) (Cardozo, C. J.)
7. "The problem of selecting a term from a collection of terms, or of selecting a collection from a set of collections, is a general, formal procedure, although its outcomes can be particular to the circumstances in which the operation is done" (Schegloff 1972: 15).
8. Moreover, let us not forget an organizationally based motivation possibly more familiar to most than Recipient Design, but equally ubiquitous, which informs how we frame and express and present our observations and their implications. That motivation is the practical as well as ideological desire to continue to work productively with and influence others within our corporate emporiums. See below.
9. That these problems may seem intractable, and beyond our best efforts at remediation, should not in any way beguile us into avoiding them. Rather, they need to be addressed, and described, and mourned over so that we do not forget that they haunt our lovely, neatly coherent accounts.

10. May 2006. For the full text of the list see Appendix B. For the full text of the email and exchanges about it, the material is archived at Anthrodesign group at groups.yahoo .com.

11. Interestingly, the first two responses to the email are emblematic of the polar positions that can be taken. The first constitutes a plea for acknowledging the richness and thick description ethnography can generate. The second, in response to the prior as well as to the original posting, cautions against baffling the newbie clients by complicating matters with talk about richness and complexity of the outcomes ethnography can contribute.

12. Design Research III, job No. RX1000015718 Location US—Sunnyvale Job Function UED Job No. RX1000015718.

13. A situation certainly not unique to either this manufacturer or this school district.

14. For a lovely display of issues of ontological methodology see Law 2004: 152–55.

References

Brun-Cottan, Françoise, and Pat Wall. 1995. "Using Video to Re-present the User." *Communications of the ACM* 38(5): 61–71.

Clifford, James. 1986. *Writing Culture: The Poetics and Politics of Ethnography.* Berkeley, CA: University of California Press.

Cussins, Charis M. 1998. "Ontological Choreography: Agency for Women Patients in an Infertility Clinic." In *Differences in Medicine: Unraveling Practices, Techniques, and Bodies,* Berg and Mol, eds., 166–202. Durham, NC: Duke University Press.

Fischer, Michael M. J. 2003. *Emergent Forms of Life and the Anthropological Voice.* Durham, NC: Duke University Press.

Geertz, Clifford. 1973. *The Interpretation of Cultures.* New York: Basic Books Inc.

Haraway, Donna. 2003. *The Companion Species Manifesto.* Chicago, IL: Prickly Paradigm Press, University of Chicago.

Johnson, Bary Alyssa. 2006. "How To Build A Better Product—Study People." *PC Magazine,* May 2006. http://www.pcmag.com/article2/0,1895,1959591,00.asp.

Law, John. 2004. *After Method: Mess in Social Science Research.* London: Routledge.

Sachs, Pat. 2005. Email exchange on the Anthrodesign distribution list.

Schegloff, Emanuel A. 1972. "Notes on a Conversational Practice: Formulating Place." In *Studies in Social Interaction,* Sudnow, ed., 75–119. New York: Free Press.

———. 2006. "Interaction: The Infrastructure for Social Institutions, the Natural Ecological Niche for Language, and the Arena in which Culture is Enacted." In *Roots of Human Sociality: Culture, Cognition and Interaction,* Enfield and Levinson, eds., 70–96, Oxford: Berg Publishers.

Traweek, Sharon. 2005. "We All Live and Work in Messy Worlds." Paper presented at the AAA Anthropology in Studies of Science and Technology: "Faultlines" seminar.

Van Maanen, John. 1979. "Reclaiming Qualitative Methods for Organizational Research: A Preface." In *Qualitative Methodology,* Van Maanen, ed., 9–18. Beverly Hills, CA/London: Sage Publications.

Wall, Patricia, and Brinda Dalal. 2005. "The Baker's Dozen: The Presence of the Gift in Service Encounters." *Ethnographic Praxis in Industry Conference Proceedings,* 100–13. American Anthropological Association.

APPENDIX A

Bulletin Request Process

DATA	PARTICIPANT	COMMENT
	Here's one supply order form I got in from one of our reps....He's leaving me a note.... other than these things he needs this.	D receives a request from a field rep for materials describing products and supplies. Requests come in b mail and fax, very rarely by phone. Those received by mail come in on blue forms. This particular form has come in with handwritten annotations from the requesting rep.
	Well he doesn't read his literature that we send him because that happens to be an Avon product and its on the Avon list. Okay, so I in turn... I am sending a copy when I send his literature, that this is an Avon product. From the future to get it from Avon. But in the meantime I have faxed this to Avon and asked it to send it to him so that we're not delaying his order for that product.	Relevant for distributed work. Multi layered documen printing- fax- copy- write- / articulating meaning of forms highlighting processes/color same document connects - carries instructions for 3 people. Redundancy. Past and future history.
	And this product, he didn't see this on the order form. Well he didn't see it on the order form because he's using the old order form. So if he looked at the new order form he'l find it there. So I am telling him this also In the meantime he will get a copy of this highlighted with the information	Date info on rep request document allows diagnostic on reason for problem. D gives remedial instruction. *Circles* 'old date' to point to problem. Gestures on paper- circles, arrows - possible retrieval method highlighting distinguishing features of different handwritings
	So in the meantime now I will take a copy of this, this is going to the clearwater rep	Highlighted 'copy' is going to go to Avon if highlighting function is to be preserved the document will be sent by mail or delivered. At this point the Company does not have a highlighting copier, nor a color fax. Document duplication records transactions among three interactants. Cycle: printed form, handwriting, fax, highlighting, handwriting, copy Then fax&mail

FB-C

APPENDIX B

Yahoo Job Ad
Location: US—Sunnyvale
Job Function: UED

Description
Yahoo! Inc. is looking for a talented Design Researcher to help drive the future of Yahoo! Mail, one of the most popular services on the Web! As a member of the User Experience & Design (UED) team, you will be part of a highly collaborative, fast-paced environment, working closely with visual designers, interaction designers, product managers and technologists. You will help define the user experience strategy, spearhead a user centered design process and develop usable, useful and compelling Web experiences.

Primary Function
Lead Design Research efforts for Yahoo! Mail and related products. Interface with Product managers and user experience designers on the vision and strategy to create products and services that best meet user needs and ensure that relevant data are collected, analyzed and interpreted to support the strategy.

Responsibilities
- Responsible for the user research, including planning and running usability studies (including rapid iterative studies), ethnographic field studies, benchmark studies, competitive evaluations, participatory design sessions, user surveys, heuristic evaluations, and similar methods.
- Provide insight and vision for the team based on researching user needs. Convert research findings into actionable items.
- Work closely with interaction designers, visual designers, product managers, marketing, technologists, and other user experience researchers to improve and define the user experience of Yahoo! Mail.
- Collaborate with other research organizations within Yahoo! (market researchers and data mining analysts) in order to create comprehensive coordinated research.
- Understand the business needs, while researching the needs of the user, in order to create solutions and opportunities for the business unit.

Qualifications
- Master's degree or Ph.D. in Human Factors, Human-Computer Interaction, Cognitive or Experimental Psychology, Cognitive Science, Anthropology, or related area (or equivalent experience).
- At least 3 years experience in user experience research/design research, conducting ethnographic research, heuristic evaluations, usability testing, benchmark testing, competitive evaluations, and questionnaire/survey design within a product development organization or large website.
- Experience researching user needs throughout the complete product development cycle of successfully launched web and/or software application products.
- Able to develop creative approaches to researching complex user experience problems and can convey ideas in tangible form.
- Must communicate clearly and effectively to varying audiences; have strong analytical skills; have excellent interpersonal skills; able to collaborate actively with others in a cross-functional team with the ability to build consensus.
- Able to switch rapidly between different projects in a fast-paced environment.
- Must be innovative, demonstrate an ability to "think out of the box", and think beyond what is asked for.
- Must pay attention to detail, yet be able to see the big picture and maximize work effort.
- Familiarity with quantitative data analysis and experience with Keynote user research tools a plus.

CULTURE AND
CORPORATE EPISTEMOLOGIES

Chapter 7

EMERGENT CULTURE, SLIPPERY CULTURE
Conflicting Conceptualizations of Culture in Commercial Ethnography

Martin Ortlieb

Introduction

As many Europeans who have traveled to the United States will tell you, when Americans greet someone casually, they generally just say "hi." They don't normally shake hands. Similarly, visitors to Germany will report that in German etiquette one does shake hands and says "*Guten Tag.*" And before my visit to Sicily, I was told that "male friends greeting each other lightly touch cheeks but without 'sound,' whereas when men greet women or women greet women, the 'sound' of a kiss accompanies the gesture."

In most cases, once we are aware of these traditions, we'll be able to get through a greeting ritual in a different country and/or culture without committing a major faux pas. Even so, these traditions change over time. For example, the "fist bump" is said to have originated in the 1960s in urban black culture, but it became more mainstream via sporting events in the 1970s (Stephey 2008). Since Michelle Obama's famous demonstration on the TV show "The View" in June 2008, the greeting has now seemingly reached public acceptance among senior public figures.[1]

If we take more complex situations, however (for example, the process of buying/selling cars, communicating privately or for business by email, or finding a date via online-dating services after an appropriate period of virtual acquaintance), the "proper," "most trustworthy," — or, for the companies offering these services, the "most profitable" — way of "doing things" and engaging with each other may be quite elusive and difficult to emulate. Cultural specifics will influence these situations, whether within a single culturally different context or, and even more so, across several cultural, national, and/or linguistic contexts. For a business in a global context, brand reputations can be lastingly damaged, or at least products are less successful than expected in a major market. The everlasting question is: Can one get the culture thing right?

This chapter looks at changing perceptions about conceptualizations of culture in the commercial world. Companies have now generally accepted that culture—"manifested" in their customers' behavior—is important to their bottom line in a globalized economy (see also Melissa Cefkin's Introduction [chapter 1] to this volume). However, how should culture be conceived? Is culture simply something difficult to pin down, "slippery" but tangible? Or is culture inherently shifting and elusive yet perceptible, emerging ephemerally out of time- and place-bound contextuality? The implications of the meeting of these philosophically rather different conceptions in the commercial environment form the basis for this article. For simplicity's sake I have created a scale of two ends: "emergent culture" and "slippery culture." They tend to not exist in pure form, but the scale serves to bring into view the differences of these—in practice and reality—messily interacting philosophical positions.

I associate these two views with two players in the customer-knowledge market. On the one hand is a group of culture-knowledge buyers (traditionally, the business decision-makers) who traditionally adhere to a "slippery concept of culture," and on the other, the expert knowledge provider (typically, the commercial anthropologist)—a relatively recent arrival in the business world—who offer insights into the businesses' customers via an "emergent view of culture."

Firstly, I would like to illustrate the two parameters. Secondly, I want to sketch out the recent theoretical development in regards to these positions. Thirdly, I attest that the traditional view by businesses of "culture as slippery" is changing and I want to show how the theoretical implications are playing out in applied instances in the industry. Fourthly, I shall give an example of a company where I see this change happening, before concluding with an outlook for multicultural commercial ethnographic research settings.

"Slippery Culture"

Let me then introduce you to "slippery culture" and give a couple of examples/case studies for illustration. Representations of that conceptualization start with the belief that culture is ontologically grounded: it is as you find it. Culture is something that is "just" hard to define and difficult to pin down, but once you get it right, the problem can be fixed, in a best-case scenario, once and for all. This is the position I call "slippery culture," and this is the view in the commercial context often taken by the "culture-knowledge receivers." Verena Stolcke (1995) defines the perhaps more extreme end of this school of thought as "cultural fundamentalism" (Stolcke 1995, quoted in Brumann 1999: S10). It describes culture as finite, distinct, and tied to specific locations of origin. "These are taken as ultimately antagonistic and incommensurable" (Brumann 1999: S10). It is the "powerful structure of feeling [that] continues to see culture, wherever it is found, as a coherent body that lives and dies" (Clifford 1988: 235, emphasis removed).

Early anthropological studies were concerned with the issue of explaining cultural evolution (despite societies maintaining "recognizability") without reference to external factors: Edmund Leach's study (1954) of the Swat Pathans localized the source of change inside culture through an overall holistic notion of culture as a spiderweb that feels movement anywhere in the web and readjusts. "His thesis was that cultural systems should be regarded as consisting of heterogeneous accumulations of different ideas which could live side-by-side until the day they were amalgamated" (Gerholm 1993: 19). But Leach did try to find a handle to explain continuity and yet difference in order to bridge the theoretical chasm of sameness and metamorphosis at the time. In this way he broached—albeit for completely different reasons—a strand of thought that was picked up by some of the post-modern critique in anthropology. The latter (for example, Marcus 1998; Clifford 1988; Overing 1985) has rightly charged much of anthropology with being focused on how-things-are while treating flux, change and historical agency rather lightly.

More recent than Leach's early try, Geertz's attempt at providing a model for the conceptualization runs as follows: Culture is an "octopus with poorly connected semi-autonomous arms" (1973: 407–8), tentacles that are generally integrated on their own, but neurally connected quite poorly with one another and to the main body. The octopus's brain manages both to get around and to preserve itself, for a while anyway, as a viable if somewhat ungainly entity (Geertz 1973). Ulf Hannerz (1992), on the other hand, avoids this discussion and proposes his own system for measuring culture: "culturality" is a compound derived by scoring on a set of criteria: among others, coherence, persistence, and social distribution of cultural values. More recently, Sarah Green, Penny Harvey, and Hannah Knox (2005: 807–8) usefully reconfigure the discussion into "community" and "network," but apart from introducing new terminology, they do not challenge the general conceptualization of culture.

Wolf = Communication

While boundedness is what the anthropological debate discussed above reacted against and, in its way, grew out of as well (see, for example, Wagner 1981; Marcus and Fischer 1986; Clifford 1997; Kuper 1999; Ess and Sudweeks 2001; Van Maanen 2001), it may be that the followers of the "slippery-culture" school of thought *want* culture to be timeless, finite, and essentialized—or expect it to be (see Flynn, chapter 2, for a description of her clients' customers). In their defense, we could argue that this view is based on much older (than anthropological ethnographic writing) traditions that viewed culture as "the natural, internally undifferentiated, and unproblematic reference units just as they had been—and *continued to be*—in most pre- and non-anthropological ethnography" (Brumann 1999: S5, emphasis added). This also throws into relief the, often implicit, correlation of "culture" and "identity." Based on assumptions specific to the development of Western thought, the individual (and therefore by implication his/her identity) is a bounded, autonomous, and pre-cultural entity that only becomes socio-cultural through its biological or social integration (see, for example, LaFontaine 1985; Shweder 1991; Handler 1994; Kusserow 1999; Sökefeld 1999; Edwards 2005). In other words, "slippery culture" implicitly assumes that one of the ways to "pin down" culture is by finding a representational individual, a living stereotype. Let me illustrate the overall position with a short case study from a project I was involved in.

Case Study #1: Hotel Chain

A major international hotel chain had redesigned their web presence in the US, and was now localizing the designs for the UK. The concept had been developed and tested in the US, but no international requirements were gathered (after all, it was originally established specifically for the US market). The hotel chain treated culture as a *variable* in the logistics of the supply chain, which can thus be solved in a straightforward manner. Localization testing therefore "only" scheduled a usability check (completing similar tasks to those given to test participants in the US) and reactions to the visual inventory as indications of place and location. Granted, the participants were selected from a relevant group of actual and potential customers, but—perhaps not surprisingly—the outcomes of the tests recommended slightly changed visuals. However, the underlying mental models of North America (on which the solution was based) and Western Europe were assumed to be practically equal and therefore unproblematic *before* the testing was executed. In other words, the approach was to *replace* the non-equal "cultural" parts and add or remove the "cultural outcrops" that had no equivalent. Hence, visible localization results were a diverging nomenclature, change of fonts, and changes in the display style of ads.

Following the "slippery" approach, justified by the obvious commercial success, it is argued that cultural difference is usually over-exaggerated. Adherents to the slippery model of culture like to point to convincing stories of localized commercial success, particularly Amazon and eBay, as examples of proof of concept. For example, the tracking of buying habits or the suggestions ("other people who had X in their basket also bought Y") on Amazon sites deliver benefit to customers in Germany as they do in France or the United States. The desire to compare products and prices in an instant is supported by Kelkoo, a European price comparison service[2], in ten European countries and beyond no matter what their "cultural" differences might be defined as. Cultural difference, in this view, can be reduced to not negligible but manageable specifics, and, more importantly, replicable ones, once identified.

Development in Other Disciplines

Culture with a capital "C", in its simplified, popularized version, has hardly changed in recent decades from the "slippery" conceptualization that views culture as something bounded and fixed (see, for example, Hofstede 1980), even though a critique of and dialogue with this until-then dominant discourse has become gradually established as part of a wider consciousness in Western thought since Clifford Geertz' *Interpretation of Cultures* (1973).[3] The disciplines of organization studies and business/management studies have long geared themselves toward an understanding of the kinds of institutions and (business) situations that applied/commercial anthropologists are now often studying.[4] These disciplines include their own versions of what "culture" is. Particularly, the older literature (see, for example, Sekaran 1983; Negandhi 1983; Roberts and Boyacigiller 1984) tends to conceptualize "culture" as a measurable (though "slippery") variable that can be integrated "into a multivariate statistical model—one independent variable amongst others which will help to explain 'behavior'" (Chapman 2001: 21).

For example, the growing field of "organizational culture" since the early 1980s employs culture as a conceptual tool in management.[5] Assuming culture is something that can be managed and potentially changed, Edward Schein's seminal paper (1984) defined the usage that continues to be influential today in Information Systems Research (for an example application, see Zimmerman, Grande, and Johnston 1994): "Organizational culture is the pattern of basic assumptions that a given group has invented, discovered, or developed in learning to cope with its problems of external adaptation and internal integration, and that have worked well enough to be considered valid, and, therefore, to be taught to new members as the correct way to perceive, think, and feel in relation to those problems" (Schein 1984: 3).

"Emergent Culture"

Let me then turn to the other side of the model: "emergent culture." The position could be summarized as a critique of conceptualizing culture as a seamless whole, arising in both anthropology and sociology. Thus, "the idea of the whole, integrated, self-contained social group and way of life gives way to a flexible, open view of culture that operates in a continually changing environment" (Van Maanen 2001: 234). Overall, the position maintains that "social reality is characterised by variability, inconsistencies, conflict and individual agency" (Brumann 1999: S1).

Further contemporary studies examine both the history of the conceptualization of culture as well as the history and the discourse about what measurements qualify something "to be" a culture. Perhaps the deconstruction of the term started in earnest with Roy Wagner's *The Invention of Culture*. He maintains that early anthropological theorizing on culture stressed integration, but it never challenged the pre-eminence of the concept (1981 [1975]: 132–59). This is echoed by Adam Kuper's *Invention of Primitive Society* (1988) in which he traces how science has tried to create a bounded vision of society and culture, but he concludes that the goal was illusory because science was only creating a mirror image to its own pre-existing concepts. The skeptical discourse on culture disputes that culture is homogeneous, coherent, bounded, stable, and structured. Lila Abu-Lughod's seminal piece (1991) inspired a whole "'writing against culture' movement" (Fernandez 1994: 161): for example, Robert Brightman (1995), Roger Keesing (1994), Arjun Appadurai (1996), and Marshall Sahlins (1994).

This idea challenged views that culture is "that thing of shreds and patches" (Lowie 1920: 441)—that is, a tangible "thing" or a composite of "things." It also broke down the correlation between culture and the individual in so far as the two being analogous representations of each other. Instead the position describes culture (and therefore identity) as no longer stable but constantly evolving and internally contested (Clifford 1997). Rather than representing each other, culture and identity relate to but do not match each other. Nonetheless, changing perspectives on one of the concepts still implies changed perspectives on the other. While the centrality of the individual as the locus of a cultural experience is documented by the sheer amount of anthropological thinking on the person (for example, Fowler 2003; Strathern 2004), the self (Myers 1986; Kondo 1990; Van Wolputte 2004), and the individual (Carrithers, Collins, and Lukes 1985; Joyce 2005), this is something that seems to be grounded more in the tradition in anthropology to base narratives on the experiences of the individual in order to maintain a "real-world" perspective when theorizing, rather than an attempt at creating derivative constructs of each other.[6]

Kuper (1999) therefore cautions about the difficulties that arise when "culture," or a substitute term for it, becomes a stand-alone explanation rather than an entity to be represented or interpreted. Culture in this view is more, as Robert Borofsky calls it, an "anthropological abstraction" (1994: 245) than a useful concept. Numerous other authors also worry about a potential reification of our culture theories. "Culture ... consists of transforming difference into essence. Culture ... generates an essentialisation of the world" (Friedman 1994: 206–7). Moreover, "the essentialism of our discourse [about culture] reflects our vested disciplinary interests in characterising exotic otherness" (Keesing 1994: 303). "In effect, the concept of culture operates as a distancing device" (Ingold 1993: 212). Michael Carrithers (1992) summarizes aptly: "The change of focus is, so to speak, from the centres of cultures and societies to their peripheries and the relations between them; and from a more or less static description of their characteristics to a dynamic one of processes in which they are involved" (Carrithers 1992: 27).

While these authors all question the development, usage, or even basic usefulness of the concept of culture, it yet serves them as a focal point for interrogation of human interaction (both in theorizing as well in the application of those theories). This follows James Clifford's quote that "there are times when we still need to be able to speak holistically of Japanese or Trobriand or Moroccan culture in the confidence that we are designating something real and differentially coherent" (1988, quoted in Brumann 1999: S1). In fact, Christoph Brumann (1999) and Sally Moore (1994) argue that culture as a concept cannot be discarded "because it is so deeply rooted in the history of ideas and in the discipline of anthropology" (Moore 1994: 373). Yet all authors seem to base their arguments on the assumption that lived cultures emerge and re-emerge in and out of themselves every moment in time while yet remaining clearly recognizable.[7] In other words, the precise form and nature of the persistence of conceptual categories—despite often substantial changes in the attributes that make up the category in the first place—is part of what is being contested and argued about: culture is "emergent." Let me illustrate with another "ethnographic" example from the business world.

Case Study #2: Internet Novice

The concept of the "internet novice user" has been written about for a long time in HCI (Human-Computer Interaction) literature.[8] Still an important category ten years after the internet got seriously underway, we know that the novices that "get into the internet" now exhibit different actual behavior than those of ten years ago. The expectations, behavioral strategies, conceptualizations, and so forth, mean that they don't do the same things that people did ten years ago. "To be sure, many of yesterday's innovations become part of tomorrow's transmitted 'culture'" (Wagner 1981: 135), but the category "internet novice user" still exists, at least as a useful framing device. The category of the internet novice user is still relevant for businesses today, even though it has changed some of its attributes. It became different, and yet stayed the same. In the same way, the Swat Pathans, or the Brits, are still important cultural reference points of (self-)description, of (self-)identification, of analysis, and comment (see, for example, Colls 2003; Kumar 2004).[9]

The logging of such changing sameness and continuing difference is something that anthropologists have developed expertise in describing and explaining. I do not want to equate "roles" with "culture" in a Parsonian sense through the above case study, but it shows the analogy of conceptualizing analytical categories.[10]

Anthropology and Commercial Interest

These insights into the changes of cultures, the ability to describe and analyze the behaviors, attitudes, and reasons as well as the origins and constitution of these behaviors made anthropologists interesting to commercial decision-makers who wanted to better understand their customers and how their services and products were used (see also chapter 1, this volume). "Suddenly people seem to agree with us anthropologists; culture is everywhere. Immigrants have it, business corporations have it, young people have it, women have it, even ordinarily middle-aged men have it, all in their own versions. ... We see advertising where products are extolled for 'bed culture' and 'ice cream culture'" (Hannerz 1996: 30). With the economic boom in 1990s, very competitive markets differentiated businesses solely by the user experience, the look-and-feel, and ephemeral "touchy-feely-ness." Companies in the technology sector, especially internet-related services—predominantly in the US, much more slowly in Europe—began utilizing specialists with insight into this "culture-thing" (see Kane 1996; Pesola 2004). "Larry Keeley, co-founder and president of the Doblin Group in Chicago ... said that 'if you just use anthropologists, you can triple your innovation effectiveness by three times.' Think of that for a moment. That's probably why corporations are hiring so many cultural anthropologists" (Nussbaum 2005).[11]

Notwithstanding the slowdown after the burst of the dotcom boom, the interest continues today: "In the first decade of the millennium, increasing numbers of anthropologists work for transnational companies ... and the discipline is fast becoming part of the business landscape" (Fisher and Downey 2006: 18; see also Fitzgerald 2006; this volume: Cefkin, chapter 1; Blomberg, chapter 8; Fischer chapter 9). As John Van Maanen notes, "while the anthropological market share in the cultural portrait business may be down, the market itself is booming" (2001: 236). Most notably, perhaps, we can quantitatively point to a rise in user-focused research that led to specific recommendations for product development and design (to name but a few: Nielsen 1999; Laurel 2003; Courage and Baxter 2004; Krug 2005; Nielsen and Loranger 2006).

Qualitatively, we could say, the 1990s boom marked a shift from product acceptability sessions to participatory design sessions and from market-propositioning focus groups to usability tests and conceptualization work with user-focused task and process flows. User-centered design (UCD) became suddenly hip and mainstream.[12] While the collaboration of anthropology and design (as disciplines) may have been particularly successful, as well as having become an accepted pairing for product development, the influence of anthropology reaches beyond "mere" design. Strategic direction, latent user-needs discovery, missed-opportunity detection and measurement, customer relations, and improvement of product "stickiness" are just some of the other—often less visible—contributions/output of commercial anthropologists.[13]

For these contributions, companies invited these knowledge-experts into their meeting rooms (either as consultants or as full-time employees) to teach them about the current (or assumed future) "culture" of their customers. Better knowledge about the people who buy and use their products enabled these companies to thus make a bottom-line impact in the market place. As the internet embraced diverse languages, countries, and so forth, the challenge for understanding the users also grew: various language groups in the same country were at stake—different countries, or even "newly discovered" customer segments in a market the companies may or may not have intended to enter. There are many success stories in this field; too many even to contemplate counting. A quick look at what kind of services and sites first established themselves more "globally" suffices: communication services in local languages (for example, gmx.de and web.de in Germany), travel and travel guides (Expedia), durable commodities like books and CDs (Amazon), news (online newspapers), or online banking. While a subsequent consolidation of companies may have reduced the number of local providers, the list illustrates the success of knowing the desires of the local market, by allowing for a culturally different user at the core of the service/product.

Recent Theoretical Development and Dialogue

Whether anthropology (as the discipline that claims authority over the "culture" notion) agrees or not, culture has become part of the social, legal, and political discourse like other popularized concepts, for example, "a people," "race," or "tribe."[14] No discussion internally can be had any longer without reference to the dialogues in wider academic and popular settings (see Brettell 1996; Dresch, James, and Parkin 2000; Watson 2001; Friedman et al. 2005). To the contrary, there is a lively debate about what form that interaction should take (see Mills 2003; Eriksen 2006; Blomberg, chapter 8).

Readings like those of James Clifford and George Marcus (1997), David Gellner and Eric Hirsch (2001), or Kate Fox (1991) are now exerting visible influence over publications beyond the disciplines of anthropology and sociology. Seen in the larger discourse of the study *of* organizations, my two outlined philosophical positions are somewhat aligning: even defendants of slippery culture admit that "getting culture right" is not quite as simple as exchanging some clear-cut building blocks or mere adjustments within a limited set of parameters. The visual "drape-over" approach (see the first case study above) to localization often works, but it does not guarantee commercial success in culturally different markets. Pure commercial success is only one parameter. Let me illustrate the pitfalls of such an approach with another case study from my own work experience.

Case Study #3: Car Manufacturer

A car manufacturer used the same drape-over approach of localization for its global website style guide, but it could not avoid the protruding cultural issues. Developed and built in the US, difficulties emerged when the design was "cross-tested" in three different "cultures" to check "potential localization issues." The US User Experience team had done appropriate testing with the US target audience, and we had access to these findings when we recruited participants in the markets to be tested and developed a protocol focusing on evaluative impression and interaction through task scenarios for participants to complete. Three research teams simultaneously embarked on the international testing. The nodes for the project came together in Germany. The team's first task was to talk to the team in Japan at the end of their day about their learnings. Then followed our own (German) testing. In the afternoon, we compared notes with the Mexican team. After more analysis, we finally had a conference call in the evening with the designers and engineers in the US in which we outlined the necessary modifications to the test prototype. The colleagues in the US updated the prototype, so we had a "new," iterated version the next morning that we could test with a modified test script.

From the tests we concluded that the "global" navigation categories failed to convince because people's concepts in the local marketplaces (Mexico, Japan, and Germany) differed: this included the categories, modes of interaction and politeness, and shopping service expectations. For example, customers in Germany expected the dealership to offer second-hand approved cars as a separate category. However, since the used-car market in the US is very different, this local market expectation and requirement had not been factored into the design. Furthermore, in Mexico, the main market activity was centered predominantly around *not*-new vehicles, thus suggesting a different structure to be necessary for the buying process despite the fact that the informative idea of the site worked well. Customers in Japan were concerned what kind of letters were used (Kanji or Kana) because they held social meaning. However, the concept of the site (the mood) did not fit with the typography used on the site. The incongruence disrupted the experience for Japanese users to an intolerable level.

The recommendations for the local markets—as representatives of international markets—were thus limited because only US user requirements had produced the design architecture. Many decisions had been taken based on insight into and feedback from only a domestic audience. The changes necessary for the appropriate "internationalization" (adding of categories for Germany, layout of content modules for Japan, different sales pitch/process for Mexico) required re-engineering that was not in the original time plan. It would have increased cost significantly or resulted in an impoverished user experience with the site (and thus the brand) for users outside the USA, thus (in part) negating the original envisioned benefit of a *global* style guide.

Need for Re-conceptualization is Recognized

There is now growing recognition also outside the anthropological discourse that a change of theoretical concepts is needed for better description of and application in practice. Victor Miroshnik, for example, looks at how cultural differences could be integrated in MNC (multinational companies) management. His measurement orients itself on the bottom line, but he changes tone: "The importance of understanding the cultures of countries in which a MNC operates—as well as the similarities and differences among these cultures—becomes clear when we look at the multitudes of modern managers' blunders in multi-national business" (2002: 525). He also identifies a more general flaw in theoretical writing: "The problem with the earlier studies between organizational cultures and performance is that they are always based on domestic firms and the USA" (542). He does not, however, mention that in the MNC arena so-called integration is still striven for through "localization," with a "master culture" setting the tone.

David Avison and Michael Myers (1995) argue for a broader use of the concept of culture in Information Systems Research: culture has no clear boundaries, is internally and externally contested, and constantly in flux. They suggest "that IS researchers should adopt a more critical, *anthropological* view of the concept" (1995: 49, emphasis added). Their point is made in response to managerial attempts to codify "culture," "to impose a 'mission statement' which would encapsulate this ethos and 'martial the troops' by means of a single 'culture'" (Gellner and Hirsch 2001: 4). Similarly, Ken Starkey (1998) critiques the homogenous, rational concept culture as entailed in the notion of "corporate culture." He uses Durkheimian social solidarity as a backdrop to highlight heterogeneity and resistance within organizations (see also Wright 1998). Emphasis is instead placed on context (Osland and Bird 2000; Weisinger and Trauth 2002). All this sounds like the growing influence of culture seen as "emergent" (for an example of this in regards to "office culture," see Tett 2005).

However, there are also attempts to bridge the gap from the side of anthropological literature. Allen Batteau (2001) examines culture as in "culture of organizations." Drawing on both anthropological and organization studies literature, he advocates more dialogue and cross-fertilization. Studies on "corporate culture" in the management literature view it most typically from above (for examples, see Deal and Kennedy 1982; Peters and Waterman 1982; for exceptions, see Rosen 1985; Young 1989). "Culture is seen as a set of referential statements available for management manipulation" (Batteau 2001: 726), the dualism of the "hard"; lines of budget, strategy, command/control, and the "soft"; values, feelings, and moral sentiments (737). He concludes that anthropology's holistic concept of culture provides a necessary critique to the more positivist upbeat business management studies notion of "corporate culture" (for more anthropological/sociological literature on organizational studies, see, for example, Gellner and Hirsch 2001; Wright 1994, 1998; Gamst 1989; Michaelson 1989; Morrill and Fine 1997; Moeran 2005; Fisher and Downey 2006).[15] Indeed, business studies has seen a shift in emphasis from function to meaning; in other words, a recognition of the limitations of the behaviorist/positivist models (that is, an influence of the literature like Clifford 1988; Clifford and Marcus 1986; Abu-Lughod 1991). As Malcolm Chapman (2001) notes, the shift also generally reflects the distinction between quantitative and qualitative research.

Finally, anthropology has started to come out of the ivory academic tower. Not only is there a burgeoning literature of studies in and of the business setting (Gellner and Hirsch 2001; Malefyt and Moeran 2003; Moeran 2006; Pink 2006; Fisher and Downey 2006; Foster 2007), more importantly for practitioners, the "ethos of non-interference" is waning (see also Blomberg, chapter 8). Accepting the inevitability of lasting change through interaction with the subjects of study in the decades following *Writing Culture* (Clifford and Marcus 1986), it has also spawned an assessment of the role of the anthropologist in the location of research and its implications and consequences (for example, Kulick and Willson 1995; Brettell 1996; Amit 2000; Erikson 2006).

Instilling "Emergent Culture" is Slow

Despite these recent theoretical changes, the implicit question that has been driving this article remains: Could not businesses that seek out the insights of expert knowledge providers of "emergent culture" be even more successful if the concept of the "customer's culture" was *more* refined and *better* applied in the light of the apparent success of the quick-fix, slippery "visual drape-over" approach?[16] This is a rhetorical question. In my view, it is not enough to focus on the products of material and popular culture unless we also understand—and present our knowledge about—our study participants' interactions and engagement with, discourses about, and goals for these very products. Armed with that ethnographically based kind of user understanding, products and services could be developed that deliver even more value for customers and profit for companies.

Hopping on the bandwagon in the early 1990s, many market-research organizations started calling all qualitative research "ethnography,"[17] and gave the pretence of doing anthropological fieldwork.[18] While ethnography became a ubiquitous buzzword (Moeran 2006: 11; Mitchell 1998), it became also more separated from anthropology. I believe that anthropology's specific focus on the "messy details of everyday life" (Holt 1994: 344) fosters an ethnographic attitude that anchors its recommendations in data from real consumer behavior. It thus debunks assumed or conjured abstractions against "life-tested" results. In this way, we could say that if "ethnographic" is relating to a *technique*, "anthropological" refers to a *way of knowing* and a *way of analysis.* It is also a skill that is difficult (if not impossible) to measure.

It does not relieve anthropology from an examination of "organizational" culture (in addition to the literature quoted above). To the contrary, the discipline should take them as equivalent instances for knowledge production as the traditional anthropological focus on, for example, ethnic groupings. Indeed, while we now know that our subjects may "talk back at us,"[19] in the political and contested fields such as commerce and industry, anthropology could meaningfully and critically engage with various "incarnations" of the concept of "culture" and at the same time offer perspectives developing and providing better services and products. This view of culture as evocative and emergent (Clifford 1997), as including aspects of rationality and resistance (Batteau 2001: 737), as well as similarity, continuity (Leach 1954; Geertz 1973), and context (Weisinger and Trauth 2002), has seen some success in the academy, but it has been hard to convince the decision makers in the business world. In the end, I agree that "where heads of state agencies or chief executive officers (and their consultants) get their master-of-the-universe ideas probably matter less than the consequences of putting such ideas into play" (Van Maanen 2001: 243). Brun-Cottan (chapter 6), Jordan (chapter 4) and Blomberg (chapter 8) all address these consequences by focusing on the outputs of ethnographically inspired insights. In the remainder of this chapter I would therefore like to offer some suggestions as to why the adaptation of this new theoretical position has been so slow in business, but also point to an example where the adaptation of a more "emergent culture"-type conceptualization is currently underway.

At the root lies the fact, I believe, that despite the success stories, the premises of the commercial buyers of culture knowledge and of the knowledge providers of culture are fundamentally different. This became apparent once the "New Economy"-bubble burst at the end of the 1990s. In the period since, a re-evaluation of the relationship between buyers and providers has taken place. After all, culture is now "available as an explanatory mechanism not only to ethnographers but to organizational members (and their many professionally interested observers such as consultants, reporters, stock analysts, social critics, politicians, competitors, prospective employees and so on)" (Van Maanen 2001: 244; see also Brettell 1996; Malefyt and Moeran 2003; Bell 2006). This assertion of difference is based on a generalized view, on the juxtaposition of the extremes, not on the often successful negotiation across them.[20]

The specialist knowledge providers—often anthropologists, but by no means only—have been trying to tell the knowledge buyers that cultures are more diverse and dynamic than the slippery model suggests. In the commercial conversations between the believers of "slippery culture" and those of "emergent culture," the latter find it difficult to convince the business de-cision makers that the cultural resistance to a given design or product isn't necessarily due to specific "bits," but to the local cultural approach which is much more encompassing and holistic. On top of the apparent juxtaposi-tion in conception as well as structural position, I therefore believe that dis-agreements about the right approach to knowing about one's customers are most often a matter of cross-communication and misunderstanding. The disagreements are persistently misconceiving the issue at stake.

It is not about different solutions, but about differing views of the problem (see also Flynn, chapter 2, this volume). Since such meta-talk is usually not employed in these situations, changing one's underlying concepts tends to be more difficult than tweaking a solution based on those concepts. This is due to the fact that the "emergent" and the "slippery" versions of culture may "co-exist," but only as long as they are not made explicit. As soon as they are, each concept coheres to different philosophical assumptions. Un-less the underlying concepts are made visible,[21] none of the participants on a project team may realize that they are working to different assump-tions. In other words, it is a conflict of conceptualization between the com-mercial buyers of culture-knowledge and the expert knowledge providers of culture. Only by rephrasing the concepts could a path be created that lets the experts and the receivers get at the problem together.

In my experience anthropologists—as the expert knowledge provid-ers—are often unwilling to accept the bounded needs of the boards, and what they see as an (over-)simplification of cultural variances. The busi-ness decision makers, on the other hand—the project managers, the board members, the knowledge buyers—often do not want to accept that the problem is more complex or more detailed than they originally conceived or would like it to be, and ought to be treated more seriously.[22] Delays in floating the product or service are therefore often much more likely originating in the different understandings of what culture "is" among the project team than in the company having no leverage to understand local culture. It is true that cost constraints often seem to forbid an approach other than a "slippery" one because it is initially cheaper than one with an "emergent" view of culture[23] that offers a more long-term ROI.[24] I would like to illustrate with a final case study the ongoing process of change after a realization of the need of investment.

A Company in Concept Change

Let me now briefly discuss a final case study of a company that is cur-rently aligning its internal conceptualization of "culture." Yahoo acted like the bulk of its industry with respect to its international cultural approach. Not altogether surprising, the company was founded on the West Coast, but almost immediately had an impact on the whole of the US, before spreading out to "ROW" (rest of world), eventually spanning the globe.[25] However, products were developed in the US, and then rolled out. When regional businesses centers were established (in the UK, Germany, France, Japan, Korea, and so on), product development was still predominantly done in the US. Though products were cross-tested in other countries/ cultures, changes mainly referred to some translation adaptations after which the product was rolled out.

It was the idea of fixing the cultural context: like fixing a technical bug, like flipping a switch, the cultural issue could be sorted. If it weren't, then several iterations would eventually approximate an acceptable local solution: addition or removal of specific functionality, positioning of the product, and/or the emphasis of certain aspects (for example, security concerns in German-speaking countries). Nothing in this is different to any comparable company.[26] But things are changing.

As the company is maturing (Yahoo celebrated its tenth anniversary in early 2005), and regional and local businesses understand their markets to a depth where they can discern differences from the US market (as well as make more-informed decisions as to why these do or do not matter), the setup for product development is changing; requirements gathering is becoming global. This difference can be noticed in the language of product managers when they talk about rolling out products/services in Europe. When I joined in 2004, they used to say that "they did the UK and France before launch." By late 2006 they start speaking of "including business, product and user requirements from the main markets in EU."[27] The needs for security of data, often anecdotally said to be the main concern of Germans, are researched also in France, and, more importantly, heard and taken seriously.

On the one hand, researchers with a specific international focus concentrate on global products across markets. Complementing this, local researchers are being employed to inform local decisions (to help local business units to make US-developed products local in an appropriate form). But in collaboration with the US-based team, they also inform global strategic decisions (What do our customers want from us and how? What standards can they expect? Where should Yahoo as a global brand go? What synergies can the business utilize? and so forth). This means that a different type of information gathering is needed to enable a more general, global requirement gathering: input from different markets *before* new or improved products are developed and rolled out. Where the aim used to be formulated as "to understand the UK," it is now described as "to understand the user needs from the UK."

Moreover, there is return benefit: the adaptation for local markets has produced products and product features that can be introduced to other markets or be incorporated into global offerings. Whether these are blogging or online-dating tools (Jones and Ortlieb 2006) or specific styles of cooperative searching for information (so-called "social search") that emerged in the Asian markets in recent years, it has hit home that a more integrated and cooperative gathering of global product requirements is not only needed, but valuable to the bottom line and future direction of the company. I must offer a caveat, however, that this kind of thinking occurs more in American—and probably specifically West-coast based—technology-oriented companies.[28] Europe has a lot of catching up to do. Companies there have yet to realize the opportunities and value in Europe's inherent multicultural setting and that tending to that can make them profit. Currently, "emergent culture" is too frequently seen as a mere cost with too little or too long of a return for its investment.[29]

Company leadership (including, but not limited to, Yahoo) begins to understand that culture difference is not solved in the manner of a flipped switch. And, of course, they understand that if local culture is understood appropriately, there is a lot to be gained: reputation, loyalty, and market share, but, more concretely, also more relevance, revenue, monetization, and profit. Products that resonate in substance, form, and/or positioning with local concepts and needs will perform better than clumsy adaptations of foreign concepts that do not ring true locally and which everybody in the local target audience recognizes as such. In other words, most users see through the drape-over approach or react to it sub-consciously. If products were globally developed, they tend to afford and allow the relevant adaptation into local contexts. For example, during the localization of the hotel chain study, one of the most despised aspects for the UK audience was the perceived Americanism of the adverts. While a "small" design issue, it distinctly—and negatively—colored the perception of all trial users of the site. The damage to the brand would have outweighed the effort spent to "get it right" hundredfold (for an example focusing on language issues, see Bowen 2008).

Conclusion

At Yahoo, this changeover of understanding "culture" will be a process that will take some time. While there is still debate over what the culture thing *is*, there is the readiness to let the culture specialists develop these requirements and the processes for gathering them. There is a readiness to listen if the expert researchers come back with a different model from the one the business managers had brought to the table and a readiness to decide afterward which approach yields the greater benefit for the business.[30] While there is pressure via a focus on time-to-market business requirements and short-term ROI, but if benefit can be demonstrated, an alternative approach to deployment may be accepted. For example, researchers are currently developing a more compact set of guidelines and methodologies for global research practices, there are case studies of a more globally integrated research approach to product development, and there is more collaboration between international product and research teams than previously.

The changes I observed at Yahoo are, overall, representative of a larger change in global commercial understanding and conceptualizing "culture"; it is slow, but it's happening. Fischer (chapter 9, this volume) labels that approach as recognizing "ethnographic knowledges.... in the plural." It may be confined to the service-oriented industries, but it is pushing the boundaries of global product development in the internet services, and it is beginning to yield results. For the foreseeable future, the working notion of "what culture is" will have to be negotiated between the knowledge buyers and the expert providers on a case-by-case basis in the face of specific market, project, and timeline requirements. But the fact that the expert knowledge providers are convincing the business buyers of such knowledge more regularly and more often makes me excited to advocate "emergent culture" in my commercial environment every time a (potentially) global product—or, in fact, any product—comes across my desk.[31]

Acknowledgments

This chapter was first conceived for and presented at the Annual Conference of the SfAA 2005 in Santa Fe. I would like to thank the "Workplace and Consumer Studies: A Dialogue" panel, organized by Melissa Cefkin, and the audience participants there for helpful suggestions. Particularly, I would like to thank Melissa Cefkin who read through various drafts and helped me substantially to advance my thinking, and the other contributors to this volume for their very useful suggestions and comments. Matthias Beer helped to research further resources and commented on early versions. Any remaining faults are my own.

Notes

1. For a comparative storyline, think also of the change of the status of the "high-five" greeting, which now even has a (US-)nationally recognized day (17 April). It has been attributed to the black community as a sign of solidarity and to soldiers during the Vietnam war but may be even older.
2. Kelkoo was founded in France in 1999 and bought by Yahoo in 2004. The name "Kelkoo" is a 'phonetic' spelling resembling the French phrase "Quel coût?", meaning "At what price?" It could also be understood as "Quel coup," meaning "What a bargain."
3. Even more so in the intellectual circles in the United States, where Geertz's ideas exerted considerable influence (Penny Harvey, personal conversation). See also Downey and Fisher (2006:19).
4. This is despite the fact that anthropology was not really intended to study those instances. Instead, it is generally accepted that anthropology grew partly out of the colonial context, if any (see, e.g., Keesing 1981; Kuper 1983).
5. However, it ought to be noted that organization studies developed more independently in the US. In Europe, research in this area is much more closely tied to sociology and psychology (see Koza and Thoenig 1995; Child 1995).
6. Indeed, anything else would be to argue in a "slippery" mode.
7. See discussion on Leach (1954) above. It is one of the contradictions in the scholarly discourse that there seems to be a theoretical *treatment* of the notion and a practical *use* of the term. While I touch on this paradox throughout, it is not the focus of this article.
8. Representatively, I reference two short articles by Jakob Nielsen, one of the most vocal usability advocates (e.g., his regular column "Alertbox"), from 1 April 1997 and 6 February 2000.
9. For more light-hearted but still insightful reading on "the English," see Paxman (1999) and Fox (2005). For "the French," you may try Rochefort (1997) or Alston, Hawthorne, and Saillet (2003). A more serious, albeit more dated, account on Europe is Edward Hall and Mildren Reed-Hall's (1990) treatise on cultural differences between Germans, the French, and Americans. The latter is part of a growing literature, both academic (e.g., Bell (2006); Osland and Bird (2000)) and popular (Lord (2005); Flippo (1996); Sears and Tamulionyte-Lentz (2001); Abbot (2004)) of ("dummy") guides to culture difference focusing on outcomes, and attributable behavior.
10. Perhaps the illustration of this point with an analogy dangerously close to (and across) the Parsonian segmentation between "culture" and "society" may raise more concerns for a US readership than for British anthropologists, who continued to see culture and society as complementary concepts that cannot be studied and understood on their own (e.g., Firth 1951). Since my background is in the latter, I hope my US-trained readers can accept the analogy.
11. On the other hand, comments like this raise questions in the community of professionals. One of the members of Anthrodesign (an email group/list for designers and anthropologists in mainly applied and/or commercial fields), Anthony Alvarez (2005), asked a question that is symptomatic: "In the bigger picture, do claims like this really help the cause of design anthropology (or ethnography in industry, a phrase I'm taking a shine to) by putting some real world numbers to it, or simply reduce it to a gimmicky formula ('Triple your brain power in 30 days!')?"
12. While there is not enough room here to go into a review of UCD (user-centric design) literature, I'd like to point to a few seminal pieces of work that have influenced the field. For good introductions to UCD processes and philosophy, see, e.g., Donahue (2002);

Cooper (2003); Norman (1998); Rubin (1984); Bias and Mayhew (1994). The books generally start with a focus on the potential users of the product/service to be designed, specifically modes and patterns of use, behavior, habits, types of use, types of users, etc.

13. I comment here only on anthropology in industry, but there are examples, stories, and case studies of how anthropologists have "found" their way into development agencies—the NHS (National Health Service) or the MoD (Ministry of Defence)—to fill similar and corresponding gaps in those institutions. Since I have no direct knowledge of these instances, other people are better equipped to tell their story (see Tett 2005; Pink 2006).

14. Susan Wright (1998) discusses the politicization of culture in and through its popularized usage.

15. There is, of course, also another strand of thought, represented, e.g. by Roger Bell (2006), that suggests that the current perception could also be solved by making cultural interpretations more "accurate." For reasons of scope and space, I shall not discuss this "slippery-culture" defence here further.

16. The association of the "slippery" concept of culture with the "quick-fix drape-over" approach is based on their congruent focus on comparison of the surface outputs (in the case of design changes, this is literally so). I am indebted to Matthias Beer for pointing me back to my own idea.

17. Other academic disciplines have done and are increasingly making use of "fieldwork" in their own ways (Dresch, James, and Parkin 2000: 1–2). The debate about who "owns" and "defines" the conundrum of how to, if at all, distinguish between "fieldwork as a method of doing research and ethnography as a means of presenting the results of that research" (Moeran 2006: 11) inside anthropology is ongoing.

18. Not all research done in this manner was pretentious and/or of low analytical quality. However, a lot of it also was. On the other hand, I would not want to claim that this was something new. Anthropologically inspired fieldwork and research techniques in qualitative research, advertising, etc., has long had close correlations (Malefyt and Moeran 2003: 12–17; Moeran 2005: 195–99; Mitchell 1998).

19. "Everyone is into culture now. For Anthropology, culture was once a term of art. Now the natives talk culture back at them" (Kuper 1999: 2). See also Brettell (1996).

20. Nafus and anderson (chapter 5) report on such negotiations by investigating a corporation's social memory as invested in tangible or material objects.

21. For example, through collaborative workshops, shared analysis sessions, or other facilitated techniques. The onus is, however, clearly on the knowledge experts to enable the teams they work with to work through these concepts and arrive at a shared understanding.

22. In their defence, "they … generally *believe* that culture is not only very 'real' but does provide the key to understanding the underlying needs, motivations and behavior of consumers" (Downey and Fisher and 2006: 19, emphasis added). Flynn, chapter 2, also usefully discusses the political dynamics and resolving of such disagreements between ethnographers and their internal clients at Microsoft.

23. Even Brumann recognizes that "the demand for unproblematically reproduced, overlarge, and ethnicized cultures" will not cease, and furthermore that "this kind of culture is often deployed or commoditised more effectively than what we have to offer as an alternative" (1999: S12).

24. The industry is always looking for definite articles that "prove" the ROI, but there are only a few well-known articles that are re-enlisted on multiple occasions: e.g., Aaron Marcus's 2002 article, *"Return on Investment for Usable User-Interface Design."*

25. In 2006, this included over thirty websites in more than twenty-five countries, including USA, Brazil, Mexico, England, Germany, France, Italy, Spain, India, China, Korea, and Japan.
26. And indeed to a lot of the theoretical positions I have been outlining in this chapter.
27. I would like to get them to say "prior to locking down specifications" rather than "prior to launch," but this is still a transformation in progress.
28. This statement is based on my knowledge of the market and the conversations I have had with people who work in this field. I should emphasize that this is tentative and not quantified at this stage.
29. It may also represent a different stage in accepted theoretical models employed in the US and Europe. (See Koza and Thoenig 1995; Child 1995.)
30. There is a shift to view "lived culture as a socially negotiated, dynamic, practically and locally situated process" (Weisinger and Trauth 2002: 309), based on ideas as proposed, e.g., by Lave and Wenger (1991) and Weisinger and Salipante (2000).
31. Post-script: Since I completed this article, I have left Yahoo. Rather than changing my verbs into the past, I felt the present tense is still the appropriate tense for the statements I'm making throughout because they hold true irrespective of my place of work.

References

Abbot, Charles. 2004. *Culture Smart! Italy: A Quick Guide to Customs & Etiquette.* Portland, OR: Graphic Arts Center Publishing Company

Abu-Lughod, Lila. 1991. "Writing Against Culture." In *Recapturing Anthropology: Working in the Present,* Fox, ed., 137–162. Santa Fe, NM: School of American Research Press.

Alston, Jon, Melanie Hawthorne, and Sylvie Saillet. 2003. *A Practical Guide to French Business.* Lincoln, NE: Writers Club Press

Alvarez, Anthony. 2005. "Big Words." Message #2672, sent on 18 November 2005 (19:35). Posting on Anthrodesign (internet forum/group). http://groups.yahoo.com/group/anthrodesign/.

Amit, Vered. 2000. *Constructing the Field: Ethnographic Fieldwork in the Contemporary World.* London: Routledge.

Appadurai, Arjun. 1996. *Modernity at Large: Cultural Dimensions of Globalisation.* Minneapolis, MN: University of Minneapolis Press.

Avison, David, and Michael Myers. 1995. "Information Systems and Anthropology: An Anthropological Perspective on IT and Organizational Culture." *Information Technology & People* 8(3): 43–56.

Batteau, Allen. 2001. "Negations and Ambiguities in the Cultures of Organization." *American Anthropologist* 102(4): 726–40.

Bell, Roger. 2006. "Paradoxes of Culture: How to make more accurate Interpretations." *Handbook of Business Strategy* 7(1): 363–68.

Bias, Randolph, and Deborah Mayhew. 1994. *Cost-Justifying Usability.* Boston, MA: Academic Press.

Borofsky, Robert. 1994. "Rethinking the Cultural." In *Assessing Cultural Anthropology,* Borofsky, ed., 243–49. New York: McGraw-Hill.

Bowen, David. 2008. "Personal View: Looking Local can Make a Big Difference on the Web." *The Financial Times,* 11 February.

Brettell, Caroline. 1996. *When They Read What We Write: The Politics of Ethnography.* Westport, CT: Bergin & Garvey.

Brightman, Robert. 1995. "Forget Culture: Replacement, Transcendence, Relexification." *Cultural Anthropology* 10: 509–46.

Brumann, Christoph. 1999. "Writing for Culture—Why a Successful Concept should not be Discarded." *Current Anthropology* 40 (supplement): S1–27.

Carrithers, Michael. 1992. *Why Humans Have Cultures.* Oxford: Oxford University Press.

Carrithers, Michael, Stephen Collins, and Steve Lukes. 1985. *The Category of the Person: Anthropology, Philosophy, History.* Cambridge: Cambridge University Press.

Chapman, Malcolm. 2001. "Social Anthropology and Business Studies: Some Considerations of Method." In *Inside Organisations: Anthropologists at Work,* Gellner and Hirsch, eds. 19–34. Oxford: Berg.

Child, John. 1995. "Guest Editorial." Special Issue: The European Perspective on Organization Theory. *Organization Science* 6: 117–18.

Clifford, James, and George Marcus. 1986. *Writing Culture: The Poetics and Politics of Ethnography.* Berkeley, CA: University of California Press.

Clifford, James. 1988. *The Predicament of Culture: Twentieth-Century Ethnography, Literature and Art.* Cambridge, MA: Harvard University Press.

Clifford, James. 1997. *Routes: Travel and Translation in the Late Twentieth Century.* Cambridge, MA: Harvard University Press.

Colls, Robert. 2004. *Identity of England.* Oxford: Oxford University Press.

Cooper, Alan, and Robert Reidmann. 2003. *About Face 2.0: The Essentials of Interaction Design.* Second edition. New York: John Wiley & Sons.

Courage, Catherine, and Kathy Baxter. 2004. *Understanding Your User: A Practical Guide to User Requirements.* San Francisco, CA: Morgan Kaufman.

Deal, Terrence, and Allen Kennedy. 1982. *Corporate Cultures: The Rites and Rituals of Corporate Life.* Reading, MA: Addison-Wesley Publishing Company.

Donahue, Karen. 2002. *Built for Use: Driving Profitability Through the User Experience.* Maidenhead: McGraw-Hill.

Downey, Greg and Melissa Fisher. 2006. "Introduction: The Anthropology of Capital and the Frontiers of Ethnography." In *Frontiers of Capital: Ethnographic Perspectives of the New Economy,* Fisher and Downey, eds., 1–30. Durham, NC/London: Duke University Press.

Dresch, Paul, Wendy James, and David Parkin. 2000. *Anthropologists in a Wider World—Essays on Field Research.* New York/Oxford: Berghahn Books.

Edwards, Jeannette. 2005. "'Make-up': Personhood Through the Lens of Biotechnology." *Ethnos* 70(3): 413–31.

Eriksen, Thomas Hylland. 2006. *Engaging Anthropology: The Case for a Public Presence.* Oxford: Berg.

Ess, Charles, and Fay Sudweeks. 2001. *Culture, Technology, Communication: Towards an Intercultural Global Village.* Albany, NY: State University of New York Press.

Fernandez, James. 1994. "Culture and Transcendent Humanisation: On the 'Dynamics of the Categorical.'" *Ethnos* 59: 143–67.

Firth, Raymond. 1951. "Contemporary British Social Anthropology." *American Anthropologist* 53(4): 474–89.

Fisher, Melissa, and Greg Downey. 2006. *Frontiers of Capital: Ethnographic Perspectives of the New Economy.* Durham, NC/London: Duke University Press.

Fitzgerald, Michael. 2006. "Intel's Hiring Spree." *Technology Review.* Cambridge, MA: Massachusetts Institute of Technology. Found at http://www.technologyreview.com/InfoTech/wtr_16340,294,p1.html.

Flippo, Hyde. 1996. *The German Way: Aspects of Behavior, Attitudes, and Customs in the German-Speaking World.* New York: McGraw-Hill.

Foster, Robert. 2007. "The Work of the New Economy: Consumers, Brands and Value Creation." *Current Anthropology* 22(4): 707–31.

Fowler, Chris. 2003. *The Archaeology of Personhood: An Anthropological Approach.* London: Routledge.

Fox, Kate. 2005. *Watching the English: The Hidden Rules of English Behavior.* London: Hodden & Stoughton.

Fox, Robin. 1991. *Recapturing Anthropology: Working in the Present.* Santa Fe, NM: School of American Research Press.

Friedman, Jonathan. 1994. *Cultural Identity and Global Process.* London: Sage.

Friedman, Jonathan, et al. 2003. "Anthropologists are Talking: About the New Right in Europe." *Ethnos* 68(4): 554–72.

Gamst, Frederick. 1989. "The Concept of Organizational Culture and Corporate Culture: An Ethnological View." *Anthropology of Work Review* 10(3): 12–16.

Geertz, Clifford. 1973. In *The Interpretation of Cultures.* New York: Basic Books.

Gellner, David, and Eric Hirsch. 2001. *Inside Organisations: Anthropologists at Work.* Oxford: Berg.

Gerholm, Lena. 1993. "The Dynamics of Culture." *Ethnologia Scandinavica* 23: 13–24.

Green, Sarah, Penny Harvey, and Hannah Knox. 2005. "Scales of Place and Networks." *Current Anthropology* 46(5): 805–26.

Hall, Edward, and Mildren Reed-Hall. 1990. *Understanding Cultural Differences: Germans, French, and Americans.* Boston, MA: Intercultural Press.

Handler, Richard. 1994. "Is 'Identity' a Useful Cross-cultural Concept?" In *Commemorations—The Politics of National Identity,* Gillis, ed., 27–40. Princeton, NJ: Princeton University Press.

Hannerz, Ulf. 1992. *Cultural Complexity: Studies in the Social Organization of Meaning.* New York: Columbia University Press.

———. 1996. *Transnational Connections: Cultures, People, Places.* London: Routledge.

Hofstede, Geert. 1980. *Culture's Consequences: International Differences in Work-related Practices.* London: Sage.

Ingold, Tim. 1993. "The Art of Translation in a Continuous World." In *Beyond Boundaries: Understanding, Translation and Anthropological Discourse,* Palsson, ed. 210–30. London: Berg.

Jones, Rachel, and Martin Ortlieb. 2006. "Online Place and Person-Making: Matters of the Heart and Self-Expression." *Ethnographic Praxis in Industry Conference Proceedings,* 214–28. American Anthropological Association.

Joyce, Rosemary. 2005. "Archaeology of the Body." *Annual Review of Anthropology* 34: 139–58.

Kane, Kate. 1996. "Anthropologist Go Native in the Corporate Village." *Fast Company* 5. Found at http://www.fastcompany.com/magazine/05/anthro.html.

Keesing, Roger. 1981. *Cultural Anthropology—A Contemporary Perspective.* Second edition. London: Holt, Rinehart and Winston.

———. 1994. "Theories of Culture Revisited." In *Assessing Cultural Anthropology.* New York: McGraw-Hill.

Kondo, Dorinne. 1990. *Crafting Selves: Power, Gender and Discourses of Identity in a Japanese Workplace.* Chicago, IL: Chicago University Press.

Koza, Mitchell, and Jean-Claude Thoenig. 1995. "Organisation Theory at the Crossroads: Some Reflections on European and United States Approaches to Organisational Research." *Organization Science* 6: 1–8.

Krug, Steve. 2005. *Don't Make Me Think: A Common-Sense Approach to Web Usability*. Berkeley, CA: New Riders.

Kulick, Don, and Margaret Willson. 1995. *Taboo: Sex, Identity and Erotic Subjectivity in Anthropological Fieldwork*. London: Routledge.

Kumar, Krishan. 2003. *The Making of English National Identity*. Cambridge: Cambridge University Press.

Kuper, Adam. 1983. *Anthropology and Anthropologists: The Modern British School*. Second edition. London: Routledge.

———. 1988. *The Invention of Primitive Society*. London: Routledge.

———. 1999. *Culture: The Anthropologists' Account*. London: Harvard University Press.

Kusserow, Adrie. 1999. "Crossing the Great Divide: Anthropological Theories of the Western Self." *Journal of Anthropological Research* 55: 541–62.

LaFontaine, Jean. 1985. "Person and Individual: Some Anthropological Reflections." In *The Category of the Person: Anthropology, Philosophy, History*, Carrithers, Collins, and Lukes, eds., 123–40. Cambridge: Cambridge University Press.

Laurel, Brenda. 1990. *The Art of Human/Computer Interface Design*. Boston: Addison-Wesley.

———. 2003. *Design Research: Methods and Perspectives*. Cambridge, MA: MIT Press.

Lave, Jean, and Etienne Wenger. 1991. *Situated Learning: Legitimate Peripheral Participation*. Cambridge: Cambridge University Press.

Leach, Edmund. 1954 [1964, 1970]. *Political Systems of Highland Burma: A Study of Kachin Social Structure*. London: Bell & Athlone Press.

Lord, Richard. 2005. *Culture Shock! Germany: A Survival Guide to Customs and Etiquette*. Culture Shock! Guides. Portland, OR: Graphic Arts Center Publishing Company

Lowie, Robert. 1924. *Primitive Society*. New York: Boni & Liveright.

Malefyt, Timothy Dewaal, and Brian Moeran. 2003. *Advertising Cultures*. Oxford: Berg.

Marcus, Aaron. 2002. *Return on Investment for Usable User-Interface Design: Examples and Statistics*. New York: AM+A. Found at http://www.amanda.com/resources/ROI/AMA_ROIWhitePaper_28Feb02.pdf.

Marcus, George. 1998. *Ethnography through Thick and Thin*. Princeton, NJ: Princeton University Press.

Marcus, George, and Michael Fischer. 1986. *Anthropology as Cultural Critique: An Experimental Moment in the Human Sciences*. Second edition. Princeton, NJ: Princeton University Press.

Michaelson, D. R. 1989. "The Current Practice of Corporate Culture: Is it True to Ethnographic Analysis." *Anthropology of Work Review* 10(3): 11–12.

Mills, David. 2003. "Professionalising or Popularizing Anthropology." *Anthropology Today* 19(5): 8–13.

Miroshnik, Victor. 2002. "Culture and International Management: A Review." *Journal of Management Development* 21(7): 521–44.

Mitchell, Marilyn. 1998. *Employing Qualitative Methods in the Private Sector*. London: Sage.

Moeran, Brian. 2005. *The Business of Ethnography: Strategic Exchanges, People and Organizations*. New York: Berg.

———. 2006. *Ethnography at Work*. New York: Berg.

Moore, Sally. 1994. "The Ethnography of the Present and the Analysis of Process." In *Assessing Cultural Anthropology*. Borofsky, ed., 362–74. New York: McGraw-Hill.

Morrill, Calvin, and Gary Fine. 1997. "Ethnographic Contributions to Organisational Sociology." *Sociological Methods and Research* 25: 424–51.

Myers, Fred. 1986. *Pintupi Country, Pintupi Self*. London: Smithsonian Institute.

Negandhi, Anant. 1983. "Cross-Cultural Management Research: Trend and Future Directions." *Journal of International Business Studies* 14(2): 17–28.

Nielsen, Jakob. 1997. "Tech-Support Tales: Internet Hard to Use for Novice Users." Online article from April 1, 1997. Posted on useit.com. http://www.useit.com/alertbox/9704a.html.

———. 1999. *Designing Web Usability: The Practice of Simplicity.* Indianapolis, IN: New Riders Publishing.

———. 2000. "Novice vs. Expert Users." Online article from February 6, 2000. Posted on useit.com. http://www.useit.com/alertbox/20000206.html.

Nielsen, Jakob, and Hoa Loranger. 2006. *Prioritising Web Usability.* Berkeley, CA: New Riders Press.

Norman, Donald. 1998. *The Design of Everyday Things.* Boston, MA: The MIT Press.

Nussbaum, Bruce. 2005. "Creating Google." Online article from 15 November 2005. Posted on Business Week Online. http://www.businessweek.com/innovate/NussbaumOnDesign/archives/2005/11/creating_google.html.

Osland, Joyce, and Alan Bird. 2000. "Beyond Sophisticated Stereotyping: Cultural Sensemaking in Context." *Academy of Management Executive* 14(1): 65–79.

Overing, Joanna. 1985. "Introduction." In *Reason and Morality,* Overing, ed. 1–28. London: Tavistock (ASA monograph 24).

Paxman, Jeremy. 1999. *English: A Portrait of a People.* London: Penguin.

Peters, Thomas, and Robert Waterman. 1982. *In Search of Excellence.* New York: Time Warner.

Pesola, Maija. 2004. "Symbols of Change Cause a Market Reaction." *The Financial Times,* April 6.

Pink Sarah. 2006. *Applications of Anthropology: Professional Anthropology in the Twenty-first Century.* New York/Oxford: Berghahn Books.

Roberts, Karlene, and Nakiye Boyacigiller. 1984. "Cross National Organizational Research: The Grasp of the Blind Men." *Research in Organizational Behavior* 6: 455–88.

Rochefort, Harriet. 1997. *French Toast An American in Paris Celebrates the Maddening Mysteries of the French.* New York: St. Martin's Press.

Rosen, Michael. 1985. "Breakfast at Spiro's: Dramaturgy and Dominance." *Journal of Management* 11(2): 31–48.

Rubin, Jeff. 1984. *Handbook of Usability Testing: How to Plan, Design and Conduct Effective Tests.* New York: John Wiley & Sons.

Sahlins, Marshall. 1994. "Goodbye to Tristes Tropes: Ethnography in the Context of Modern World History." In *Assessing Cultural Anthropology.* Borofsky, ed., 377–94. New York: Mc-Graw-Hill.

Schein, Edward H. 1984. "Coming to a New Awareness of Organizational Culture." *Sloan Management Review* 25(2): 3–16.

Sears, Woodrow, and Audrone Tamulionyte-Lentz. 2001. *Succeeding in Business in Central and Eastern Europe: A Guide to Cultures, Markets, and Practices (Managing Cultural Differences).* Oxford: Butterworth-Heinemann.

Sekaran, Uma 1983. "Methodological and Theoretical Issues and Advancements in Cross-Cultural Research." *Journal of International Business Studies* 14(2): 61–74.

Shweder, Richard. 1991. *Thinking Through Cultures.* Cambridge, MA: Harvard University Press.

Sökefeld, Martin. 1999. "Debating Self, Identity and Culture." *Current Anthropology* 40(4): 417–47.

Starkey, Ken. 1998. "Durkheim and the Limits of Corporate Culture: Whose Culture? Which Durkheim?" *Journal of Management Studies* 35(2): 125–36.

Stephey, M.J. 2008. "A Brief History of the Fist Bump", Online article from 05/06 2008. Posted by Time Magazine. http://www.time.com/time/nation/article/0,8599,1812102,00.html

Stolcke, Verena. 1995. "Talking Culture: New Boundaries, New Rhetorics of Exclusion in Europe." *Current Anthropology* 36(1): 1–24.

Strathern, Marilyn. 2004. "The Whole Person and Its Artifacts." *Annual Review of Anthropology* 33: 1–19.

Tett, Gillian. 2005. "Office Culture." *The Financial Times* Weekend Magazine, 21 May.

Van Maanen, John. 2001. "Afterwords: Natives 'R' Us: Some Notes on the Ethnography of Organisations." In *Inside Organisations: Anthropologists at Work*, Gellner and Hirsch, eds., 233–61. Oxford: Berg.

Van Wolputte, Steven. 2004. "Hang on to Your Self: Of Bodies, Embodiment and Selves." *Annual Review of Anthropology* 33: 251–69.

Wagner, Roy. 1981 [1975]. *The Invention of Culture*. Chicago, IL/London: University of Chicago Press.

Watson, Tony. 2001. *In Search of Management: Culture, Chaos and Control in Managerial Work.* London: Thomson.

Weisinger, Judith, and P. Salipante. 2000. "Cultural Knowing as Practicing: Extending our Conceptions of Culture." *Journal of Management Inquiry* 9(4): 376–90.

Weisinger, Judith, and Eileen Trauth. 2002. "Situating Culture in the Global Information Sector." *Information Technology and People* 15(4): 306–20.

Wright, Susan. 1994. *Anthropology of Organisations*. London: Routledge.

———. 1998. "The Politicization of 'Culture.'" *Anthropology Today* 14(1): 7–15.

Young, Ed. 1989. "On the Naming of the Rose: Interests and Multiple Meanings as Elements of Organizational Culture." In *Organization Studies* 10(2): 187–206.

Zimmermann, J., S. Grande, and S. Johnston. 1994. "Adding Value by Working Differently: Enabling the Learning Culture." In *Transforming Organizations with information Technology: Proceedings of the IFIP Wg8.2 Working Conference on information Technology and New Emergent Forms of Organizations*, Baskerville, et al., eds. IFIP Transactions, vol. A–49: 437–50. Amsterdam: North-Holland Publishing Co.

ANOTHER LOOK

COMMENTARIES FROM
CORPORATE RESEARCH AND THE ACADEMY

Chapter 8

INSIDER TRADING

Engaging and Valuing Corporate Ethnography

Jeanette Blomberg

Inside Out

Melissa Cefkin, in her introduction to this volume, frames the discussion by asking the rhetorical question, "What are we doing there?" The readers of this collection of essays are provided a glimpse into the "what" of her question through the reflexive ethnographic accounts of the authors. The equally important and often hotly contested "we" and "there" of Cefkin's question are also offered up for our scrutiny. Undoubtedly something is going on in corporate arenas by people who variously refer to themselves as ethnographers or user researchers or experience modelers or a myriad of other designators, and they toil in a variety of relations to the corporations who provide the sites for the research and/or its sponsorship. At least one of the authors of each of the chapters in this volume is a PhD anthropologist and almost all have worked in and for corporations for a number of years. But the burgeoning field of corporate ethnography referred to by Cefkin and others in this volume is being populated by people who hail from any number of backgrounds (design, computer science, engineering, communications, human factors, marketing, business, and so on), and most learn the "trade" on the job in the contexts in which they work. And so it is imperative that we inquire specifically about those contexts and the opportunities they afford for the theory-building and game-changing aspirations of the authors of this volume, not to mention the instrumental desires of their projects.

My own experience working inside corporations for over two decades has made me aware, sometimes painfully, of how the possibilities for "what we are up to" are shaped, constrained, and signified by the specifics of who we work with, how we are funded, and what we are asked to produce. This is a concern that a number of the contributors to this volume also ponder from their particular vantage points, and one we need to keep in mind as we attempt to answer the question "What are we doing there?" and consider whether a coherent practice and discourse are coalescing from the multiple sites of ethnographic praxis. I am cautious in my views here and wonder if there really is something common and persistent that joins the "we" and the "there." A number of the authors maintain that it shouldn't be mere technique or method, but something more like worldview or relationship to the subjects of inquiry. But as always these notions are very difficult to define, pin down, or discriminate and rarely satisfy either our corporate colleagues or our academic friends. In the end perhaps it doesn't matter that there is a coherent "what" as long as what we are doing in any particular instance makes sense to us and to the array of people, organizations, and institutions that have a stake in it. And that holds for all of us, and always has, whether we are professors, product developers, consultants, teachers, or corporate ethnographers.

I will return to the concern about the coherence of the ethnographic project in corporations at the end of my commentary, but now I'd like to reflect on what the contributors to this volume are saying about the question "What are we doing there?" by addressing three themes that run throughout the volume: (1) insight and action through engagement, (2) valuing ethnography, and (3) situating ethnographic projects.

Insight and Action through Engagement

In some ways there is nothing new in the observation that we gain insight by engaging directly with the subject(s) of our inquiry. After all, this has been a hallmark of ethnography since before it had a name as explorers and missionaries brought back new insights from their encounters with people in far-off lands. And one of the emblematic practices of ethnography is participant observation where new understandings emerge in the context of doing and acting, and not just asking or observing. But for many of these authors, direct engagement is not only about gaining new insights and perspectives on the activities in focus, but also about enabling actions through the enrollment of others who are indispensable to getting something—almost anything—done inside these corporate contexts.

This issue of engagement is perhaps most directly explored in the chapter 3 by Darrouzet, Wild, and Wilkinson, who demonstrate the value of direct involvement by the subjects of study, in their case the employees of the VA hospitals. Importantly, they are enlisted not only in the characterization and analysis of hospital practices, but also in the design and implementation of specific interventions. Their approach to what they call participatory ethnography recognizes the importance of and evidences a respect for different knowledges (for example, nurses, doctors, administrators, and researchers), also a cornerstone of both ethnographic practice and cooperative or participatory design as developed in Scandinavia (Kensing and Blomberg 1999). In the complex organizations where these authors work, they have concluded that it is important to enable organization members themselves to engage in a reflective practice coupled with a progressive change agenda.

Although not the main focus of Brun-Cottan in chapter 6, she shares with the reader her pleasure in returning to the site of one of her studies to engage with a participant. Brun-Cottan is interested expressly in getting the participant's reaction to some technology design ideas, but importantly for Brun-Cottan this is an opportunity to check back to see if her characterization of the work rang true. As Brun-Cottan recounts, while her characterization of the work may have presented few surprises, this moment of participatory reflection was the occasion for Brun-Cottan's realization that some of the embodied experiences or, as Brun-Cottan refers to them, "dance steps," in her "ontological choreography" had been left out of the earlier accounts. This omission prompts Brun-Cottan's worry that in the rush to draw the instrumental lines between ethnographic insight and technology intervention, the complexities and intricacies of "informants" lives often are ignored.

Aligning Organizational Actors

Corporate ethnographers repeatedly find themselves in webs of interdependent relations with a whole host of organizational actors, not just those nominally referred to as the subjects or informants of their studies. And perhaps born out of necessity, considerable effort is often required to align these organizational actors to achieve the instrumental goals of the ethnographic project (more on the instrumental orientation of most corporate ethnography in the next section). Flynn (chapter 2) points to the necessity and importance of engaging with product developers, in her case sometimes successfully mediated through personas, where her insights only can be made "real" and actionable if translated and taken up by specific product teams. And to accomplish that Flynn must navigate intricate and sometimes convoluted organizational histories and entrenched corporate interests. Flynn's analysis reminds us that success in corporate settings is often directly dependent on establishing and harnessing relationships with differently positioned organizational actors.

In chapter 5, Nafus and anderson explore how representations on walls, flip charts, and white boards (however fleeting), and the repeated articulations and annotations of words and phrases jotted down in proverbial brainstorming sessions, enroll product developers, managers, and fellow researchers in emergent agendas and far-away places. Like Flynn's personas, these material representations provide the focus and the occasion for talk about connections between the sites of ethnographic inquiry and the interventionists objectives that are always coming in and out of view.

In reading these chapters I was reminded of the lessons we learned early on in the formation of our work-oriented or practice-based approach to technology design at Xerox PARC (Suchman el al. 1999). These lessons were born out of the frustrations and inadequacies we felt in not being able to say in just so many "bullet-pointed" design recommendations what our developer and computer science colleagues should be designing to transform (for the better?) the work and the organizations we studied. You couldn't just throw your "insights" over the wall and expect them to take hold in these other places or move their inhabitants to act. Our work required not only an engagement with those who participated directly in our research projects, be they lawyers, engineers, technicians, or office workers, but also with the developers, technical infrastructure stewards, managers, sponsors, and others who would be essential for success as measured in a variety of ways (more in the next section on how measurement regimes shape the work or corporate ethnographers). One strategy we adopted was to create what we called "case-based" prototypes that through engaged interactions provided the opportunity for work practitioners, developers, and managers alike to assess the meaning of the sociomaterial assemblages represented in the prototype. These case-based prototypes configured "working practices, hardware and software—in a way that construct[ed] a partial alignment across the heterogeneous shop floors of industrial research and development on the one hand, and various sites of work and technology use on the other" (Suchman et al. 2002). And as Flynn, and Nafus and anderson deftly portray, these material representations are always constituted in and inseparable from interactions with their interlocutors. In Nafus and anderson's words there is no "point-to-point translation" from ethnographic study to design, but instead only a sometimes messy, engaged romp with uncertain outcomes, necessarily involving those other interested and implicated coconspirators.

Externalizing Analytic Practice

Nafus and anderson's account highlights the highly distributed and iterative quality of the analytic work that characterizes ethnographic research in many corporate settings. In these situations analysis of the activities in focus (for example, street life in Brazil, the use of product documentation among software development, chip assembly in manufacturing plants, and so forth) are not easily separated from the planned or hoped for interventions simultaneously in view. In this sense prototyping practice and other representational practices of design that often occur concomitantly with analysis "simultaneously recover[s] and invent[s] work requirements and technological possibilities that make sense each in relation to the other" (Suchman et al. 2002).

While there has been a long-standing concern in anthropology and other social sciences that interventionist agendas run the risk of compromising the integrity of the analytic lens, the projects reported upon in this volume suggest the contrary. The interventions themselves can be revelatory in the quest to understand what's going on in particular settings. In our efforts to understand the document practices of civil engineers engaged in the design of a bridge (Suchman 2000a, 200b; Suchman et al. 2002; Trigg et al. 1999), we found that our engagements with the civil engineers and our computer science colleagues around the evolving prototype were precisely the moments when our understanding of certain entailments of the work of civil engineering emerged.

Similarly, the project rooms that Nafus and anderson describe become not only the settings to enroll others in their projects, but the sites for a distributed and embedded analytic activity focused around the materialized representation of events, actions and locales at the center of their studies. In some sense through these practices of "project rooms" and prototyping, the analytic activity is externalized enabling participation by differently positioned organizational actors. And in this messy mixing of expertise, points of view, and interests; those assembled contribute to, as well as take from, the encounter what they can given where they are organizationally and experientially positioned.

Success for the ethnographic project in corporations importantly involves the ability to align, through mediated engagements, many differently positioned organizational actors from study participants, to fellow researchers, to product developers, to name but a few.

 ## Valuing Ethnography

A central, although sometimes just-under-the-surface, assumption that underpins much, if not all, of the work of corporate ethnographers is that ethnography is good for something or at least it has to be argued to be good for something. Moreover that something must be valued by the corporate sponsors (for example, design a better product, invent the next big thing, reach new markets for products or services, increase the effectiveness of employees, strengthen the brand). Brian Noble (2007: 340) defines the instrumentalism characteristic of modern institutions as "actions that deliberately mobilize or enroll resources (human, tangible, intangible, technical, and so forth) to produce effects that usually, but not necessarily, entail specifically imagined ends." The ethnographic projects reflected upon by the authors of this volume clearly evidence this instrumental orientation.

Flynn's reflections on doing ethnographic research for Microsoft display the instrumental aim of the projects with which she was aligned: "inform development of … product families" and, specifically, to "cut production costs by moving 80 percent of product documentation away from paper and compact disc formats to the web." In arguing that a "bird's-eye view" understanding of complex organizations is not really possible, Darrouzet, Wild, and Wilkinson instead proffer the value of their project as increasing the ability of organizations to figure things out themselves and take action as a result. Through their participatory ethnography they enable organizations in which they work to get better at a grounded and engaged analysis of their own practices.

Brigitte Jordan (chapter 4), while acknowledging that her corporate sponsors often don't know exactly what they are looking for from her ethnographic studies, cautions that in the end they expect an outcome that arguably will contribute to improvements in their organization. This value might initially be expressed in general terms like "improve 'operational efficiency,'" but as Jordan's project continued she together with her collaborator Lambert had to engage in an ongoing fashion with their sponsors as their sponsors' appreciation for the ethnographic project evolved, and sometimes with little warning abruptly transformed.

The ethnographic projects that inform Dawn Nafus and ken anderson's (chapter 5) reflections on "the materiality of ethnographic practice within a large technology firm" have as one of their objectives to inform opportunities for new technology designs though an understanding of street life in different settings (for example, Brazil and China). Similarly Françoise Brun-Cottan's (chapter 6) sponsor was interested in novel uses for new document machine technologies just introduced to the market. In both cases the investments made in these projects were expected to lead to better or more innovative technology informed by an understanding of other people's work and lives.

Finally, Martin Ortlieb in his exploration of contrasting notions of "culture" (chapter 7), provides case-study examples of how ethnographic insights are being harnessed to adapt websites to an international marketplace. Furthermore, his argument for why it is important to get conceptualizations of culture "right" is for greater effectiveness at designing internet services for diverse, international audiences. As he writes, "Armed with that ethnographically [emergent] based kind of user understanding, products and services could be developed that deliver even more value for customers and profit for companies." The overwhelming instrumental orientation of these ethnographic projects often obliges corporate ethnographers to expend a good deal of effort articulating just what ethnography is good for in terms that can be understood by a diverse set of corporate actors. As a personal note, I find myself engaged more than I like in these discourses of the value of ethnographic research to the corporate agenda.

While this instrumentalism permeates the corporate landscape, the vehicles through which ethnography delivers its value vary within different corporate settings and include technology designs or prototypes (Flynn, Nafus and anderson, Brun-Cottan); new methods or approaches (Darrouzet, Wild, and Wilkinson; Jordan; Flynn); and new conceptualizations of the problem space (Ortlieb). As Nafus and anderson write, "It is never clear what ethnographic knowledge is speaking to—sometimes it shapes physical technologies, sometimes business strategy, but also occasionally social science itself."

The timeframes for the realization of business impact vary considerably from one project to the next and within different corporate settings. In some instances, value realization is a component of the project itself and cannot be easily distanced from the research, for example, when an ethnographic project is coupled with website design and development as was the case in the projects reported by Ortlieb. At the other extreme, ethnographic projects might only profess a benefit that will be realized within years, for example, when an ethnographic project contributes to a new model of business performance that promises to "transform" the effectiveness of service businesses, as is the situation in my own organization. Ethnographic projects need not argue for only a single value or outcome, but routinely contribute on multiple fronts, directly and over time. This is certainly true for some of the projects reported on in this volume.

Alongside the relatively tangible promises of the ethnographic project are more intangible benefits, some of which are illustrated by the contributors to this volume. Flynn discusses the role of the ethnographer in "reframe[ing] priorities, values and even relationships" within the corporation. Darrouzet, Wild, and Wilkinson argue for the value of their approach in creating new relationships through which corporate knowledge can be constructed. Nafus and anderson reveal that at Intel, "The goal is to 'change the conversation', that is, change the terms of discourse about technologies and their value to people." Jordan's project not only professes to provide her sponsors with a better understanding of how RFID tags might be integrated with their manufacturing practices, but also with codifying a set of methods and practices to enable greater participation by ethnographically trained researchers. Ortlieb is concerned not only with helping to inform the design or his company's websites, but also with changing the way organizational actors understand the notion of culture. For him this later objective will also contribute to better websites and offerings for his company's increasingly internationalized marketplace.

Lucy Suchman (1999) observed after many years working at Xerox PARC that perhaps the greatest contribution anthropologists and ethnographers working in corporate settings can make, and their biggest challenge, is opening up the spaces within specific locations for new voices and new knowledge to engage with and define corporate agendas. Echoing Suchman, Flynn offers that "[our] power as ethnographers lies in being able to reframe priorities, values and even relationships within those landscapes of production" and that the real struggle for corporate ethnographers is in providing the contexts for the "production, dissemination, and adoption of ethnographic knowledge."

In light of this challenge, and as we explore answers to Cefkin's question "What are we doing there?" we should take to heart Daniel Miller's worry that too often we are just contributing to rather than refiguring the discourses, techniques, and tools of our new interlocutors (designers, marketers, business reengineers [Miller, 2001]). In my experience one of the biggest and ongoing challenges of working inside corporations is getting our corporate colleagues to adopt a different relationship to the subject(s) of our (and their) desires, be they customers, markets, worker productivity, organizational effectiveness, or new technology. As a participant in an EPIC 2006 panel, "Considering Ethnography in Various Business Settings: What is Success?" I speculated that this particular difficulty in broadening participation in and changing the character of corporate discourse was one of the reasons corporate ethnography seemed to be rediscovered every couple of years. We are still struggling to refigure the discourse inside corporations and as such find ourselves in this state of perpetual becoming—now more than a quarter of a century since Xerox PARC hired it's first anthropologist (chapter 1; Blomberg 2006).

Situating Ethnographic Projects

A number of the papers in this volume make reference to the constraints in time, money, and focus that characterize ethnographic projects in corporate settings and some bemoan how this reduces the value of the ethnographic project. Jordan specifically grapples with the consequences of restrictions often placed on ethnographic projects in corporate settings. She suggests that corporate settings place new requirements on ethnography leading "us to think less of long-term, deep methods, and rather of economical, tightly focused tactics that produce the results the situation requires (and no more)." She associates long-term, deep methods with a kind of ethnographic ideal that characterizes academic projects historically and within our memory. Jordan argues however that even with the constraints placed on corporate ethnography it can deliver and provide value in corporate arenas. I would like to question what I think is an underlying assumption in some of these arguments, that if there was more time or money or freedom corporate ethnographers would be able to do better ethnography and as such provide even more value. My argument is not that there would be no difference in these projects, but that the ability to deliver value in terms recognizable by the corporations who sponsor the work is not principally gated by these factors of time and money, but instead by the relationships developed within these corporations through which ethnographic insights and sensibilities can have impact. I would submit that a day on the streets in Sao Paulo as viewed through the lens of decades of anthropological and sociological theory and perspective, when connected to the "right" organizational actors, can have significant impact on corporate agendas of technology production or market penetration, even in terms that might warm the hearts of corporate ethnography's most ardent critics. In my view our emphasis should not be on whether corporate ethnographic practices live up to some ideal, but rather on the "appropriate" pairings of opportunities (of access, funding, participants), research problems, and desired outcomes. This might inform not only "what" we do, but also the accountabilities we have to our discipline, collaborators and sponsors, and to social theory. Furthermore, these same choices based on access, funding, and research questions are made by those working outside corporate contexts as is evidenced in articles published in respected journals that feature ethnographic projects.

This brings me back to a point made at the beginning of my commentary, that these ethnographic projects in corporations should be examined in their own terms and should be held accountable within the context of what they are trying to achieve (for example, change the conversation in corporations or design a better web experience). There is no formula that would suggest, for example, that to internationalize a website you must conduct this many interviews, observe for this many hours or spend this many weeks on analysis. Or, at the other extreme, to advance social theory you need spend this many months in the field or this many months analyzing fieldnotes. Making advances in social theory or contributing to the disciplines from which corporate ethnographers originate, is less about whether the ethnographic projects tend to take place over days, weeks, or months or even have an explicit interventionist objective, than whether the ethnographers have the proclivity, are afforded the time, or are rewarded to participate in theory-making and discipline-advancing activities.

As alluded to earlier and called out by Cefkin in chapter 1, the chapters in this volume focus not so much on the ethnographic analysis and insights that were the presumed basis for value creation of their projects—through which the utility of the ethnographic project was displayed—but instead the authors reflect on their experiences working inside corporations, a kind of ethnography of doing ethnography in corporations. Is there something more to my observation that ethnographers working inside corporations are more likely to write about and focus on their experiences there (see table 8.1), than specifically about the ethnographic insights that result from their studies (that is, street life in Brazil, document practices among office workers)?

	Ethnographers working in or for corporations	Ethnographers working in academic institutions
Accounts of ethnographic practice	**Primarily and this volume**	**Few examples**
Ethnographic accounts of the activities and practices of others	**Few examples**	**Primarily**

Table 8.1 Focus of publications.

While there are no doubt proprietary issues that hinder publication of the specific results of these studies, if my observation is correct there is most likely more to it than that. Chief here is that the "deliverables" to which these ethnographers are accountable bear little resemblance to ethnographic accounts that might find an audience in academically oriented journals. Instead the outputs are more likely to be personas, use scenarios, prototypes, experience models, design recommendations, or feature and function lists. The effort to write ethnographic accounts that speak outside the settings of their production is often unrewarded. There are undoubtedly ethnographic texts to be written, enhanced significantly by the insider access granted to corporate ethnographers. But the paucity of such writing in my view is less about the quality of the ethnographic research or of the ethnographers involved and more about the lack of institutional support for the production of such texts. The utilitarian requirements of these projects, coupled with the substantial intrinsic rewards garnered by those who engage in them, means there is little space for such labor.

This then brings me to an issue that is indirectly touched on by some of the chapter in this volume, particularly those by Flynn and Brun-Cottan, and one that in my view plays a significant role in shaping our views of corporate ethnography. Ethnographers working in corporate settings are enmeshed in reward and measurement regimes that favor one set of activities over some others. It is not necessarily the case that the work ethnographers are doing in these corporate settings doesn't lend itself to contributing to theory or discipline discourses, but there often is little to be gained for doing so. When ethnographers working in corporate settings find themselves in contexts that reward publishing, advancing theory, and participation in academic discourses they make significant contributions (c.f., Blomberg et al. 1996; Button and Sharrock 1996; Cefkin et al. 2007; Nardi 1993, 1996, 2000; Orr 1996; Suchman 1987, 1995, 1999, 2000a). The point is not that making a contribution to academic discourse is dependent only on reward structures as there are undoubtedly examples of contributions from those who work in contexts where publishing is not valued, but that corporate sponsorship or employment should not imply that the research is of lesser quality and not suitable for scientific contribution.

In this regard perhaps we should ponder whether and in what ways the authors of these chapters are being rewarded for their labor in writing them and whether their corporate sponsors and colleagues would find their specific reflections of value. Would Flynn's colleagues be interested in her discussion of the politics of organizational life as it relates to the ability of ethnographic knowledge to deliver value? Would Jordan's corporate sponsors be occupied by her proposition that new forms of ethnographic practice are emerging through the experiences of ethnographers working in corporate settings? Would Nafus and anderson's exploration of the place of materiality in ethnographic practice excite their technology design partners? Would Brun-Cottan's cautionary tale about what gets left out of corporate tellings about the lives of study participants worry her product-development collaborators? And finally, would Ortlieb's argument for the value to corporations, and those they serve, of new (more informed, enlightened) notions of culture be likely to inspire? I don't know the answer to these questions, but I pose them to reflect on my earlier observations that "What" we are up to is shaped by who we work with, how we are funded and rewarded, and what we are expected to produce. I would speculate that in many cases the contributions to this volume are a labor of love and signal a personal commitment of the authors. Acknowledging the risks inherent in the project of corporate ethnography, but also its intellectual potential, the authors find a desire to explore the "What" in Cefkin's central question.

Outside In

My appeal that we judge the projects of corporate ethnographers on their own terms and not in relation to some ideal of ethnographic practice does not excuse me or us or them from asking the question that I would assert is never far from the thoughts of corporate ethnographers everywhere, including the authors in this volume: "In whose interests do we act and with what responsibilities to those who participate in our projects?" Cefkin highlights the importance of issues of ethics and responsibility to those who participate in our studies, pointing out that while the contributors to this volume "avoid ... self-flagellating hindsight" and a "mea culpa tone," they cannot ignore the ethical dilemmas their varied projects present. None of us, wherever we are located, can escape consideration of how what we do effects those with whom we collaborate to produce our accounts and endeavor to convey their promise. This concern is central to Brun-Cottan as she develops the notion of layered ontologies of meaning and significance. While the corporate ethnographic project invites critical reflection, at the same time those who dedicate themselves to embedding ethnographic sensibilities within corporate settings, with all the compromises and struggles involved, might also be applauded for these efforts. Brun-Cottan joins with others (Beck 2002; Blomberg et al. 1997; Nardi and Engeström 1998; Star 1999) who have found that their accounts of the situated, embodied accomplishments of workers throughout the organizational hierarchy provide management with "a clear way of seeing the knowledge and competence" of their employees. While there is nothing in these corporate settings that necessarily implores a concern for the lives of the people who are the focus of our studies, the impulse of many who work in these settings is to make a difference not only to the bottom line of the companies they work for, but also for the various people who are effected by the choices made there.

Acknowledging that there are both challenges and opportunities to "do the right thing" in these corporate settings, we are still left with the question of whether the range of things corporate ethnographers are up to cohere in a meaningful way and if we should insist that they do. Ultimately corporate ethnographers must identify concrete channels through which impact and value can be realized and understood in terms recognizable by the corporations in which they work, but their greater contribution may be in changing the conversation inside corporations, and providing voice for perspectives and people not often heard. Returning to the three themes that organized my commentary, insight and action through engagement, valuing ethnography, and situating ethnographic projects, we might rightly conclude that corporate ethnographers who actively engage with those who stand to gain (or lose) from their projects, who recognize the value in changing the terms of the debate inside corporations, and who find ways to participate in discourses that expand our understandings and not simply corporate profits should be encouraged and applauded. In response to Cefkin's question "What are we doing there?," the authors in this volume can say they are doing exactly that.

References

Beck, Eevi. 2002. "P for Political—Participation is Not Enough." *Scandinavian Journal of Information Systems* 14: 77–92.

Blomberg, Jeanette. 2006. "Between Hype and Promise: Two Decades of Becoming." *Ethnographic Praxis in Industry Conference Proceedings*, 76–77. American Anthropological Association.

Blomberg, Jeanette, Lucy Suchman, and Randy Trigg. 1997. "Back to Work: Renewing Old Agendas for Cooperative Design." In *Computers and Design in Context*, Kyng and Mathiassen, eds., 268–87. Cambridge, MA: MIT Press.

———. 1996. "Reflections on a Work-Oriented Design Project." *Human-Computer Interaction* 11: 237–65.

Button, Graham, and West Sharrock. 1996. "Project Work: The Organisation of Collaborative Design and Development in Software Engineering." *Computer Supported Cooperative Work* 5(4): 369–86.

Cefkin, Melissa, Jakita Thomas, and Jeanette Blomberg. 2007. "The Implications of Enterprise-wide Pipeline Management Tools for Organizational Relations and Exchanges." *Proceedings of Group '07*, 61–68. ACM Press.

Kensing, Finn, and Jeanette Blomberg. 1998. "Participatory Design: Issues and Concerns." *Computer Supported Cooperative Work* 7(3–4): 163–65.

Miller, Daniel. 2001. *Consumption: Critical Concepts in the Social Sciences.* London/New York: Routledge.

Nardi, Bonnie. 1993. *A Small Matter of Programming: Perspectives on End User Computing.* Cambridge, MA: MIT Press.

———. 1996 *Context and Consciousness: Activity Theory and Human-Computer Interaction.* Cambridge, MA: MIT Press.

Nardi, Bonnie, and Vicki O'Day. 2000 *Information Ecologies: Using Technology with Heart.* Cambridge, MA: MIT Press.

Nardi, Bonnie, and Yrjö Engeström, eds. 1998. "A Web on the Wind: The Structure of Invisible Work." Special Issue. *Computer-Supported Cooperative Work* 8(1): 1–8.

Noble, Brian. 2007. "Justice, Transaction, Translation: Blackfoot Tipi Transfers and WIPO's Search for the Fracts of Traditional Knowledge Exchange." *American Anthropologist* 109(2): 338–49.

Orr, Julian. 1996. *Talking about Machines: An Ethnography of a Modern Job.* Ithaca, NY: Cornell University Press.

Star, Susan Leigh, and Anselm Strauss. 1999. "Layers of Silence, Arenas of Voice: The Ecology of Visible and Invisible Work." *Computer Supported Cooperative Work* 8(1–2): 9–30.

Suchman, Lucy. 1987. *Plans and Situated Actions: The Problem of Human-Machine Communication.* Cambridge: Cambridge University Press.

———. 1995. Special Issue: Representations of Work. *Communications of the ACM* 38(9).

———. 1999. "Working Relations of Technology Production and Use." In *The Social Shaping of Technology,* second edition, MacKenzie and Wajcman, eds., 258–65. Buckingham: Open University Press.

———. 2000a. "Organizing Alignment: A Case of Bridge-Building." *Organization* 7(2): 311–27.

———. 2000b. "Embodied Practices of Engineering Work." *Mind, Culture & Activity* 7(1–2): 4–18.

Suchman, Lucy, et al. 1999. "Reconstructing Technologies as Social Practice." Special Issue. *American Behavioral Scientist on Analysing Virtual Societies: New Directions in Methodology* 43(3; November/December): 392–408.

Suchman, Lucy, Randy Trigg, and Jeanette Blomberg. 2002. "Working Arefacts: Ethnomethods of the Protopye." *British Journal of Sociology* 53(2): 163–79.

Trigg, Randy, Jeanette Blomberg, and Lucy Suchman. 1999. "Moving Document Collections Online: The Evolution of a Shared Repository." *Proceedings of the European Computer Supported Cooperative Work Conference,* 331–50.

Chapter 9

EMERGENT FORMS OF LIFE
IN CORPORATE ARENAS

Michael M. J. Fischer

Stem Cells for the Regeneration of Ethnographic Life?

Corporate arenas form one of the key sites—along with cousin-sites in the technosciences (biological, informatic, material sciences), financial arenas, environmental understandings, and media environments—for the development of new anthropologies and ethnographic practices to reflect upon, inform, and reconstruct the changing worlds and emergent forms of life in which we live. Sometimes referred to with "tags" such as "second-order modernization," "reflexive social institutions," "flexible" labor and production forces, "learning organizations," and multiple, flexible, and continually retrainable selves, macro-social theory has long been sketching large and small shifts for which corporate arenas are key ethnographic production sites.

These "production sites" of emergent, sometimes uncomfortable and bizarrely self-misrecognizing forms of life have long been target arenas for a variety of overlapping fields of social research and intervention, including Taylorism, social architecture (such as Margarete Shütte-Lihotzky's widely disseminated "Frankfurt kitchens" and kindergarten pavilions [Reisman 2006: 43–44, 53–55], or the open-office formats passed back and forth between Germany and the US [Schwarz 2002]), applied anthropology, work-practice studies, organizational behavior, occupational psychology, consumption studies (Sunderland and Denny 2007), and STS (science, technology, and society). Patricia Sunderland and Rita Denny remind us of the interconnections between the advertising industry and many of the University of Chicago's famous anthropologists and sociologists in the 1940s and 1950s, beginning with the founding of SRI (Social Research, Inc.) by W. Lloyd Warner, Bill Henry, and Burleigh Gardner, and continuing into the 1980s via anthropologist Steve Barnett's role in New York, and business school anthropologists such as John F. Sherry, Jr., and Grant McCracken. Sid Levy (of symbolic analysis fame), Erving Goffman, Lee Rainwater, Anselm Strauss, Herbert Gans, Gerald Handel, Carl Rogers, David Reisman, Robert Redfield, Everett Hughes, and Herbert Blumer are some of the marquee names that float by, reminding of the ties between consumer research, popular-culture analysis, and qualitative method development.

But there is also a specific history, or lineage, of contemporary ethnographic work within and for corporations, outlined in Melissa Cefkin's invaluable overview (chapter 1), beginning in the late 1970s at Xerox PARC, first with the hiring of anthropologist Eleanor Wynn, and a few consultants such as Brigitte Jordan, and then with the famed Work Practice and Technology Group led by Lucy Suchman. The equally famed IRL (Institute for Research Learning), founded and promoted by John Seely Brown with grants from the Xerox Foundation, was a sister initiative, with some such as Brigitte Jordan having joint appointments. Others in the present volume who worked either at PARC or IRL, or as subcontractors to IRL, include Jeanette Blomberg, Melissa Cefkin, Chris Darrouzet, Helga Wild, and Susann Wilkinson.

Among the distinctive features of this lineage of ethnographic work, as it continues to evolve in the fascinating self-analyses in this volume, are the "ethnographically sensitive deliverables" rather than ethnographies per se: the idea that the consumer is buying an ongoing set of interactions (of which ethnographic feedback is a component) rather than a stand-alone deliverable; that internal "culture wars" or deeply embedded perspectival and presuppositional differences (between designers and strategists, among product teams, ethnographers, and clients) need to be made visible for negotiation; that such culture wars can become embedded in product outcomes ("artifacts have politics"); that collaboration itself is an intense field of political competition for resources, status, and power; that, in the IRL mantra, work, learning and change are social and informal rather than rule governed, and require ethnographic awareness; and, perhaps, that the dissemination of ethnographic sensibilities as general common sense might be analogous to the Web 2.0 notion of engaging distributed wisdom, rather than relying on command-and-control expertise that is inevitably narrowed and generative of indifference, resistance, and brittleness.

The corporate worlds invoked in this volume are neither generic nor insignificant: Intel, IBM, Microsoft, the VA, Yahoo, and consulting firms such as Veri-phi are major players in life today, and are fitting hosts for culturing new forms of ethnography that are not only responsive and accountable to multiple audiences, but are productive of multiple forms of results. The calls for collaboration, polyvocality, benefit to subjects, and other "ethical" forms of anthropological practices have long been articulated within the profession, but find particularly compelling and challenging configurations in corporate arenas. Among these, sooner or later the bottom line of contribution to profitability, if not totally determining of the conditions for the possibility for research, comes into play. At the same time another competing condition for the possibility of the research requires that ethnographic research not be absorbed into the pure instrumentality of short-term cost-benefit relations subordinated to current management practices, lest it lose its distinctive ability to contribute fresh perspectives and thereby earn its keep. If accountability to business needs and to professional charges are two audiences, other audiences include the local workforces as well as the clients, customers, or users of the corporate services and products. Multiple audiences require multiple forms of production and products. The calls for experimental forms of writing within anthropology have been constant since Bronislaw Malinowski (realist translation of cultural worlds), E. E. Evans-Pritchard (structural problematics), Max Gluckman (legal case study formats), Victor Turner (social dramas revealing structural conflicts), Laura Bohanan (repetition of situations with deepening layered understandings), Gananath Obeysekere (psychoanalytic case-study formats), Claude Levi-Strauss (hermeneutic-structuralist semiotics), and Clifford Geertz (hermeneutic-interpretive and stoic-ironic philosophical formats), to mention but a few. But corporate worlds elicit yet again new forms not just of literal writing (reports, memos, proposals, protocols, white board notes, fieldnotes), but also of performative interventions (films, videos, wikis, websites, meetings, discovery tactics, creating new channels of communication) that have both immediate effects and leave variable "half-life" traces in the social text (as Paul Ricoeur famously formulated it, and Geertz popularized it).

The popularization of ethnographic methods in a variety of fields beyond anthropology proper might be analogized, as suggested above, to the contemporary spread of the digital media and especially the so-called Web 2.0 principles of collective production (including the critical tagging of entries with their degrees and sources of verifiability, and their background notes on disputes, lacunae, and need for further input). In other words, can the spread of an ethnographic sensibility become part of a general common sense that would allow the construction, evolution, or mutation of new flexible "smart" institutions of so-called second-order modernization to replace old, brittle bureaucratic forms of command and control?

And recursively then, what can the access to corporate arenas teach us in re-theorizing how we think about the social worlds we participate in, that surround us, and that produce much of the texture of our lives, whether or not we actually work within their legal, organizational, and conventional confines? Complexity is a disciplining first feature of such theorizing, not as a vague hand-waving refusal to detail, but on the contrary as a yoga of being able to accommodate, control for, repurpose, work around, patch, leverage, retool, and coach. Indeed the executive and life-coaching industry is a small index of the mutations from earlier efficiency, psychotherapy, operations research, and management languages (Ozkan 2007). It would be interesting to speculate on the cultural possibilities latent in these worlds, both as reflected in such creative writing as by Douglas Coupland's sardonic *Microserfs*, and the engaging science fiction stories in *Infinite Loops* (Constantine 1993), written by artificial-intelligence and media-lab types. There are indeed hints at such extended possibilities in this volume's chapters.

Of Media and Retooling Genres

Each of the chapters in this volume provides a different retooled genre of reflection on the "betwixt and between position of ethnography in firms" (Nafus and anderson, chapter 5).

Flynn provides a topological analysis of the dynamics of identification (slyly hinting at their now-you-see-it-now-you-don't Moebius-like Freudian and Lacanian possibilities) in the construction of short-hand "personas" of typical users, in the impression management (Goffman 1959) enforced by organizational insistence on an individualism belied by collaborative necessities, and in the fierce political competition for resources, status, and power that goes under the idealizing notion of collaboration. Genre-wise, Flynn's essay hints at a cross between these Lacanian topologies of displacements, hiding of things in the open, and cracks in the mirror scenes (of projecting wholeness where there are but partial understandings) on the one hand, and on the other hand experimental knowledge about interrelations of, and conflicts between, roles gained in small group psychology and family systems therapy settings. (In such systems therapy, whether in dysfunctional families or in manipulation of task leaders or emotion leaders in small groups, one can introduce a shift in "scripts" or "functional role" for one player and watch how the scripts and roles of other players reconfigure.)

More than this, she suggests that ethnographic knowledges need to be analyzed in the plural quite as much as the products produced by Microsoft. Ethnographic knowledges emerge in process (not as fixed end points), shifting from perspective to perspective, from communication circuit to circuit, highlighting the frictions and unintended transductions across circuits. Microsoft, thanks to Douglas Coupland (1994) and others, is already a rich cultural arena of folklore, and Flynn also exploits this richness (Microsofties, Microsoft builds for Microsoft, mind-share, "user-experience" teams) in a way that others might well want to follow in order to build into our everyday discourse about corporations as a quite different model than that of *The Organization Man* of the 1950s (Whyte 1956), or the wacky driven nerds of Coupland's novel, or Scott Adam's *Dilbert* corporate-life comics. There is life here, indeed a variety of emergent forms of life in Wittgenstein's sense of pragmatic actions leaving legacies of socialities, or Riceour's sense of social action leaving legible traces. Flynn reminds us that it was not only Robert Moses who showed us that artifacts have politics (Winner 1986), but also more everyday objects and technologies do as well. Here Flynn reminds us that collaboration is not a fuzzy feel-good ideal, nor just something that people of good will work at, but is a highly fraught field of competitive politics.

Flynn provides a critique here on the culture of individualism socially engineered and disciplined at Microsoft, and the self-recognition generated by management that one needs anthropologists to help with vigilance against assumptions about customer needs, technological uses and behaviors. The creation of personas to represent ideal typical customers is ambivalently a useful shortcut and a potential source of misrecognition, but behind it stands a deeper triangular conflict, and set of almost Lacanian misrecognitions among product teams who identify with customers (who they often once were), anthropologists (looked down on by the techies, but looked to by customers to help with the over-identification of the techies with their particular product and with the customer), and customers (who need to integrate non-interoperable products from Microsoft, hence the joke: Microsoft builds products for Microsoft rather than for real customers). The primary puzzle remains, on the one hand, the long corridors of identical offices, insistence on creativity from the lone mind looking at or through the screen, and only catch-as-catch-can spaces to collaborate, enforced by annual reviews with no discounting or addition for group work. On the other hand, there are the productive Microsoft groups that need to actually put products together (and of course as the innumerable jokes go, fix the bugs later).

Darrouzet, Wild, and Wilkinson provide the closest example of the case-study genre, but with great effect they retool the case study to articulate a performative function for ethnography, one that teaches people within the largest health care system in the US, the VA, how to do their own participatory ethnography as well as participate in design for a reorganization of work processes. A historical trace is acknowledged as helping provide an opening: the leaders of reorganization of the VA under Kenneth Kizer in 2005–6 had heard of, and believed in, "the IRL mantra about work learning and change being mainly social and informal." What professional ethnographers provide is the staging, a mise-en-scène and safe space, for discussions that people otherwise have as corridor talk, gossip, or other means of social control and leverage, but which benefit from open acknowledgment and negotiation in non-personalized ways that open possibilities rather than reinforce barriers. "Ethnography done well is also about growing relations among people ... and from this generate a refreshed model of that con-joint 'reality' that can be reflected and acted upon." These are three critical and separate notions: growing relations, periodically and regularly "refreshing" (as for a computer screen), and externalizing for not just reportage but for acting upon. Speaking *about* others, Darrouzet, Wild and Wilkinson remind us (nicely reformulating Johannes Fabian 1983), needs to be backed up by speaking *with* others. The case study of bed control and patient discharge is a vivid demonstration of how a flow chart would not be the same. A telling small item is that of the bed control nurse wisely not trusting the computer, where staff can hide beds or push them off to the next shift, not out of maliciousness but out of system dynamics. Even more telling, is the lovely analogy from the chief of clinical staff that the professional ethnographic process gave the organization "an opposable thumb," the externalized mise-en-scène for critical reflection and making it possible to build consensus for organizational change.

A third genre tweaking: Jordan might be read as annotating a Non-Disclosure Agreement (NDA), a kind of document that is becoming a negotiated tool of access for academic anthropology in its claims to have relevance both for analysis of, and providing return benefit to, corporate forms of life. Jordan does not invoke the legal genre of NDAs. I am drawing a parallel or comparison between the formal, prescriptive, and proscriptive NDA and the constantly renegotiated agreements and redefinitions that emerge in the course of fieldwork. I am intrigued by the internal walls and "no-go" zones within corporations as well as between corporations and potential rivals. A recent stark example: having bought an iPhone, I found not only were AT&T representatives in some places not allowed to touch them or have access to billing and accounting records, but even between a corporate office of AT&T in Cambridge, MA, and its supervisors in Texas certain information was not allowed to be directly passed in order to correct a glitch in the billing system. All the supervisor was willing to do was provide hints until his representative figured out a patch or workaround himself. At issue are various kinds of barriers, with differential porosities, to the free flow of information, sometimes to protect profits, sometimes to protect information turf and power relations, and sometimes just unintended inefficiencies in work practices.

Non-disclosure agreements not only sit betwixt and between intellectual property (IP) requirements and academic scholarship (ideally premised on free flow of information), but also might be used as a way to open up the increasingly troubled nature of Institutional Review Boards (IRBs) in academic scholarship. IRBs were originally instituted in medical research to protect experimental subjects, but through "mission creep" due to fear of litigation, university lawyers and administrators have increasingly abandoned protecting First Amendment rights and freedom of research in favor of extending the term "experimental subjects" to all human beings (and animals in the case of IRBs for animal research), less to protect them than to protect the university institutions from lawsuits. Not surprisingly, this concern for the ethics of research is asymmetrically applied more to less well funded disciplines (ethnography, sociology, history) than to well-funded, high-stakes disciplines (biotechnology, human genome projects, human diversity genome projects) where researchers acknowledge ELSI (ethical, legal, and social issues) concerns in principle but argue ferociously for the right of inquiry wherever it leads. At issue are fascinating complex economic and legal, as well as cultural presuppositional pressures and counterpressures, that bear ethnographic detailing, beyond any simple abstract solutions or easy emotional indignation.

Internal pressures of corporate anthropologists might provide some insight and guidelines about the dynamics of what is truly important to corporations and what can be negotiated in innovative ways. The brief case examples here of chip manufacturing in Costa Rica and Malaysia are suggestive, both of methods ("follow the lot"), and of the often complementary need for rapid versus deep ethnography. It is fascinating how parts of the intellectual property restriction dynamics apply to Intel's own anthropologists working within the corporation attempting to contribute to its own better management, just as they would to an outside consultant or anthropologist. One is reminded that access always has elements of serendipity, personal relations, or location in the institution, but it is also fascinating how invisible or unrecognized critical work (face to face communication between shifts, reconciling machine data and on-the-ground data, and so forth) are further screened out by these blocks to externalized reflection, and even if revealed during discovery processes, are repackaged and black boxed in management reports. Considerable sophistication, tact, and restraint is required to negotiate these constraints even in the context of desirous corporate sponsors and willing anthropologists who come with different presuppositions, and capacities to "hear." The case-study examples in their archive of situational experiences demonstrate the power of ethnographic detailing over abstract acknowledgment of difficulties: it is the eventual successes, not the frequent barriers, that are most enlightening about situational configurations and possibilities.

Nafus and anderson perform a welcome anthropological retooling of some tropes and moves in Science, Technology and Society (STS), as well as social memory studies, by taking white boards and other intermediate artifacts (things, material-semiotic objects, boundary objects) as indexes both of the postmodern firm's shifting assemblages, instabilities, and sudden strategy corrections; and also of the notions of complexity and of the very media of what constitutes research and feedback. What is particularly important here is again the ethnographic detailing of how material artifacts themselves become mediators in understanding heterogeneity and instability, and how "this in turn means producing, sustaining, and destroying many boundary objects, that is, things in which many have shared stakes but on radically different terms and often to different ends." Again this is, as with the performative processes described by Darrouzet, Wild, and Wilkinson, about making active a process that "invites people who did not perform the field research into the production of knowledge," and about making possible a great deal of decentering work and reconfiguration. These processual ethnographic sensibilities are important both in translations from researchers to designers, or producers to marketers, or company to customers; but also in the extended social lives that videos, notes, photographs, diagrams, and quotes can have beyond the immediate projects and contexts of their production. As they say, complexity has directionality, "knowledge does not just circulate, but is consistently made to appear as if it were new, regardless of its origins," and so this itself will call for the subsequent need for an opposable thumb of ethnographic processes to reconsider and configure anew.

Brun-Cottan provides two short case studies in which she, like Flynn, hints again at a Lacanian duality—"I understand what she said, but what did she mean by it?" ("You are trying to get rid of people")—as well as triangular misrecognitions (between music teacher, IT support, and product marketing), but she tracks us also into a sharper focus on processual dramas and choreographies (like Jordan, and Nafus and anderson), where the ephemera of intervening in "artful and principled ways" is what often counts much more than the final report. The opening anecdote about the psychic dissociation and belated recognition by the anthropologist of Dee's worry about job loss and devaluation of her work life reminds of the persistent tropes of anxiety from the early worries about automation in the 1950s to perennial worries about working for humanitarian aid or development projects, or even academic ethnographies of quasi-isolated groups: Am I contributing to the destruction of this way of life? Just who in the end are you working for, despite your intentions and those of your employer? It is, of course, not only engineers and marketers, but also anthropologists, who are caught up in larger structures than themselves. The second anecdote about the music teacher who wanted to use a web platform to download music compositions and upload student compositions as a teaching tool and shareware with other schools is a more intricate icon of our times. He found he didn't have the rights to download, couldn't change the operating system settings to enable the uploads (fixed so that users couldn't overload and choke the system), and in general faced that hydra-headed monster of passwords, permissions, privacy protections, and code that defeated many a good educational project in the early days of the digital-media revolution, and that continues to bedevil companies, schools, and consumers. As with the large amount of necessary invisible work in paperless offices (Schwarz 2002) and in Jordan's examples, users must hire support staff to help them negotiate the interesting, changing, and maddening complexities. In Brun-Cottan's preliminary example of the document-management system for a specialty large-scale construction machine manufacturer, one of the proprietary and secrecy issues is the access to the technology of the one company by another by virtue of providing a service. One can begin to imagine the burden of licensing, NDA, and other legal instruments, as well as informal work arrangements, that both facilitate and slow our techno-scientific lives.

Like other chapters in this volume, Brun-Cottan explores the dilemmas of, on the one hand, having to mine data to fit instrumental communication, and, on the other hand, having to demonstrate that the ethnographic value is not in such formats, but in what people do as opposed to what they say they do, in cultural presuppositions that they act out even in contradiction to what they profess, in unpacking the meaning of abstract pronouncements and value statements, in showing the ramifications of small things having large impacts—all things that are quite "hard" and empirical, and thus precisely not massageable into "soft" statistical or stereotypical short cuts.

Ortlieb deploys lightning fast sound-byte "case studies" as analogies in a demonstration that not only do ethnographic knowledges need to be pluralized (as in Flynn), but so do the formation of cultures: consumer cultures, organizational cultures, working class cultures, and professional cultures are as different kinds of categories as are national, ethnic, religious, or linguistic ones. In some sense, as Cefkin points out in chapter 1, Ortlieb is in conversation with Sunderland and Denny exploring the fixed categories that businesses often fantasize of, but can never quite seize, versus the always-in-process indexical cues with which actors constantly unweave and reweave the variations that give cultural meaning. Sunderland and Denny's funniest case is of their struggles with ethnic consultants who think they need to discipline their market, fixing it, lest it evaporate (and, ipso facto, evaporating, if not their jobs, their fantasized comparative advantage in getting advertising contracts) into the general marketing that consumers often turn out to desire instead. Ortlieb, with super quick, light strokes, reminds that global advertising campaigns have (since Coke in the 1970s, and Lever Brothers even earlier) had to learn over and over that not all commodities translate uniformly. Lever Brothers for many years held a monopoly over many rural products in India because of its vast army of outlets providing localized feedback. What is interesting about the campaigns and their morphing forms is not so much whether cultures are relatively fixed or not, but how the marketing itself reveals the differentials and shifts in common sense and desire in different places, market niches, and status hierarchies. Used-car markets in Germany, Mexico, and Japan function differently, and used car markets in turn are quite different from the dynamics of e-services such as Yahoo. The history Ortlieb indexes is from old product acceptability to participatory design, from focus groups to usability studies, and from anthropological-designer collaboration to exploring latent user needs, product stickiness, and alternative business strategies. What next needs exploring is how the vast databases generated by Yahoo, Amazon, eBay, and other e-services are changing the landscapes of possibilities and product formation, of subjectivation, and citizen formation. All those tough ethical questions highlighted by Brun-Cottan are returning in intensified forms that Lever Brothers' information hoards could never have anticipated.

Beyond Method

Beyond the rich work on which this volume lifts a corner of the curtain, lies the question, To what extent can we in academia exploit the access of our colleagues in the corporate world to generate richer understandings of their fields of production, beyond what business school case studies or investigative journalists provide? Are the NDAs of employment too confining for this, and how could we make it otherwise? Could corporate anthropologists ever be allowed to produce the equivalent of such studies of the biotech industry as those by Barry Werth, Paul Rabinow, Kaushik Sunder Rajan, or Melinda Cooper; of the IT world such as those by Gabriella Coleman, Chris Kelty, or Hal Abelson, Ken Ledeen, and Harry Lewis; or (from the legal world) Lawrence Lessig; or of the financial world as those by Donald MacKenzie? Or is that request less in conflict just with

NDAs, and rather more in conflict with the new ethnographic products being developed, and should we rather look to more volumes like this one that can build up an archive of situated experiences, ethnographies of social context, and social dramas of collaborative politics?

The conceptual contributions of corporate ethnographers, as registered in this volume, are significant. Not only are such terms as "complexity" thematized in several of the chapters in interestingly grounded and different ways, that make them ripe for study and analysis. The varieties of ethnographies tailored to different purposes are invoked and illustrated: light and deep ethnography, rapid ethnographies, management-school ethnographies, and para-ethnographies. Ethnography as a frame of mind (not just discrete methods and tools) is transformed by its uses. While it can be instrumentalized (for good and ill, for profit, and for screening out information important to the company's bottom line had a bit more time been invested), it also transforms the notion of epistemological encounter, making it performative: ethnography as everyday consciousness, and as making social interaction into a model for reflection and action, not just a role-playing game (as in earlier performative genres for worker motivation, family therapy, or conflict mediation).

Answers to these substantive and conceptual questions will emerge as the practice deepens and evolves. Extraordinary that in 2004 Intel should have been reported to have spent five billion dollars on ethnographic research, or that as many major corporations as listed in Melissa Cefkin's introduction (chapter 1) should have anthropologists on staff. One way, I have suggested in my readings of these essays, is to ask the epistemological question about whether the genres of writing, presentation (could be film, slide shows, whiteboards, workshops, quotes, anime), and reflection, in their variety, can help us push our questioning further, opening up new layers of configuration and interaction, insight, and even entertainment and pleasure.

References

Abelson, Hal, Ken Ledeen, Harry Lewis. 2008. *Blown to Bits: Your Life, Liberty and Happiness after the Digital Explosion.* Boston: Addison-Wesley.

Coleman, Gabriella. 2005. "The Social Construction of Freedom in Free and Open Source Software: Hackers, Ethics, and the Liberal Tradition." PhD Dissertation, University of Chicago.

Constantine, Larry, ed. 1993. *Infinite Loops: Stories about the Future by the People Creating It.* San Francisco, CA: Miller Freeman.

Cooper, Melinda. 2008. *Life as Surplus: Biotechnology and Capitalism in the Neoliberal Era.* Seattle: University of Washington Press.

Coupland, Douglas. 1995. *Microserfs.* New York: Harper-Collins.

Fabian, Johannes. 1983. *Time and the Other: How Anthropology Makes its Object.* New York: Columbia University Press.

Goffman, Erving. 1959. *The Presentation of Self in Everyday Life.* New York: Doubleday.

Kelty, Chris. 2008. *Two Bits: Free Software and the Social Imagination after the Internet.* Durham: Duke University Press.

Lessing, Lawrence. 1999. *Code and Other Laws of Cyberspace.* New York: Basic Books.

———. 2001. *The Future of Ideas: The Fate of Commons in a Connected World.* New York: Random House

———. 2004. *Free Culture: How Big Media Uses Technology and the Law to Lock Down Culture and Control Creativity.* New York: Penguin.

MacKenzie, Donald. 2006. *An Engine, Not a Camera: How Financial Models Shape Markets.* Cambridge, MA: MIT Press.

Ozkan, Esra. 2007. "Executive Coaching: Crafting a Versatile Self in Corporate America." PhD dissertation, MIT (STS). Cambridge, MA.

Rabinow, Paul. 1995. *Making PCR.* Chicago: University of Chicago Press.

Reisman, Arnold. 2006. *Turkey's Modernization: Refugees from Nazism and Atatürk's Vision.* Washington, DC: New Academia.

Schwarz, Heinrich. 2002. "Techno-Territories: The Spatial, Technological and Social Reorganization of Office Work." PhD dissertation, MIT (STS). Cambridge, MA.

Sunder Rajan, Kaushik. 2006. *Biocapital: The Constitution of Postgenomic Life.* Durham: Duke University Press.

Sunderland, Patricia, and Rita M. Denny. 2007. *Doing Anthropology in Consumer Research.* Walnut Creek, CA: Left Coast Press.

Werth, Barry. 1994. *The Billion Dollar Molecule: One Company's Quest for the Perfect Drug.* New York: Simon and Schuster.

Whyte, William H. 1956. *The Organization Man.* New York: Simon and Schuster.

Winner, Langdon. 1986. *The Whale and the Reactor.* Chicago, IL: University of Chicago Press.

CONTRIBUTORS

ken anderson is at Intel Research where he conducts ethnographic research of human cultures and social practices to inform corporate strategy and technology development. His specialties are in globalization, identity, and urban studies.

Jeanette Blomberg is an anthropologist who has worked in corporate research for over 20 years. She is currently a member of the Service Research group at the IBM Almaden Research Center. Prior to her current position, Jeanette was a founding member of the pioneering Work Practice and Technology group at the Xerox Palo Alto Research Center (PARC), a director of experience modeling research at Sapient Corporation and an industry affiliated professor at the Blekinge Institute of Technology in Sweden. Jeanette received her PhD from the University of California, Davis, where she was a lecturer in cultural anthropology and sociolinguistics.

Françoise Brun-Cottan is a senior research scientist who has spent more than a decade as a work place ethnographer and interaction analyst at Xerox PARC. She now consults for libraries as well as large corporations, and also produces personal oral histories and memoirs for/with individuals.

Melissa Cefkin is a member of the Services Research group at IBM. A Fulbright award grantee with a PhD in anthropology from Rice University, Melissa has experience in research, management, teaching, and consulting. With a particular interest in the performative dimensions of work and identity, she is dedicated to pursuing a critical understanding of the intersections of anthropological practice within business and organizational settings. Melissa was previously a director of user experience and member of the Advanced Research group at Sapient Corporation. Prior to that, she was a senior research scientist at the Institute for Research on Learning (IRL).

Chris Darrouzet is cofounder and principal of Water Cooler Logic, Inc., a consulting firm. He was a senior research scientist at the Institute for Research on Learning in Menlo Park in the 1990s, prior to which he worked on technical staff at several major computer companies in Silicon Valley. He earned his PhD in anthropology from the University of North Carolina, Chapel Hill, in 1985, having conducted his thesis research on social and cultural in change in Papua New Guinea.

Michael M. J. Fischer teaches at MIT and Harvard and has been a practitioner, observer, and theorist of changes in anthropological and ethnographic methods in fields from religion and social change to science studies and corporate consultancies. One of his recent essays on this subject is "Culture and Cultural Analysis as Experimental Systems," which will be a chapter in his forthcoming book, *Anthropological Futures.*

Donna K. Flynn is a Senior Manager in Microsoft's consumer experience strategy group. She has led strategic research projects and user experience research teams on a wide range of business and consumer users, and specializes in international ethnographic approaches. Donna received her PhD in anthropology at Northwestern University in 1997. As a Fulbright scholar, she investigated impacts of cross-border trade movements and smuggling on West African border communities. She then went on to work in applied research on economic development and microfinance, leading projects at the International Center for Research on Women, the US Agency for International Development, and the World Bank. Prior to joining Microsoft in 2003, Donna was a senior manager of user experience for Sapient Corporation in San Francisco.

Brigitte Jordan has carried out ethnographic research for more than thirty years in academic and corporate settings. Now working as a freelance consultant, she previously held an appointment as a principal scientist at Xerox PARC and at the Institute for Research on Learning. Her special interests and expertise lie in the adaptation of ethnographic methods to physical, hybrid, and virtual ecologies. Many of her publications can be found at her website www.lifescapes.org.

Monique H. Lambert is principal investigator of clinical practices research in Intel Corporation's Digital Health Group. Monique's research focuses on the dynamics of work, technology, and organization in complex organizations. Monique's most recent research includes clinical workflow and work-practice studies of acute-care nursing in the inpatient environment, and telehealth and chronic-care nursing in disease management, home-care, and community-health organizations in the outpatient environment. Monique's prior research includes ethnographic operations research of Intel's high-volume chip-manufacturing, assembly/test, and warehousing/

distribution facilities, and ethnographic research of Mars mission design at NASA's Jet Propulsion Lab. Monique holds BS and MS degrees in materials science and engineering from the University of Illinois at Urbana-Champaign and the University of Washington at Seattle, respectively, and a PhD in engineering from Stanford University with a specialization in organization science.

Martin Ortlieb is a design anthropologist who has been applying qualitative, quantitative, and ethnographic research methodologies to develop far-reaching strategic and tactical solutions for products and services in a broad range of industries, from snack food via cameras and mobile telephones to lots of work in the WWW. He has worked in multi-disciplinary teams, and has taken an active role in extending collaborative approaches. He gained his PhD from the University of Manchester on working with Northern Finnish dairy farmers. Even then he was fascinated by how adept the farmers were in adopting new technology and how they had done remote banking before the internet was even invented. Martin recently joined Google as a senior user experience researcher in Europe.

Dawn Nafus is an anthropologist at Intel Research in Portland, Oregon. She holds a PhD from the University of Cambridge, and is interested in discourses of "the technological," cultural notions of time, migration and mobility, and gender and technology. She has done research in Russia and the UK.

Helga Wild was introduced to qualitative methods and ethnography as member of the Institute for Research on Learning after a decade in experimental neuropsychology. She worked as researcher and project manager for the Institute, looking into the connection of work, learning, and space in a number of corporate projects. She founded Water Cooler Logic, Inc., with Chris Darrouzet to deliver an organizational-change and improvement approach that embodies the principles of social learning. She has delivered the Water Cooler Logic approach in over forty projects focusing on complex management issues within a large government agency.

Susann Wilkinson began her study of work places and work practices in 1982 in the oil and chemical refineries of east Texas. She has since conducted action research on the roles of regulatory agencies, industry, professionals, and financing bodies, in the emergence of new medical technologies. Her current focus on work-practice analysis and promoting organizational and social learning was inspired by association with the former Institute for Research on Learning and Water Cooler Logic, Inc.

INDEX

and space, 44, 56n1, 140; versus individualism, 44, 230
collaborative ethnography, 9, 65
commercial ethnography, 186, 197, 198, 202, 203, 204. *See also* corporate ethnography
commoditization of anthropology, 21, 159. *See also* corporate ethnography
communities of practice, 67, 91, 101, 165, 166
competition as organizational practice, 44–46, 54. *See also* collaboration
Complexity and Group Processes: A Radically Social Understanding of Individuals (Stacey), 71
complexity, 25, 62–63, 67–71, 230; and anthropology, ethnography, 72, 89, 92n7; as detailing of boundary objects, 234; as field of negotiations, 230; and systems thinking, 68–70
complexity science(s) and theory, 63, 68, 69, 71, 92n4
Computer-Human Interaction (CHI), 7
Computer-Supported Collaborative Work (CSCW), 7
Connerton, Paul, 141, 153
Constantine, Larry, 230; *Infinite Loops*, 230
consumption or consumer studies, 11, 227; compared to workplace studies, 13, 19–20, 31n16
context as aspect of culture, 186, 196, 198, 200, 203
Conversation Analysis, 165
Cooper, Alan, 46; *The Inmates Are Running the Asylum*, 46
Cooper, Melinda, 236
corporate ethnographers. *See* practitioner(s), ethnographic
corporate ethnography: and anxieties of discipline

formation, 19–22, 154, 220, 224; emergence of, 3, 13–17, 96, 213; institutionalization of, 4, 6–8, 95–96, 154, 155; in reformulating anthropological praxis, 22–23, 27, 129, 221, 224. *See also* commercial ethnography; commoditization of anthropology
Coupland, Douglas, 230, 321
Creating Breakthrough Ideas (Squires and Byrne), 6
creativity, 29n6, 153; organizational, 70, 92n5
CSCW (Computer-Supported Collaborative Work), 7
Csikszentmihalyi, Mihaly, 29n6
cultural analysis, 7, 12, 42
culture knowledge buyers, 186, 187, 198, 199, 202
culture knowledge providers, 186, 193, 197, 198, 199, 202, 204
culture, conceptualizations of, 19, 69, 186, 187 198, 218; in anthropology, 190–91, 196, 198; in the commercial world, 26, 186; in other disciplines, 189. *See also* "emergent culture"; "slippery culture"
culture, organizational, 41, 44, 69, 189, 196, 198, 235; of Intel, 97, 107, 127; of Microsoft, 44; of VA, 74. *See also* business o corporate culture
cultures as different kinds of categories, 235
Cussins, Claris, 163
customer experience versus corporate perspective, 43–4

D
Damiris, Niklas, 92n6
Damon, Frederick, 92n7
Darrah, Charles N., 29n9
Darrouzet, Chris, 10, 138, 214, 218, 219, 224, 228, 231, 232, 234

value of ethnography, 27, 55, 87–89,
    217–19, 235. *See also* ethnographic
    value
values and "anti-values", 107, 127,
    131n13
Van Maanen, John, 190, 193, 198
Veri-phi, 228
Veterans Health Administration, 24,
    62. *See also* VA.
Viant, 5
visual anthropology, 11

W

Wagner, Roy, 153, 190, 192; *The
    Invention of Culture,* 190
Wakeford, Nina, 8, 30n11
Wall Street, 17
Warner, William Lloyd, 228
Wasson, Christina, 30n10, n18
Water Cooler Logic (WCL):
    perspectives of, 64–65, 72, 85, 90;
    phases, processes and practices,
    66, 75, 78, 86, 89–90. *See also* Co-
    design, Discovery
Wayne State University, 30n8
WCL. *See* Water Cooler Logic
Web 2.0 (collective production), 229
web.de, 193
Weisinger, Judith, 205n30
Wenger, Etienne, 6, 67, 69
Werth, Barry, 236
West, Paige, 30n20
Wetherell, Margaret, 92n1

Whyte, William H., 231
Wild, Helga, 10, 24, 92n6, 138, 214,
    218, 219, 228, 231, 232, 234
Wilkinson, Susann, 10, 24, 138, 214,
    218, 219, 228, 231, 232, 234
Wittgenstein, Ludwig, 231
Work Practice and Technology
    Group, 228
work practices and processes, 76,
    83, 99
work-practice studies, 7, 11, 29, 5,
    227
workaround(s), 106, 122, 125, 232
workplace studies, 7, 11, 13, 176;
    compared to consumer studies,
    12, 19–20, 30n16
World Bank 131n14
Wright, Susan, 204n14
Writing Culture (Clifford and
    Marcus), 20, 197
writing, anthropological debates,
    138
Wynn, Eleanor, 4, 228

X

Xerox Foundation, 5, 228
Xerox PARC, 4, 5, 216, 220, 228
Xerox, 4, 29n7, 83

Y

Yahoo, 228, 236
Yanagisako, Sylvia, 65
Yates, Simeon J. 92n1

247

Janet
David C.
Michael